Brave Women

A celebratory event at a girls' school in Daikundi Province, Afghanistan. Photo credit: Muzafar Ali, 2007

Julia Zulver • Kiran Stallone
Editors

Brave Women

Fighting for Justice in the 21st Century

Editors
Julia Zulver
Wallenberg Academy Fellow
Swedish Defence University
Stockholm, Sweden

Kiran Stallone
Independent Researcher
Bogotá, Colombia

ISBN 978-3-031-70701-8   ISBN 978-3-031-70702-5 (eBook)
https://doi.org/10.1007/978-3-031-70702-5

© The Editor(s) (if applicable) and The Author(s), under exclusive license to Springer Nature Switzerland AG 2025

This work is subject to copyright. All rights are solely and exclusively licensed by the Publisher, whether the whole or part of the material is concerned, specifically the rights of translation, reprinting, reuse of illustrations, recitation, broadcasting, reproduction on microfilms or in any other physical way, and transmission or information storage and retrieval, electronic adaptation, computer software, or by similar or dissimilar methodology now known or hereafter developed.
The use of general descriptive names, registered names, trademarks, service marks, etc. in this publication does not imply, even in the absence of a specific statement, that such names are exempt from the relevant protective laws and regulations and therefore free for general use.
The publisher, the authors and the editors are safe to assume that the advice and information in this book are believed to be true and accurate at the date of publication. Neither the publisher nor the authors or the editors give a warranty, expressed or implied, with respect to the material contained herein or for any errors or omissions that may have been made. The publisher remains neutral with regard to jurisdictional claims in published maps and institutional affiliations.

This Palgrave Macmillan imprint is published by the registered company Springer Nature Switzerland AG.
The registered company address is: Gewerbestrasse 11, 6330 Cham, Switzerland

If disposing of this product, please recycle the paper.

Foreword

Stories and solutions to violence, war, and oppression too frequently add women as an afterthought. If they are told at all, reports of women's experiences in these circumstances are usually those of suffering and silence, of pain and passivity. They focus on rape and abuse, on helplessness and victimhood. These stories are simultaneously important and inaccurate. They are important because acknowledging the crimes committed against us is not automatic. It was only 11 years ago when I stunned a room full of Libyan ministers and justices just by uttering the word rape. For them, rape was a crime committed by the victim, a burden to be carried in their silence and shame. We have fought and we will continue to fight for recognition of the violence committed against our bodies.

But the burden we bear goes beyond this violence. In the Liberian civil wars, it was women who had to keep the community alive: we hid our husbands and sons; we searched for food and water; we made sure life went on. When the time came, we also mobilized for peace. We sought peace despite the fact that we had one of the worst dictators in Africa who had created what could more or less be described as a police state. It was dangerous, but the worst that could have happened to us had already happened in war. So, we protested, we did sit ins, we organized sex strikes, we non-violently held peace negotiators hostage when talks were getting nowhere.

Accounts of violence and of war that omit these stories, or frame us as passive victims caught up in something we did not start and too complicated for us to finish, are inaccurate and perpetuate the same marginalization that harms women both in peace and in war. This book is a platform for our truths and our actions in the pursuit of peace, equality, and rights, to be spoken and heard. A dozen stories line these pages, but there are millions globally. These are stories of our resilience, our resistance, our bravery.

It is important to remember that these are not new stories. While there is perhaps more recognition for historical women's activism in the West, such as the suffragette movement in the United Kingdom or the role of women in the civil rights movement in the United States, when people hear about women protesting in Africa, they seem to think that it is a new phenomenon. They do not remember the 1929 Aba Women's Riots in Nigeria, for example. Twenty-five thousand women protesting against increases in colonial taxes on the market, before the age of cell phones or social media. But it has been men who have written history, and so it is men who feature in it.

The twenty-first century is a crucial and turbulent moment for us, and we must not allow for our voices and our battles to be written out of it. There is conflict in the Middle East and in Europe, in Africa and in Asia. In Latin America, levels of violence make many places into zones of war. Women are mobilizing in all these locations to fight for our rights. In the United States and Europe, South Africa and Brazil, women continue to fight against domestic violence, for indigenous rights, and against racial injustice.

Our fight does not start and end in time with the gunfire. In Liberia, when we silenced the guns 20 years ago, we were expected to go back to housework. After the peace agreement was signed in 2003 a minister congratulated me, but said it was time for me to return home and take care of my children. I refused. An agreement is only the start of peace, and we had to make sure that every point was adhered to. Women's bravery and activism do not end with men signing a piece of paper, just like wars do not end with men signing a piece of paper. I still do not want to say that we have peace in Liberia because peace to me is not the absence of war, but the presence of dignifying conditions. We continue to fight to make the lives of women in Liberia better. The same can be said throughout the stories etched into this book, whether they hail from contexts of war, peace, or, frequently, the area in between.

What makes these chapters so important is that we have written them. We have written them in collaboration with our allies, but they tell our stories, from our perspectives. It is often the case that women's activism flies under the radar, especially when the activists are also marginalized because of their poverty, race, sexuality, or ethnicity. Many of us do not have the tools or opportunities to share our stories beyond our immediate environment, but it is crucial that we do. Recognition of our struggles brings value, wider awareness, and legitimacy to what we do. Hopefully, it can also inspire women elsewhere to rise up and stand up for their rights. I remember going to Israel and Palestine to screen the documentary *Pray the Devil Back to Hell* about our movement in Liberia. It became part of the inspiration for Women Wage Peace, who have worked since 2014 to try to unify Israeli and Palestinian women to pursue peace together. Now, more than ever, inspiration and solidarity are needed in the Middle East.

We must be united in our battles. The relationships forged by Women Wage Peace between Jewish and Muslim women are the types of relationships required to progress our collective and contextual struggles. One of the main reasons for the success of our movement in Liberia—the Women of Liberia Mass Action for Peace—was the fact that it drew together Christian and Muslim women. We knew that all Liberian women were needed to find peace, no matter their religion, age, class, or tribe. And we know that all Liberian women now deserve better and equal lives. We used to say, "Does a bullet know a Christian from a Muslim?" It became one of our slogans. We appealed to our shared struggles and to our similarities, but we never went into communities to tell them how to carry out their activities. This is the kind of solidarity that we need in the twenty-first century, and this is the kind of solidarity represented in this book. Not only does each story reflect on how unity across difference was constructed in each context, but the chapters themselves, co-written by activists and academics, embody the solidarity we have forged with our allies from across the world, who support our activism and collaborate to find ways to further our objectives in intellectual, policy, and advocacy spheres.

Solidarity is a key component of our activism. Another is diversity. We must be united across difference, but we must also respect and be attuned to the difference. As women we share many similar struggles. But, as imparted in these chapters, many of us also experience marginalization because of our religion or race, our ethnicity or class. Think about Doña Ines, whose story is inscribed in Chap. 3 of this book. She faces discrimination on account of her indigeneity as well as her womanhood. Different contexts call for different strategies and different objectives. There are no one-size-fits-all solutions. Perhaps the most pivotal contribution of this book lies in its attention to a wealth of contexts from the perspectives of those who live, unite, and advocate in each context. It celebrates diversity and solidarity, difference and shared struggle.

The lessons learned from this book should extend from the most local forms of women's activism to the highest reaches of policy-making. I have long criticized the copy-and-paste approach of UN peacebuilding. What this book shows is that contextual analysis is always required, but that women's activism and bravery is pervasive and holds incredible potential. Our job, as activists and academics, is to advocate for our rights, for gender justice, and for equality, and also to open spaces in which the potential of women and girls can be unlocked. There is no archetype for how this can be achieved. But the stories woven through these pages can inspire. In itself, this book creates a space, an opportunity to learn. By telling our stories, we can hope to motivate more brave women to fight for justice in the twenty-first century.

Leymah Gbowee

Founder of Gbowee Peace Foundation Africa.
Co-Founder of the Women of Liberia Mass Action for Peace.
2011 Nobel Prize Laureate.

Acknowledgments

Over many years, we have found ourselves drawn to work with, write about, and support brave women. Where does this interest—this vocation—come from? Upon reflection, we are convinced that it comes from the exceptional examples of bravery—in its multiple and everyday forms—we were fortunate enough to learn from in our childhood homes. To our mothers Geraldine and Linda: we learned from you what it means to be brave women. Thank you for showing us every day what it means to confront and overcome adversity with grace, strength, and humor. And to our grandmothers—Margaret, Kathryn, Sally, and Eleanor—and all of the women in our families who came before them, creating a legacy of strength and inspiration.

We thank all the authors who contributed to this volume. First and foremost, we thank them for their patience; this project began during the pandemic and survived ongoing lockdowns, international moves, new jobs, new babies, the submission of PhDs, among many other important life changes. We extended the timeline many times, and we are grateful for the contributors' ongoing commitment to *Brave Women*. Beyond our own delays, we are aware that women activists, advocates, and academics have multiple responsibilities—to their communities, organizations, families, and jobs—that make demands on their time. Thank you for giving us some of this precious resource—we are certain that sharing your voices will inspire others around the world. A special thanks to Leymah Gbowee, who kindly agreed to participate, serving as a north star to set the tone of the volume.

We thank our editor Rebecca Longtin, who believed in this project and accepted our proposal—we are thrilled to have found a home with you at Palgrave. We are also grateful to the anonymous reviewers, whose generous words of support about our manuscript pushed the project forward.

Earlier iterations of this project included Hilary Matfess—thank you for your thought partnership, creativity, and honesty. During writing, we were lucky enough to have the support of amazing research assistants—Ila Zelmanovitz Axelrod and Angus Williams—who answered our late-night emails and never failed to provide exceptional inputs. Thank you to Cora Thomas for helping make connections with brave women.

Thank you to Leigh Payne, who has been an academic mentor, moral compass, and, importantly, friend, throughout our academic journeys. Our gratitude also extends to our colleagues at Ladysmith, where we know we can always go for feminist encouragement and friendship.

Importantly, thank you to our partners, Manuela Sáenz and Álvaro Garza Galván, for your love and support (and patience!) during our many academic and non-academic projects.

Finally, we are grateful for each other, as writing partners, academic co-conspirators, and best friends. In an industry that rewards competition and individualism, working together has become our secret weapon. Sharing work, credit, and responsibility is our small act of subversion, highlighting our belief that it's always best to find your academic coven (as Mirya Holman would say) and stick together. Thank you also to our third coven member—Samuel Ritholtz—for your friendship and for always standing by us.

Julia's work on this book was funded by the European Union's Horizon 2020 research and innovation program under the Marie Skłodowska-Curie Grant Agreement No. 838513 and the Knut and Alice Wallenberg Foundation.

Contents

1 Introduction — 1
Kiran Stallone and Julia Zulver

2 Silences That Speak: Deciphering the Unsaid While Protecting Women in Colombia — 11
Yirley Velazco and Kiran Stallone

3 Inés Fernández and the Me'phaa Ambassadors in Guerrero, Mexico: As Related to Julia Zulver by Inés Fernández and the Ambassadors — 23
Inés Fernández and Julia Zulver

4 Ancestrality and the Fight for the Right to Self-Representation: The Political Struggle of Enslaved People's Great-Granddaughters in Brazil — 37
Ivone de Mattos Bernardo, Malu A. C. Gatto, and Debora Thome

5 "My biggest achievement...was to be myself." Trans Activism in Peru — 59
Ana Flavia Chávez Pedraza and Janice Gallagher

6 Practices of Love and Care in the Women's Advocacy Network, Northern Uganda 71
Fatuma Abiya and Erin Baines

7 Feminist Activism in Exile: Burundi's *Mouvement Inamahoro* 93
Marie Louise Baricako and Miriam J. Anderson

8 The Politics of Care in the Fight Against Domestic Violence: Community-Coordinated Safety and Collective Care in South Africa 109
Tarisai Mchuchu-MacMillan and Emma Louise Backe

9 Transformative Activism: Women's Peace Efforts Within Conflict-Affected Populations in Georgia 127
Ekaterine Gamakharia and Magda Cárdenas

10 "I'd rather create my own table than sit where I am not wanted." A Conversation Between Stella Naw and Jenny Hedström About Myanmar 143
Stella Naw and Jenny Hedström

11 Pretty Purposed: A Social Justice Partnership for Black Girls in Virginia, United States 163
Nishaun T. Battle and Bianca Myrick

12 Conclusion: Brave Women in Afghanistan and Beyond 177
Farkhondeh Akbari, Kiran Stallone, and Julia Zulver

Index 187

Notes on Contributors

Fatuma Abiya holds a Bachelor's of Law from Ugandan Christian University and set to begin a graduate degree in Peace and Conflict Studies at the University of Notre Dame. She is a women's rights advocate and member of the Youth Advocacy Network-Uganda who advocate for children born of sexual violence during wartime. She is an intern with the Transformative Memory International Network, youth volunteer for the Women's Advocacy Network, winner of the Research-Network for Women, Peace and Security's Women's Rights Activist award (2022), and survivor of the conflict in northern Uganda.

Farkhondeh Akbari is a Postdoctoral Research Fellow at Monash University where she researches inclusive peace, diplomacy of non-state armed actors, feminist foreign policy and the women, peace, and security agenda. She has recently written on diplomatic engagements and the Taliban's gender-apartheid regime in Afghanistan. Farkhondeh completed her PhD in diplomatic studies at the Coral Bell School of Asia Pacific Affairs at the Australian National University. Her thesis examined the required characteristics for non-state armed actors to engage in meaningful diplomacy and looked at the cases of the Taliban in Afghanistan and Khmer Rouge in Cambodia. She has work experience at the Department of Political Affairs at the United Nations Headquarters in New York, the Afghanistan Independent Human Rights Commission, and the Afghanistan Independent Directorate of Local Governance in Kabul. Farkhondeh leads a grassroots non-for-profit NGO in Afghanistan taking a bottom-up approach to development and peacebuilding in Afghanistan, focusing on women's empowerment. She is also an activist, using her scholarly research to advocate for women's rights and the rights of marginalized ethnic groups in Afghanistan.

Miriam J. Anderson is an Associate Professor in the Department of Politics and Public Administration at Toronto Metropolitan University and Visiting Fellow at the Centre for Women, Peace and Security, LSE. She researches non-state actors and international security, specializing on women's participation in peace processes and in post-peace accord politics. Anderson has authored two books: *Windows of Opportunity: How Women Seize Peace Negotiations* (Oxford University Press, 2016) and *Transnational Actors in War and Peace: Militants, Activists, and Corporations in World Politics* (Georgetown University Press, 2017). Her work has also been published in *International Studies Review, Global Studies Quarterly, Politics & Gender*, and *International Negotiation* as well as in various edited volumes. From 1999 to 2002, she served as Human Rights Monitor for the Organization for Security and Co-operation in Europe (OSCE) Mission to the Republic of Croatia. Dr. Anderson holds a PhD from the University of Cambridge.

Emma Louise Backe is a PhD candidate at the George Washington University (GW) in affiliation with the University of Cape Town. She also holds a Master's in Medical Anthropology and Global Gender Policy from GW and a BA in Anthropology from Vassar College. Emma's dissertation research focuses on the politics of crisis and care for survivors of intimate partner violence (IPV) in Cape Town, South Africa, in particular what dynamics of care, healing, and recovery look like through a survivor-centered, trauma-informed lens. Emma's work is informed by feminist, activist medical anthropology, with a focus on mental health, gender-based violence, and care assemblages. Her work has been published in *Medical Anthropology Quarterly; Cultural Anthropology; Feminist Anthropology; Violence Against Women;* and *Culture, Medicine and Psychiatry* and is supported by the Wenner Gren Foundation, the Social Science Research Council (SSRC), and the American Association of University Women (AAUW). She's also served as a rape crisis advocate, community educator, and policy activist around gender-based violence, sexual harassment, and institutional accountability to and for survivors within Washington, DC, through her work with Collective Action for Safe Spaces (CASS), DC Rape Crisis Center and Peace Corps.

Erin Baines is an Associate Professor at the School of Public Policy and Global Affairs at the University of British Columbia. Her research focuses on the transformative possibilities of stories and storytelling in and after war, and the practices and politics of social repair. She is author of *Vulnerable Bodies: Gender, the UN, and the Global Refugee Crisis* (Ashgate, 2017) and *Buried in the Heart: Complex Victimhood and the war in northern Uganda* (Cambridge, 2017). Erin is a co-principal investigator of the Transformative Memory International Network, an interdisciplinary space for graduate students, scholars, activists, and artists to exchange, create, and challenge hegemonic, normative approaches to memory in the aftermaths of mass political violence.

Marie Louise Baricako is the President of the transnational Burundian feminist organization, Mouvement Inamahoro: Women and Girls for Peace and Security. She has held leadership roles in organizations and networks concerned with peace and security, human rights, women's rights, and leadership focused on Africa and on Burundi, in particular. These organizations include FEMWISE Africa (AU Women's Mediating Network), the African Women's Leaders Network (AWLN), the International Leadership Foundation (ILF), Femmes Africa Solidarité (FAS), the Burundi Action Group (BAG), an initiative of Burundian, regional and international NGOs that advocate for peace, security, and human rights in Burundi. She played an active role in the African women engagement in Durban that was instrumental in the African Union's adoption of the Gender-parity principle in 2002 as well as the African Union Heads of State and Government Adoption of the Solemn Declaration on Gender Equality in Africa in 2004. She supported Burundian women peace activists to ensure they had a voice in the 1998–2000 Arusha peace negotiations. Marie Louise Baricako contributed to support actively, as Chair of the Board of FAS, the beginnings of the Mano River Women's Peace Network (MAROWPNET) in 2001 when the region of Liberia, Sierra Leone, and Guinée was in turmoil. She also played a crucial role in the operationalization of the Women Situation Room during the Senegalese Elections in 2012, when electoral violence was threatening to break. Baricako holds a PhD in English literature and was Head of English Department at the University of Burundi.

Nishaun T. Battle is the author of *Black Girlhood, Punishment, and Resistance: Reimagining Justice for Black Girls in Virginia*, by Routledge

Publishing. She is an Associate Professor at Virginia State University. Nishaun is the Principal Investigator of the STOP School Violence grant, funded by the U.S. Department of Justice. She has written extensively on Black Girlhood, with her most recent article published in 2021, entitled "Black Girls and the Beauty Salon: Fostering a Safe Space for Collective Self-Care" in the journal *Gender & Society*. Additional academic achievements include being accepted into the first cohort of the Mellon Fellow funded grant, "Democratizing Knowledge" and a participant of the Intersectional Qualitative Research Methods Institute at the University of Maryland-College Park, and currently a consultant for the Howard University Social Justice consortium funded by the Mellon Foundation. Dr. Battle is a Self-Care coach and Wellness consultant, who helps other academics create their own unique self-care routines and she also hosts self-care workshops. Additionally, Dr. Battle helps educators who have social justice and wellness-based research, gain clarity on their ideas by merging their research, wellness, and unique skillset, and experience to help others in their communities and society. Dr. Battle provides mentorship and mentorship training with organizations centering social justice, leadership development, and holistic wellness for Black girls and girls of color in the surrounding Richmond, and Petersburg, Virginia areas, is a board of Directors member for a youth-based non-profit organization for young girls, Pretty Purposed, and is a consultant for MENTOR Virginia, a nationwide mentoring program that provides free technical assistance to youth-based non-profit organizations based in Virginia.

Magda Cárdenas is an international consultant and researcher on women and peacebuilding. She holds a PhD in Political Science from Umeå University. Her research focuses on women's role in conflict resolution and peacebuilding in different conflict settings, including Georgia, Myanmar, and Colombia. Her works have been published in the *Journal of Peace Research*, *Women's Studies International Forum*, *Civil Wars*, *European Journal of Politics and Gender*. Magda has also been consultant for UN Women on the themes of women's participation in peace efforts, mediation, and women's mobilization in non-violent movements. Cárdenas worked with the Colombian government for seven years as an advisor for justice and gender issues.

Ivone de Mattos Bernardo, a seasoned social worker, has dedicated her career to championing human rights, notably within Quilombola communities. Serving on the board of ACQUILERJ (Association of Quilombola Communities of the State of Rio de Janeiro) and CEDINE (State Council for the Rights of Black People) from 2009 to 2021 and 2010 to 2020, respectively, she leads as Coordinator at CONAQ (National Coordination of Quilombola Articulation). Ivone's impactful journey includes a pivotal role as Coordinator of Municipal Policies for Racial Equality in Magé-RJ from 2012 to 2018. There, she crafted and implemented policies across various sectors, fostering partnerships with government bodies and civil society to drive affirmative action. In her current capacities, as CONAQ Coordinator, she continues to advocate for public policies, actively engaging with social movements to ensure the promotion and protection of rights.

Inés Fernández is an Indigenous Me'phaa woman from Guerrero, Mexico. Originally from a rural, mountainous community, she was attacked by Mexican soldiers in 2002. When she reported the case to local authorities, she was called a liar, and her case was not properly handled. With the support of a local human rights organization, she took her case to the Inter-American Commission of Human Rights, which eventually passed it to the Inter-American Court of Human Rights. In 2010, the Court ruled that the Mexican State was guilty of violating Inés' rights. In 2022, Inés and a group of other women from her community opened a community center where other Indigenous woman suffering gender-based violence can access psychological and legal support in their own language.

Janice Gallagher is an Associate Professor of Political Science at Rutgers University, Newark. Her research addresses how an active civil society affects the provision of justice and the rule of law. Departing from institutional explanations of judicial change, her work emphasizes the societal embeddedness of judicial actors. She examines the micro-processes of how organized citizens matter in determining judicial outcomes, bringing activists and advocates into the picture as agenda setters and incentivizers for judicial accountability and human rights compliance. Her first book, *Bootstrap Justice: The Search for Mexico's Disappeared* (2023, Oxford University Press), has won multiple prizes, including APSA's award for the best Human Rights-themed book (2024), and LASA's Mexico Section best social science book (2024). Prior to joining Rutgers, she was a Postdoctoral Fellow at the Watson Institute for International and Public Affairs at Brown University. She has conducted extensive fieldwork in

Mexico and Colombia, and previously worked as a human rights accompanier in Colombia. She received her PhD from the Department of Government at Cornell, and an MA in Teaching from Brown University.

Ekaterine Gamakharia is the Head of Women Fund Sukhumi and has more than 20 years of experience working on gender equality, women, peace, and security in Georgia with non-governmental and international organizations. As an advocacy manager and researcher at her organization, she has led policy advocacy on gender-specific human security needs of the IDPs and conflict-affected women living close to the Administrative Boundary Line with Abkhazia and other regions of Western Georgia. She has authored several policy papers and analyses, which were further used as an evidence-based information for advocacy with government officials at the local, national, and international levels. Ekaterine has been actively involved in different dialogue and forums with conflict-divided societies from Abkhazia and South Ossetia and is dedicated to peace processes and conflict transformation in Georgia.

Malu A. C. Gatto is an Associate Professor of Latin American Politics at the Institute of the Americas at University College London (UCL). She was previously a Visiting Fellow at the Kellogg Institute for International Studies at the University of Notre Dame, a Global Fellow at the Woodrow Wilson Center for International Scholars, and a post-doctoral researcher (Oberassistentin) at the Department of Political Science of the University of Zurich. Malu's work explores questions about political behavior, representation, policy-making, and gender and politics with a regional focus on Latin America, especially Brazil. Her work research has been published in *Comparative Political Studies*, the *British Journal of Political Science*, *Party Politics, Democratization, and Politics & Gender*, among others. She has completed her doctoral studies at the Department of Politics and International Relations at the University of Oxford (DPhil, 2016). She also holds an MSc in Politics Research (2012) from Corpus Christi College, University of Oxford, and a BA (2011) from Barnard College, Columbia University.

Leymah Gbowee is a Liberian peace activist and the winner of the 2011 Nobel Peace Prize for her work on protecting the rights of women and girls in conflict and for ensuring that women are able to participate in peacebuilding processes. Gbowee led the non-violent Women of Liberia

Mass Action for Peace movement that was key in ending Liberia's civil war in 2003.

Jenny Hedström is an Associate Professor in War Studies at the Swedish Defence University. Her research concerns the relationship between households, gender, and warfare; gender, transitions, and peacebuilding; women's activism and resistance; and ethics and methods when researching war, with a focus on civil wars in Myanmar.

Tarisai Mchuchu-MacMillan is an African-feminist, advocate, and crime- and violence-prevention specialist focussed on violence against women and violence against children. Tarisai is the Executive Director of MOSAIC Training Services and Healing Centre for Women, an NPO that advocates for preventive laws and policies to be advanced to effectively reduce gender-based violence, in particular domestic, sexual, and intimate partner violence. Tarisai has received numerous awards and recognitions for her work such as her selection as a finalist in the 2011 Shoprite Checkers Women of the Year Good Neighbours Against Crime. She was listed as one of the Mail and Guardian 200 Young South Africans (you should have lunch with) and the Mail and Guardian Prominent Women in 2011. Tarisai was as a recipient of the 2012 Nedbank's Regional Business Women Achiever Award for Social Entrepreneurship. She also was the national delegate to the 2014 U.S. Department of State's International Visitors Leadership Program on Youth and Community Conflict Resolution. In 2016, she was the Vital Voices South African Ambassador in the Global Freedom Exchange programme ensuring that women and children's rights are upheld and received extensive training on human trafficking, gender-based violence, and prevention programming. She received the Black Management Forum's 2019 award for 'Most Progressive Young Professional'. Tarisai is a Mandela Washington Fellow, 2022. Tarisai is now the Vital Voices Flag Bearer for Cape Town, a mentorship programme for women empowerment held annually on International Women's Day. She has also participated in public speaking events such as the TEDxUCT conference with her talk, "Strong Communities, Fewer Criminals." Tarisai designed the SAFE-PR programme currently being piloted by MOSAIC, which is the main subject of the chapter. The SAFE-PR project is focussed on ensuring that women's rights to safety in relationships, homes and communities is advanced by strengthening duty bearers and first responders who make up the security, justice, and psychosocial support services system in response to domestic violence (DV) and intimate partner violence (IPV). MOSAIC coordinates localized multi-stakeholder platforms made up of first responders to domestic violence and intimate partner violence in communities and works with them to increase capacity to respond through a gender transformative lens by building relationships among local multi-stakeholder frontline responders in a coordinated manner that enables better service response for victims of DV/IPV, ensuring that protection orders protect and further harm is prevented. Tarisai completed her BA (2006) and LLB (2010) degrees at the University of Cape Town and is an Advocate of the High Court of South Africa.

Bianca Myrick is a mother, daughter, sister, connector, and network weaver. She is the founder and executive director of Pretty Purposed, a non-profit organization dedicated to inspiring communities to empower young women and girls through mentorship and enrichment programming. As a former fifth and sixth grade educator, Bianca had a passion for working with youth and saw a need in her community where girls could use support beyond the academic curriculum. Her teaching career fostered a development of healing-centered practices, coupled with social emotional learning and youth-centered project-based experiences that are now an integral part of Pretty Purposed programs. Bianca is also executive director of the Virginia Association of Environmental Education, where they empower and uplift educators that support environmental literacy, justice, and equitable outdoor access. As the owner of Bianca Myrick Consulting, she is able to support individuals, organizations, and businesses, specifically in the areas of youth development, which fuels her work as a consultant for Mentor Virginia and Mentor National. She is a 2010 graduate of Virginia State University, where she now serves as an adjunct professor in the Department of Teaching and Learning, teaching other students about the non-profit sector, human service work, and philanthropy. Bianca also has a Master's degree in public administration from Virginia Commonwealth University. In addition to being a grassroots non-profit leader, she dedicates her time advocating for funding for Black and Brown-led organizations, as a founding board member of Collective 365. Bianca's ultimate goal is to continue advocating for women, girls, and families through her work as a non-profit leader, domestic violence speaker and advocate, and her consulting career. She resides in Chesterfield County, Virginia, with her son.

Stella Naw is a former Deputy Minister for International Development of the National Unity Government of Myanmar. As an independent political writer and commentator, her writings have been published in various Burmese national and international media platforms including in the Diplomat and Foreign Policy concerning Myanmar's peace and conflict, and land and resource issues. Stella has also worked as an international rights advocate for inclusive peace and justice in Burma/Myanmar. One of the projects Stella has been working on for the past few years is her role as an impact strategist for an Indigenous Kachin environmental film called "Above and Below the Ground," a film capturing leadership of Indigenous Kachin women to protect a traditional river from a Chinese-backed mega-hydropower project in her ancestral land. With her research interests being non-Western peacebuilding, decoloniality/decolonization, and Indigenous feminism, Stella works toward social justice and transformation change.

Ana Flavia Chávez Pedraza has a Bachelor in Journalism and a Master's in Equality and Gender from the Universidad Jaime I in Spain. Ana Flavia is the Founder and President of the Peruvian Trans Movement of Arequipa. In this role, she oversees between 40 and 50 cases of discrimination against trans women every month, providing them access to support, shelter, and psychological and legal services. She is also the Founder of the first Peruvian-Venezuelan LGBTQ Shelter in Peru, which receives more than 900 LGBTQ individuals every year, especially in times of political and social conflict.

Kiran Stallone holds a PhD in Sociology from the University of California, Berkeley, and an MSc in Latin American Studies from the University of Oxford. She analyses gender and civilian agency in war and conflict. Through her work, she contributes to peacebuilding and conflict resolution efforts by providing research and recommendations that address the complexities of armed conflict violence. In addition to her academic research, Kiran also regularly works as a consultant on gender and development projects. She has led and supported gender research and data collection work in Colombia, Ecuador, Ethiopia, Nigeria, Tajikistan, and Kyrgyzstan. She is a Senior Researcher at Ladysmith.

Debora Thome is a political scientist, writer, and feminist activist, with research on gender and access to spaces of power, representation, candidates, and political ambition, based in Brazil, doing her post-doc in

Fundacao Getulio Vargas (FGV), Sao Paulo. She was a visiting scholar at Columbia University and is a Professor at the Columbia Women's Leadership Network. After a 15-year successful career in journalism, since 2014, she has been working with advocacy, training, and research on women and leadership, both in the private sector, third sector and in politics. She trained more than 600 women candidates in different Brazilian cities and was also a UN Women Consultant. Thome wrote several books for children and adults concerning gender and politics.

Yirley Velazco is a community leader and women's rights activist based in El Carmen de Bolívar, Colombia. She is the founder and legal representative of Asociación Mujeres Sembrando Vida, an organization that provides support to women survivors of sexual and domestic violence in the Montes de María region. Yirley has dedicated her life to protecting other women from violence and equipping them with the tools to lead dignified lives in areas impacted by violence and conflict.

Julia Zulver is a Wallenberg Academy Fellow at the Swedish Defence University (Försvarshögskolan). Previously, she was a Marie Skłodowska-Curie Research Fellow at the UNAM in Mexico and Oxford in the UK. Her research focuses on feminist responses to backlash in different contexts of violence. Her book—*High-Risk Feminism in Colombia*—is available from Rutgers University Press and in Spanish from Ediciones Uniandes. Julia prioritizes making her research accessible to diverse audiences, and frequently publishes opinion and analysis pieces. She is a Senior Researcher at Ladysmith, where she leads the Women, Peace and Security + Portfolio.

List of Photos

Photo 1.1	Julia Zulver and Kiran Stallone during a fieldwork trip to interview women's organisations in Cauca, Colombia	9
Photo 2.1	Yirley Velazco in Colombia	13
Photo 3.1	Inés Fernández, Julia Zulver, and Prisciliano Fernández outside Noemí's house in Ayutla de los Libres	34
Photo 4.1	Ivone discusses candidate support initiatives with other activists in an event in Belém, Brazil, where Malu and Débora learned about Ivone's work to promote the election of Quilombola women	43
Photo 5.1	Ana Flavia participates in a body mapping exercise at the 2024 IGLI meeting in Mexico City where she and Janice met	66
Photo 6.1	An example of WAN's bead and needlework. Gulu, Uganda	77
Photo 7.1	Marie Louise Baricako and Miriam J. Anderson on a Zoom call	96
Photo 8.1	Tarisai Mchuchu-Macmillan and Emma Louise Backe	113
Photo 9.1	Eka Gamakharia speaking with women at a workshop about women's rights in Georgia	137
Photo 10.1	A painting created by Maji Nu Ra (15 years old), living in an IDP camp in Kachin State, Myanmar	159
Photo 11.1	Bianca Myrick, founder of the Pretty Purposed program	171
Photo 12.1	Farkhondeh Akbari in Bamiyan, Afghanistan, in 2019. She stands in front of the empty niches of Bamiyan Buddha, a symbol of Hazara heritage, destroyed by the Taliban in 2001	180

CHAPTER 1

Introduction

Kiran Stallone and Julia Zulver

> *Everything we know about war we know with 'a man's voice.' We are all captives of 'men's' notions and 'men's' sense of war. 'Men's' words. Women are silent.*
> Svetlana Alexievich (*2017*), *The Unwomanly Face of War*

What does it mean to be a brave woman? In 2020, we saw Belarusian women take to the streets dressed in white to oppose the violent dictatorship that had been in power for 26 years. In 2021, our television screens showed the Fall of Kabul, and the takeover by Taliban fighters, who, overnight, began to reverse decades of women's empowerment. In response, and despite the risks, women demonstrators took to the streets in Kabul to demand their rights to work, education, and political participation. And in late 2022, we saw Iranian women fight for freedom, cutting their hair and burning their headscarves as they called for women's rights in the context of brutal repression. These are but a handful of the myriad examples of women transgressing what is societally expected of them. They go out into

K. Stallone
Bogotá, Colombia

J. Zulver (✉)
Swedish Defence University, Stockholm, Sweden
e-mail: julia.zulver@fhs.se

© The Author(s), under exclusive license to Springer Nature Switzerland AG 2025
J. Zulver, K. Stallone (eds.), *Brave Women*,
https://doi.org/10.1007/978-3-031-70702-5_1

the streets, they post on social media, and they protest governments and make demands for change. Around the world, we see women *being* brave. They do so at great personal risk, and often when the potential benefits of being brave are infinitesimally small.

We also see women telling their stories. Their stories are powerful and important, yet they are often told by academics, journalists, or policymakers who are not necessarily involved in the day-to-day struggles for women's rights. While women activists may be featured for a snippet of the global news cycle, we rarely hear about their lives and work in depth: how did they end up on the frontlines, protesting for their rights? What happens when the cameras and news crews go home? Who are these brave women who protest and tell their stories even when they face deadly threats, and what makes them dedicate their lives to activism? What are the challenges they encounter, and how do they overcome them?

Around the globe, women continue to stand up to repression, violence, and authoritarianism to make demands for their rights. Against the odds and often risking their safety, such women continue to dedicate their lives to the vision of a more gender-just future. This type of mobilization should not be taken for granted or overlooked, yet it is too often all-consuming, unpaid, or underpaid, and disappointing and disillusioning. This book focuses on these brave women activists and gives the public a unique opportunity to hear their stories, told in their own words.

Historically, there is a long tradition of women who have written directly from their experiences on the frontlines of conflict. Such women include Ida B. Wells-Barnett, a woman leader during the civil rights movement in the United States, who used her skills as a writer to shed light on the experiences of marginalized Black women and bring their knowledge to light in the early nineteenth century.

More recently, Nadia Murad—a Yazidi human rights activist who escaped sexual slavery at the hands of ISIS and went on to tell the world her story—writes: "my story, told honestly and matter-of-factly, is the best weapon I have […]" (Murad 2017, 306). In her case, she uses her story as a way to bring her former captors to justice. For others, it is a way of not forgetting or a way to ensure that what happened to them never happens to anyone else. There is power in storytelling. It is often the case, however, that women from marginalized backgrounds—women from rural areas, poor women, disabled women, racial and ethnic minority women—do not have the opportunities to share their stories beyond their immediate social circles. As feminist academics, we believe that it is our responsibility to elevate brave women's stories. We must learn from them.

When we envisioned this book, we wanted to find a way for the women we work with in our own academic research to tell their stories, instead of us doing it for them. In discussion with these women, we decided to play with the traditional academic form in a way that facilitates storytelling. Each chapter in this book was written by a pair of activists and academics who have partnered together to tell compelling accounts of what the struggle to advance women's issues looks like on the ground. It takes the reader around the world to learn about—and to learn from—brave women.

The book includes the work of Yirley, a woman who faces brutal death threats for helping other women by reporting cases of sexual violence in the aftermath of Colombia's armed conflict. It also features in-depth access into what it means to be a woman risking her life to protest against repression after the military coup and subsequent crackdown on rights in Myanmar. The chapters take readers from Burundi to Afghanistan, from an Afro-Brazilian women's movement trying to regain their rights to their land to women's efforts to prevent domestic and intimate partner violence (IPV) in South Africa. They weave together stories from across the globe to show the rich diversity of women's struggles for rights, while also touching on the similarities that activists face in different contexts.

The chapters are written from a personal perspective, so that each woman's story connects with a diverse audience around the world. Intentionally, the chapters avoid the typical jargon of academic texts and are instead accessible to anyone interested in learning about women's rights activism in global conversation. We include a range of experiences so that we can learn about what unites the women's movement at a global level.

By telling stories, we also fulfill a broader goal: to move away from pink-washed or ahistorical narratives about women's public participation. Indeed, we highlight the issues that women's movements face on a day-to-day basis and discuss how they are able to overcome these difficulties in different contexts and over time. Overall, the book draws out the shared challenges that women's movements around the world face, while also highlighting their unique characteristics in their particular political and social contexts. It provides a unique vision into what it means to fight for women's rights in the twenty-first century.

Women's Mobilization for Rights Around the World

The women who narrate the chapters, although from vastly different backgrounds, face sustained but distinct gender challenges in their efforts to advance gender equality in their home countries. In places where women have achieved significant rights in their legal systems, such rights have only translated to a partial gender equality on the ground. In other words, even though the law supports them in their work to achieve gender equality, the women's accounts in the book reveal that society lags behind and continues to marginalize them and bury their efforts. Women leaders from South Africa and the United States underscore what it is like to operate in these gray zones and what strategies they engage in to overcome these challenges. Conversely, in countries where women lack important equality rights under the laws of their countries, women activists must carefully navigate both state and societal oppression in order to advance their agendas. These struggles and women's creative solutions to them come through via the narratives of women fighting for rights in Myanmar, Uganda, Burundi, and Georgia.

The book focuses on key themes, in order to underscore the ways in which women operate in distinct spheres across the globe. The chapters explore critical questions about how and when women mobilize, but also shed light on more specific nuances of mobilization. We do not expect all readers to be familiar with broader academic debates, and so, in what follows, we outline in general terms the themes that each of the chapters discusses.

Gender, Agency, and Mobilization

The chapters are driven by an understanding that gender and agency are inter-connected. Agency is broadly "understood as the capacity to realize one's own interests against the weight [of] custom, tradition, transcendental will, or other instances (whether individual or collective)" (Mahmood 2005, 206). A focus on agency goes against many prevailing narratives that frame women as weak and passive victims in the face of patriarchal power, violence, or war. It is true, of course, that women do suffer different kinds of violences than men. With that said, focusing on women's ability to respond to these power dynamics highlights the ways in which they can make own decisions and choices in spite of efforts to repress or silence them.

In line with this idea of agency, the women in the chapters that follow are weighed down by different customs and traditions that inspire their struggles. In Brazil, Ivone de Mattos Bernardo leads a movement to achieve recognition for Quilombola territories and advocates for the representation of Quilombolas in elected office in a country with a violent history of slavery and ongoing practices of racist discrimination. In the United States, Bianca Myrick created Pretty Purposed to counter "adultification," a type of discrimination faced by Black girls when they are treated more harshly than their white counterparts.

Many of these women activists are also operating in spaces in which they are, were, or have been considered victims of violence. Victimhood and agency have long been considered antithetical concepts, but the women activists in the pages that follow show that even in the face of extreme violence, victimhood and agency intertwine to produce both mobilization and activism. In post-conflict Uganda, Fatuma Abiya and the women of the Women's Advocacy Network (WAN) unite and advocate for justice and reparations against the weight of societal discrimination for their former links to armed combatants due to abduction into forced marriage. As victims *and* survivors, these women have developed creative initiatives in order to bring attention to their justice and reparations mission. In Burundi, Marie Louise Baricako is at the head of Inamahoro, a movement to create peace and security for women and girls among the Burundian refugee population. The struggles of these women and their respective movements reveal that their victim identities do not hold them back—to the contrary, they use them to drive their movements forward.

Gender and Intersectionality

Intersectionality is another theme that is evident from reading these chapters. The chapters on women's mobilizations across the globe demonstrate that we must not only examine how women mobilize *as women*, but that we must also look at how gender "intersects" or interacts with other identities that women possess. They underscore the conclusions of seminal feminist scholars who have discouraged us from accepting the assumption that women are "a coherent group or category" (Mohanty 1988, 344). Put differently, gender is not a singular identity that stands alone. Scholars have instead pushed us to focus on its "interlocking" (Collins 1986) or "intersecting" (Crenshaw 1990) nature. Gender can intersect and interlock with race, sexuality, and class, among many other factors. Across these chapters, we see how gender intersects with these other facets of identity in order to shape both the barriers and the strategies that women use to mobilize.

In practice, this lens allows us to see that the women who tell their stories in this book are not just confronting gendered power inequalities. Rather, they are fighting for rights at the nexus of different identities based on gender, race, ethnicity, geography, ability, sexuality, and age, among others. For example, in Chap. 3, we see how Doña Inés faced discrimination not only because she is a woman, but also because she is an *Indigenous* woman. The chapter highlights, however, how she has strategically crafted her activism precisely around her Indigenous womanhood in order to achieve justice. In South Africa, Tarisai Mchuchu-MacMillan leads an NGO that offers care for women survivors of intimate partner violence (IPV) by drawing on tactics used during the Apartheid era to establish solidarity and sisterhood. And in Peru, we see how Ana Flavia has created a safe space for Trans women who face violence and discrimination because of their gender identity. Adopting an intersectional approach facilitates an understanding that fighting for women's rights is sometimes inextricable from fighting for other forms of justice.

Gendered Continuum of Violence

Finally, this book also sheds light on the continuum of violence across contexts. The chapters examine women's activism in both war and peace scenarios and reveal that gendered violence sits along a continuum (Cockburn 2004). What this line of academic thinking highlights is that women's experiences of violence do not stop the day that a peace accord or ceasefire is signed. In the same way that women and their bodies are often used as battlegrounds to be conquered during war (for example, through the use of rape as a strategy by a warring group), these gendered dynamics of conflict continue into the so-called post-conflict moments. War and violence cause upheaval that can actually bring women empowerment gains (Berry 2018) in terms of their access to political or civil society empowerment positions. Yet it can also bring about new and morphing forms of violence, for example, as men return home from war to find that their female partners have taken on new roles in the family. Even in countries that are not officially at war, chronic patterns of violence and insecurity have different impacts on women. Again, the case of Doña Inés cannot be understood without providing the context of militarization, narcotrafficking, and organized crime in her home state of Guerrero.

Another example can be found in the Colombian case: while Colombia signed a peace accord in 2016, the violence that Yirley suffers in her activism is ongoing. As she and Kiran outline in their chapter, since the official end of the conflict between the FARC guerrillas and the government, other armed groups are expanding their hold on communities and territories across the country. One of the most brutal ways that we have seen this violent expansion is through the attacks and killing of social leaders (rights defenders). Thus, for Yirley, the "end of the war" did not bring about peace as she had imagined or hoped, but rather, it has produced continued threats and violence, many of which are gendered and target her *as a woman*.

A Methodology of Activist and Academic Collaborations

As discussed above, one of the unique features of the book is that each chapter is co-authored by an activist- academic pairing. The activist is the central character, narrating the story of their movement, their country, and their struggle for rights through their personal experiences of activism. The academic brings structure to the chapter, framing the activists' work in the broader political and historical context of their country and, where relevant, drawing on academic insights to explain mobilization phenomena and women's strategic activism on the ground. Together, each pair provides insights into the lived experiences of being a woman activist in high-risk contexts. They reflect on how they became involved in their activism, how it has changed and developed over time, what gains and opportunities they have achieved, and what challenges they still face in a world that continues to be shaped by gendered power inequalities.

Increasingly, academic literature has documented that women are not merely passive victims when it comes to wars, armed conflicts, or fragile security settings. Indeed, women are activists and agents at the forefront of the struggle for change, for democracy, for rights, and for justice. Yet, when it comes to sharing these experiences with a global audience, many women operating from the grassroots do not have access to the necessary language skills, audiences, or media outlets to ensure their messages are heard or that their work is recognized. While certain activists have taken on important public leadership roles—Malala Yousafzai or Nadia Murad, for example—they are but the tip of the iceberg when it comes to inspirational stories about women's bravery, determination, and protagonism in their communities. For example, Doña Inés comes from an isolated community, prefers to speak in her indigenous Me'phaa language, and rarely has access to mobile phone service. Yet her fight for Indigenous women's rights to live free from violence led her to sue the Mexican government at the Inter-American Court of Human Rights, and her story is one that will inspire audiences from a variety of backgrounds.

All the chapters in this book are collaborations, in that they were written based on in-depth conversations between the activist and the academic. In some cases, the activist directly participated in writing. In all cases, they were involved in in-depth discussions where they recounted their story to an academic partner. The extent to which each activist actively participated in the writing was negotiated on a case-by-case basis. Some of the women were more comfortable sharing their stories orally. Others wanted to be active writers. In all the chapters, however, important conversations were held about how to tell these stories in a fair, equitable, and reliable way. Indeed, each of the academics has a long history working with their activist counterparts. While these bonds, developed over time, do not necessarily overcome the power differentials that exist between the pair, they do generate trust. These are not extractivist narratives that resulted from "going into the field," taking information, and leaving. Typical academic scholars "are expected to advance theories, talk authoritatively about facts, and develop precise methodological practices that produce answers" (Fox 2021, 155). But such scholarship does not always represent the complex reality and emotions that are involved in research and fieldwork (Fox 2021). These chapters go beyond "authoritative" academic research to depict relationships and tell stories. The activists developed long-standing relationships with the women they interviewed before and during the process of creating this book. The resulting trust that developed is fundamental when it comes to telling these stories with the empathy and respect that they deserve.

As the editors of this volume, we feel proud to have facilitated a space in which the brilliant, brave women with whom we work can tell their stories beyond their own communities. We recognize that being offered this opportunity to elevate and share stories is a privilege. It is also a responsibility. Telling a story requires that there is an audience who is listening. What we, as audience members, do with the stories we are told matters. As Nadia Murad wrote in a social media post in April 2022: "mine is only one story…We must keep listening to survivors and providing them with tangible support" (2022). Each chapter tells a story, but also highlights what *else* needs to be done, what actions need to be taken. Thus, this book also serves as a call to action, so that women who have had to be brave for so long can enjoy some reprieve from their ongoing struggles (Photo 1.1).

Photo 1.1 Julia Zulver and Kiran Stallone during a fieldwork trip to interview women's organisations in Cauca, Colombia

References

Alexievich, Svetlana. 2017. *The Unwomanly Face of War.* New York: Penguin Random House.

Berry, Marie E. 2018. *War, Women, and Power: From Violence to Mobilization in Rwanda and Bosnia-Herzegovina.* Cambridge: Cambridge University Press.

Crenshaw, Kimberlé. 1990. "Mapping the Margins: Intersectionality, Identity Politics, and Violence Against Women of Color." *Stanford Law Review* 43, no. 6: 1241–1299.

Cockburn, Cynthia. 2004. "The Continuum of Violence." In *Sites of Violence: Gender and Conflict Zones,* edited by Wenona Mary Giles, and Jennifer Hyndman, 24–44. Berkeley: University of California Press.

Collins, Patricia Hill. 1986. "Learning from the Outsider within: The Sociological Significance of Black Feminist Thought." *Social Problems* 33, no. 6: 14–32.

Fox, Nicole. 2021. *After Genocide: Memory and Reconciliation in Rwanda.* Madison: University of Wisconsin Press.

Mahmood, Saba. 2005. Politics of Piety: The Islamic Revival and the Feminist Subject. Princeton: Princeton University Press.

Mohanty, Chandra. 1988. "Under Western Eyes: Feminist Scholarship and Colonial Discourses." *Feminist Review* 30, no. 1: 61–88.

Murad, Nadia. 2017. *The Last Girl: My story of captivity, and my fight Against the Islamic State.* London: Virago.

Murad, Nadia. 2022. Instagram post (April). @nadia_murad.

CHAPTER 2

Silences That Speak: Deciphering the Unsaid While Protecting Women in Colombia

Yirley Velazco and Kiran Stallone

INTRODUCTION

In February 2000, armed paramilitaries blocked the exits of the town of El Salado in Colombia's Montes de María region, around three hours from the country's Atlantic Coast. After preventing civilians in the town from leaving, the paramilitaries invaded the area and began to slaughter townspeople in the central football field. They played drums as they carried out what remains today one of the largest and most violent massacres in the history of Colombia's armed conflict. At least 60 civilians died that day, according to Colombia's Center for Historic Memory (CNMH 2009). At the time, Yirley Velazco was just 14 years old. During the massacre that killed many of her friends and family members, Yirley was taken by force into a building near the football field, where she was raped along with other women from the town.

After the massacre in El Salado, Yirley realized that women victims of sexual violence were not being recognized in reparations processes.

Y. Velazco
El Salado, Colombia

K. Stallone (✉)
Bogotá, Colombia

© The Author(s), under exclusive license to Springer Nature Switzerland AG 2025
J. Zulver, K. Stallone (eds.), *Brave Women*,
https://doi.org/10.1007/978-3-031-70702-5_2

Indeed, she said people did not even speak about it. She decided that her life's work would be to help women survivors of conflict-related sexual violence, domestic abuse, and other marginalized community members in need. In 2005, she created her organization, Mujeres Sembrando Vida (Women Sowing Life), to support women victims of sexual violence in the Montes de María region. Over the years, she has helped more than 300 women to escape violence and domestic abuse. This help comes in many forms. Yirley helps women by guiding them through the reporting process to appropriate treatment from the authorities, working with them to establish financial independence, and providing health services and guidance on health issues like contraception.

I (Kiran) first met Yirley in 2021 when I wrote about her activism for The Guardian (Stallone and Janetsky 2021). At the time, I was working on my Ph.D. and was looking at the different ways in which women show agency in armed conflict situations in Colombia. Since that visit, I have stayed in contact with Yirley via WhatsApp messages and calls and eventually returned to El Carmen de Bolivar for another research trip in 2022. At the end of the visit, Yirley agreed to be interviewed for this chapter. Sitting on the top of a lookout with a panoramic view of Colombia's Montes de María mountains, we began to talk about how she understands her work and past experiences. Although she has been through extreme violence and hardship, Yirley is lovely to be around. She finds joy and laughter in everyday moments and has a seemingly endless reserve of energy to go about her hectic days.

For this chapter, I interviewed Yirley and she entrusted me to write her story on her behalf. She has participated collaboratively throughout the process in follow-up interviews and approved of a translated version of the chapter before publication. My conversations with Yirley were semi-structured, and as a result, we covered a number of different topics. The subsequent sections highlight the key themes that resulted from that conversation (Photo 2.1).

Different Silences: "Silence is a strategy to save our lives, but silence also speaks."

Yirley directly experienced the violent massacre described above in El Salado in 2000. She survived an infamous period of the Colombian conflict during which the Revolutionary Armed Forces of Colombia (FARC)

2 SILENCES THAT SPEAK: DECIPHERING THE UNSAID WHILE PROTECTING... 13

Photo 2.1 Yirley Velazco in Colombia

were locked in war with the government and the Autodefensas Unidas de Colombia, also known as the AUC paramilitaries. Both of these groups have since signed peace agreements with the Colombian government and have largely demobilized. Although this portion of Colombia's conflict ended, the Montes de María region where Yirley lives and works has not witnessed peace. Today, various armed groups control the Montes de María region, particularly the Clan del Golfo. These groups rose in the aftermath of the paramilitary and FARC demobilization, and they continue to wreak havoc on local populations.

Yirley works with survivors of domestic and armed conflict violence on a daily basis. She spends a great deal of time in the car going from place to place to meet with women survivors of violence and communities in need. She hops out of her bulletproof jeep and into the stifling heat of Montes de María to meet with community members and learn about their needs. Her days are often spent guiding women through reporting and administrative processes to ensure their protection, safety, and well-being. In response to the harms they experienced, Yirley has found that some women choose to remain silent. Over the years, she has learned to analyze and understand that women engage in different types of silences after experiencing trauma.

Silence is not typically associated with agency. Instead, it is often construed as the "inability to voice" (Guillaume 2018, 480). My conversations with Yirley, however, revealed that the inability to voice may overlap directly with strategy. Although not all situations warrant silence, Yirley explained that in some cases it is necessary to "be a little bit silent when faced with situations in which we know that if we speak out it will be worse." For women living in domestic violence and armed conflict spaces in Colombia, the strategic use of silence for this purpose makes sense. She elaborated: "There are many women who choose to keep quiet to save their lives, to protect not only themselves but the rest of their families." Yirley explained that "sometimes speaking out, speaking out can cost us our lives, speaking out about everything that has happened to us can cost us our lives." She gave the example of a man who harmed his wife and came after the women of Mujeres Sembrando Vida for attempting to help the woman. In areas that lack appropriate protection and support from local authorities, speaking out can lead to such targeting by perpetrators. As a result, some women may choose to develop their own responses as a form of protection in highly restricted situations.

Strategic silence for protection aligns with women's experiences in many other conflicts. For example, Sarac (2023, 7) finds that for some Yazidi women captured by ISIS, "their silence was not enforced by ISIS; rather, the women chose to remain silent." Speaking out could have caused them to be killed or violently abused by ISIS, and silence therefore represented a "security strategy" (Sarac 2023). In such instances, silence is not passivity, but is an active strategy of self-protection. Indeed, Hume and Wilding (2020, 14) note that "a decision not to engage […] can be a quietly critical act and not merely evidence of passivity." Despite the risks, Yirley does her best to help women in precarious situations so they do not have to resort to silence for protection.

Yirley also helped me to understand that the "absence of voice" (Guillaume 2018, 477) does not necessarily imply repression. In some cases, she explained that there are "people who, through their silence, have been able to rise above [the violence they experienced]." Recalling prior trauma may be a healing experience for some and may help them to process the violence and move forward, but it can also re-traumatize and re-victimize women if they are not ready or even if they simply do not want to speak about the past. In this way, silence can become a productive "coping strategy" to help women recover by bringing about "social forgetting" and moving beyond prior traumas without talking about them (Mannergren Selimovic 2020, 10). This is another example of the silences that exist after traumatic harm.

But silence may not be productive for everyone. Indeed, Yirley explained that there are women who "through their silence, have died" and experienced suffering. She offered her own experience as an example. She explained that she remained silent after the massacre in El Salado and kept her own harms to herself, but that this response was ultimately not helpful for her:

> I was silent for a long time. [...] I started to distance myself from my family, I started to treat my family badly and I started to treat myself very badly. And then, when I began to go through the process and ask myself, 'What am I doing?' I started to talk; I started to talk about [what I had been through]. I started to share my story, and, well, I began to heal. So, silence was very bad for me.

Yirley explained that she was silent because she feared that the perpetrators would return, and she was afraid they would harm her or her family. But she explained that she was moved to speak when she realized that the violence she faced was not being recognized: "When I began to see the injustices and to see that nothing was said about sexual violence, nor about the other violence that women had experienced, that's when I decided to speak out." Speaking out is what she does today on a daily basis through her work as the leader of Mujeres Sembrando Vida, and this has transformed her life.

Yirley also described silences that seemed to me like a test. She gave the example of the town of El Salado, where the massacre occurred, and she said that many in the town remained in silence to test and see whether or not anyone would actually respond to them: "Why are these people silent?" She explained that it was as if the townspeople were using the silence as a performative tactic in order to get people to notice them and that some authorities and entities did indeed notice and respond.

Mannergren Selimovic (2020, 11) calls such silences "enabling silences" or silences that are used to exert "authority in the face of power." By using silence in a performative way to test and get a response, people are using silence as a tool.

Yirley explained that she comes across other types of silences as well in her daily work. One type of silence occurs when people lack knowledge about their rights and do not know how to access the entities that have the capacity to help them. In rural contexts where conflict and domestic violence are prevalent, many do not know that speaking up might bring about a change and instead remain silent because they lack information about "how to demand [their rights], how to knock on doors, and how to reach the entities [that can help them]."

I also asked Yirley if people also remain silent because they are angry, and she said yes. She said people are angry and they feel that they lack power (*impotencia*). Yirley told me that authorities often fail to respond appropriately to women who have suffered violence. They stigmatize them. And as a result, women remain silent out of frustration and powerlessness because the authorities do not respond to them in a dignified manner. In this way, such authorities prevent women from sharing their stories. Mannergren Selimovic (2020, 2) calls such silences "disabling silences," or silences that are used to "erase events and agents from memory and discourse." By silencing women and preventing them from sharing their stories, their histories are erased.

"THE WORK I DO HAS NOTHING TO DO WITH *POLITIQUEROS*": DISTANCING FROM POLITICIANS IN ORDER TO CONNECT WITH COMMUNITIES

During our conversations, and also while watching Yirley work with remote local populations, I noticed that she repeatedly starts her meetings with communities by telling women that she is not a politician. She would gather the community together and state this right up front, almost as if it were some sort of preventative mechanism. When I asked her about this, Yirley explained that there is a reason for this frequent clarification:

> It's very important to me that it's clear to people that the work I do has nothing to do with *politiqueros*. One thing is politics as such and another thing is the *politiqueros* who go to the communities only when they need them. No, we do social work every day, 24 hours a day–every day we go into

the communities. On many occasions we do what the State does not do. [...] For me it is very important for the people to understand that [what we do] has nothing to do with these *politiqueros*, that the work we do will be available to them every day. If they come looking for us, we are going to be there [for them] every day.

Yirley repeatedly used the word *politiqueros* to refer to people who engage in *politiquería*, or meddling in politics using tricks or false promises for one's own benefit or to eliminate a rival (ASALE 2023; DEM 2023). There is no direct translation to English. Yirley explained that the communities she works in are frustrated with many local politicians because "they are tired of so many promises, so many lies, so much corruption." She explained that these politicians make bold promises to help the community with the provision of health services, youth education, basic services, employment, and housing. And they do not follow through. As such, Yirley makes sure to distance herself from these politicians to avoid "losing credibility." She finds it necessary to distance herself from them in order to connect with local communities and emphasize that unlike the politicians who pass through and make empty promises, her organization will be there for them every day. As a result, distancing herself from them became a strategy and an important part of her interaction with community members.

Unlike the *politiqueros* who do not follow through on their promises, Yirley explained that Mujeres Sembrando Vida goes to communities and supports locals in direct and impactful ways. In addition to accompanying women survivors, Mujeres Sembrando Vida organizes mobile health brigades to reach marginalized communities; they provide them breakfast; they put on clothing drives to redistribute clothes.

At the same time, however, Yirley shared that she makes an effort to connect with politicians and other local leaders who *are* well-intentioned:

> They are not all bad. [...] There are some politicians who have been there when we have needed them and it is also important that they know the work and that some of them are encouraged to accompany us, to support us.

She emphasized the importance of making alliances with such individuals and calling on them in times of need, such as when a woman victim of sexual violence is not getting the help she needs in a hospital. Overall, Yirley possessed a clear understanding of the local political scene and seemed to have positioned herself in a way that made it possible for her to distance herself from the negative aspects and also create alliances with those who could help advance the causes of her movement.

OBSTACLES TO GENDER-BASED ACTIVISM IN VIOLENT SETTINGS

Yirley's work does not come without risk. Over the years, Yirley has received approximately 500 threats related to her work with women, including threats against her family. While the authors of such threats are not always known, many come from armed actors in the area. In Colombia, social leaders and human rights defenders like Yirley are targeted at the highest rate in the world (Front Line Defenders 2022). Social leaders are broadly defined as individuals who "represent[s] the interests of local vulnerable communities" (Prem et al. 2018, 8). For her work with women and the aid she provides survivors, Yirley clearly falls under this category.

In addition to threats against her life, Yirley has also received rape threats. Rape threats in the context of social leadership are a particularly gendered type of threat. Such threats resonate with findings from a recent article I wrote with Julia Zulver (Stallone and Zulver 2024). For the project, we interviewed 20 men and 20 women human rights defenders working in different conflict regions throughout Colombia. Our findings revealed that women human rights defenders were more likely to face rape threats than men in similar leadership positions. In fact, none of the men we interviewed faced such threats. Unlike men, women were also told to go home and occupy themselves with housework. We called these "stay at home" threats. In Yirley's case, she said that she had been told that she should be at home taking care of her family instead of accompanying women and *jodiendo la vida* (fucking up life).

Such patterns reveal the restricted mentalities and violent gender discrimination of threat makers operating in particular contexts (Stallone and Zulver 2024). It shows they hold *machista* and patriarchal attitudes about women's places in society. Many war contexts like the area where Yirley lives and works are patriarchal, meaning that patriarchal norms that exploit and dominate women "are anchored and perpetuated in social relations, institutions, and practices that assert gendered hierarchies" (Kreft 2022, 655). This is evident from the content of the threats and their particularly gendered nature about women's place in the world.

To protect herself in the face of such violent threats, Yirley has bodyguards with her and has been issued a government protection scheme that includes a bulletproof vehicle. She explained that a local women's rights organization called SISMA Mujer helped her to secure these protection mechanisms and that the process of obtaining this protection was very difficult and complicated. Even more problematically, the bodyguards leave at night, when Yirley and her family members are all at home. This is an example of how the Colombian state has failed to fully provide for Yirley's needs and those of her family members.

Confronting Her Perpetrator: "I forgive you with my soul."

As I mentioned above, my multiple conversations with Yirley took many twists and turns. We ended by talking about what it was like for her to confront one of the men who was behind the massacre in El Salado. At a Truth Commission event in 2020, Yirley sat down with Uber Enrique Banquez Martínez, informally known as "Juancho Dique," one of the paramilitary commanders found responsible for the massacre in El Salado.

Yirley explained that she chose to meet with Banquez and to finally tell him that she forgave him for what he did. However, she also made it clear to me that this act of forgiveness was something she did because she felt ready: "I felt like I needed him to tell me what really happened, to hear the truth from him."

She underscored the importance of respecting individuals who are not ready and that forgiveness is an individual act:

> I cannot do it on behalf of the other victims. Each person lives his or her pain in a different way. Here everyone goes through their own healing process or their own forgiveness process–however they want to do it. There are some who do not believe in forgiveness and that is valid, but I, Yirley Velasco, do believe in forgiveness and that is why I decided to sit down with him and I told him to his face: I forgive you with my soul. Not with my heart, because the heart stops at some point, but with my soul. And if you are asking me for forgiveness just to have your picture taken or to be in the news–I'm not. I'm really forgiving you.

The moment when Yirley publicly forgave Banquez has been written about widely by media outlets, and there is even a video of the meeting between the two (Rozo and Arizo 2020). In the video, Yirley is seated at a table with Banquez and another woman survivor. Banquez explains that he can sleep better after requesting forgiveness from victims and that it takes a weight off his shoulders. He requests a hug from Yirley. She hugs him back.

But Yirley told me that once the cameras went off, Banquez came out with an excuse: he told her that even though he was the commander and he was present that day during the massacre, "I couldn't keep track of all the guys that went with me. It was like a flock of sheep. Some of them stray." Even though he admitted to overseeing the massacre, this was a way of distancing himself from the rapes that occurred during it. This is a typical chain of command argument that perpetrators around the globe have used to avoid responsibility, and Yirley unfortunately faced it at this event that was created to be a healing space. She said this made her feel many different emotions, including powerlessness (*impotencia*), anger, and disappointment.

After she publicly forgave Banquez, Yirley said many people criticized her: "How could you possibly sit with a paramilitary and forgive him?" But for Yirley, this process was not about him. It was about her. Prior to the meeting, she said several people tried to "put words in her mouth," but she did not let them. She decided that she would say what she felt like saying in the moment, and this was the result. She told me that she did not do this for the Truth Commission, nor did she do it for the perpetrator: "I [was] doing it for myself. For me. It [was] my healing process."

Concluding Thoughts

In 2016, the Colombian government finalized negotiations with the FARC and produced a peace agreement. It then put this agreement before the Colombian people. The Colombian people shocked the world by voting against the agreement. The government ultimately pushed the peace agreement through Congress after this nationwide rejection and began to implement the negotiated terms, but many Colombians continue to oppose negotiated outcomes with armed actors. Indeed, Yirley told me she has met many people who don't believe in peace and that although she supported the peace process, many criticized her for it. Nonetheless, for Yirley, "peace is built by each one of us from our hearts. We build peace with the work that we do every day."

Today, Yirley considers herself a survivor, and she prefers to distance herself from the term "victim." She explained to me that for her, "a victim is a person who experiences those cruel events that we have had to live through in this country." She sees the victim label as ongoing and problematic when a person cannot seem to overcome the victim label and gets stuck in it, assuming that everything should be given to them because of their victimization. Instead, she shared that "the idea is to rise up, the idea is to move forward." She explained that today, she considers herself a survivor:

> The truth is that I stopped being a victim– I became a survivor and for me, a survivor is that person who fights day by day, who knows what she is entitled to and who demands her rights, but at the same time not only her rights, but also the rights of other people.

Yirley explained to me that she finds healing within her work and that it fills her with happiness, satisfaction, and hope: "This is the work that gives my life meaning." Despite all of the hardship she has been through, Yirley has crafted a life project that helps hundreds of other women. She, like the many other women analyzed in the chapters of this book, has overcome the odds to demonstrate and embody what it means to be a brave woman activist.

References

ASALE. 2023. "Politiquería." In *Diccionario de americanismos*, edited by Asociación de Academias de la Lengua Española.

Centro Nacional de Memoria Histórica. 2009. *La Masacre de El Salado: Esa Guerra No Era Nuestra*, CNMH.

DEM. 2023. "Politiquería." In *Diccionario Del Español de México*. Available: https://dem.colmex.mx/ver/politiquer%C3%ADa.

Front Line Defenders. 2022. *Frontline Defenders Global Analysis: 2022*. Dublin and Brussels. Available: https://www.frontlinedefenders.org/sites/default/files/1535_fld_ga23_web.pdf.

Guillaume, Xavier. 2018. "How to do things with silence: Rethinking the centrality of speech to the securitization framework." *Security Dialogue* 49, no. 6: 476–492. https://doi.org/10.1177/0967010618789755.

Hume, Mo, and Polly Wilding. 2020. "Beyond Agency and Passivity: Situating a Gendered Articulation of Urban Violence in Brazil and El Salvador." *Urban Studies* 57, no. 2: 249–66.

Kreft, Anne-Kathrin. 2022. "'This Patriarchal, Machista and Unequal Culture of Ours': Obstacles to Confronting Conflict-Related Sexual Violence." *Social Politics: International Studies in Gender, State & Society* 30, no. 2: 654–77. https://doi.org/10.1093/sp/jxac018.

Mannergren Selimovic, Johanna. 2020. "Gendered Silences in Post-Conflict Societies: A Typology." *Peacebuilding* 8, no. 1: 1–15. https://doi.org/10.1080/21647259.2018.1491681.

Prem, Mounu, Andrés F. Rivera, Dario A. Romero, and Juan F. Vargas. 2018. "Killing Social Leaders for Territorial Control: The Unintended Consequences of Peace". In *Documentos de Trabajo 016385*. Bogotá: Universidad del Rosario.

Rozo, Camila Luque, and Alfredo Arizo. 2020. "En video I Por primera vez, 'Juancho Dique' pide perdón a víctimas de El Salado". *El Heraldo*, February 15, 2020. https://www.elheraldo.co/region-caribe/en-video-por-primera-vez-juancho-dique-pide-perdon-victimas-de-el-salado-701917.

Sarac, Busra Nisa. 2023. "Silence as agency: Yazidi women's security strategies during ISIS rule." *European Journal of Politics and Gender*, 1–16, https://doi.org/10.1332/251510821X16736275994312.

Stallone, K., & Zulver, J. M. (2024). The gendered risks of defending rights in armed conflict: Evidence from Colombia. *Journal of Peace Research*, 0(0). https://doi.org/10.1177/00223433231220261

Stallone, Kiran, and Megan Janetsky. 2021. "'I'm not alone': survivors organise against sexual violence in Colombia." *The Guardian*, July 22, 2021. https://www.theguardian.com/global-development/2021/jul/22/im-not-alone-survivors-organise-against-sexual-violence-in-colombia.

CHAPTER 3

Inés Fernández and the Me'phaa Ambassadors in Guerrero, Mexico: As Related to Julia Zulver by Inés Fernández and the Ambassadors

Inés Fernández and Julia Zulver

INTRODUCTION

We are often told stories where the powerless are ignored, marginalized, or further victimized by those actors who hold social, economic, and political power. However, every once in a while, the Davids win the fights against the Goliaths. It is these stories of *lucha* (struggle) and resistance to which we need to pay attention. Such is the case of Inés Fernández, an Indigenous Me'phaa woman from rural Guerrero, Mexico. Abused by agents of the state, Inés managed to take her case to the highest court in

I. Fernández
Guerrero, Mexico

J. Zulver (✉)
Swedish Defence University, Stockholm, Sweden
e-mail: julia.zulver@fhs.se

© The Author(s), under exclusive license to Springer Nature Switzerland AG 2025
J. Zulver, K. Stallone (eds.), *Brave Women*,
https://doi.org/10.1007/978-3-031-70702-5_3

23

the region and come out successful. Her unremitting quest for justice took her far beyond the town limits of Ayutla; she was able to tell her story of violence—and resistance—before some of the most important legal decision-makers in Latin America. A woman of small stature and few words, Inés represents *fuerza* (strength) and *lucha* (struggle) for her rights and the rights of other women fighting for a life free from violence in rural Mexico.

I met Inés and her family in 2022, in the context of a broader research project about women's high-risk leadership in Latin America. My research wanted to understand how particular leaders are able to generate charismatic bonds with the communities in which they work and why they continue in their struggles despite the great personal costs this can entail. After speaking with a local human rights organization that has a long history of working with Inés, I decided to go and meet her for myself.

In this chapter, I relate the stories that Inés, her family, and her friends told me over a week spent together in their town. Together, we made tortillas over an open fire, walked around the town plaza in the late afternoon, and ate *pozole* in the midday heat. As I was holding my interviews, these intimate interactions allowed me to see Inés' leadership in action. One day, I accompanied Inés and her team to a tiny Indigenous town, high in the mountains. I watched as she gave a workshop about domestic violence to a group of townspeople at the local Commissary's office. I also saw how local women quietly approached her afterward to ask their questions, out of the eyes of their husbands. She was able to connect with them, to reassure them, and to provide them with answers to their questions. For them, Inés is a beacon of hope—a woman like them, who was able to get justice in an unjust world.

Inés does not particularly care to speak Spanish; she feels much more comfortable in her native language, Me'phaa. We mainly communicated through her daughter, with Inés speaking her language and I speaking Spanish. As we got to know each other and feel more comfortable, Inés sometimes switched into Spanish to emphasize a point, or when her daughter was not around to translate for her. Collectively, we decided that I could document her story for this book, but that I would also facilitate the translation of the chapter into both Spanish and then Me'phaa.[1] At the time of writing, her daughter recently finished the translation of the

---

[1] To access the chapter in Me'phaa, visit: www.juliazulver.com/ines

chapter. Soon, I will print and bind copies and take them back to Inés, so that her story, her memory, her *lucha* will be documented for further generations of women in her town in words that they understand.

This chapter documents Inés' history as a brave woman fighting for her rights in a hostile environment. It begins by talking about her history of abuse and how she then embarked on a decades-long fight for her rights. Then, the chapter focuses on understanding Inés' motivations for leadership and how her *lucha* has changed the opportunities for Indigenous women in her community. The chapter concludes by outlining Inés' ongoing struggles for gender justice in Mexico.

A History of State Abuse

The Mexican state of Guerrero has a long and complex history of violence. Indeed, when Inés was assaulted by the military, soldiers were deployed throughout the mountains to fight organized crime and narcotrafficking. From the *guerra sucia* (dirty war) in the 1960s and 1970s to the war on drugs in the 2000s, the state has maintained a militarized presence throughout Guerrero. Indeed, throughout her legal process, Inés highlighted "the complicity of the army with municipal governments, organized crimes, and paramilitary groups" to show that her experience of violence was linked to the state not only as an act of omission, but indeed "by commission" (Hernández Castillo 2019, 640).

In this context of militarization: "women's bodies have become territories to be invaded, violated, and incarcerated" (Hernández Castillo 2019, 636). For Segato, women's bodies become a strategic objective in the war on drugs (Segato 2013). Beyond using women as a way to signal territorial domination, militarized actors tend to violently push back against those women who dare to transgress their established—gendered—social orders. As Hernández Castillo writes: "in the case of women who participate in movements of resistance, sexual violence constitutes not only a form of punishment for challenging gender roles, but also a message in the semantics of patriarchal violence" (ibid., 636). Elsewhere, I have written that when women openly make demands for *women's rights*, they further expose themselves to violent punishment (Zulver 2022).

Beyond violence related to organized crimes, the state remains one of the most dangerous for women; eight municipalities have declared an "Alerta de Violencia de Género" (gender violence alert) due to the high number of feminicides that take place in their territories (Centro de Derechos Humanos de la Montaña 'Tlachinollan' 2019). The human rights organization Tlachinollan notes, however, that feminicide is only one of the multiple forms of gendered violence that occurs in the state. They highlight how obstetric violence, human trafficking, forced marriage, sexual violence, torture, and disappearances—in a context of discrimination and prejudice against women, as well as a lack of access to justice—impact Indigenous women in particular. The state has maternal mortality rates that are two and a half times the national average.

It is in this context that Inés suffered violence and subsequently began her struggle for justice.[2] In March 2002, Inés was in her house in the small mountain village of Barranca Teocuani, Guerrero. Her husband Fortunato had gone out to tend to his livestock. Inés was in the kitchen with her small children, making them juice. In that moment, a large group of government soldiers arrived at her house. Three entered the house, without her permission, and began to interrogate her at gunpoint (in Spanish, a language she did not speak at the time) about some meat that they assumed her husband had stolen. When she did not answer them, one soldier sexually assaulted her while two others watched. Her young daughter, Noemí, witnessed the brutal attack; she grabbed the other three children and went running to her grandmother's house.

Inés was incredibly and understandably distressed after these events. Her Indigenous culture is known to be socially conservative. She was afraid that if she told anyone about what had happened to her, that she would be stigmatized or even punished. What if they thought that she had somehow encouraged the soldiers? What if people said that it was her fault? After thinking it through, however, she decided to tell her husband. Together, they discussed what her options might be.

Inés told me that she was afraid: "the soldiers had guns" and she worried that they might attack her again. Yet, Inés and Fortunato decided that they needed to report the crime that had taken place against her. After unsuccessfully trying to report the case to the local authority, they decided to speak to members of an Indigenous civil society organization of which they were members, la Organización del Pueblo Indígena Me'phaa (OPIM).

---

[2] The details about Inés' case come from interviews and were complemented with information from Centro de Derechos Humanos de la Montaña 'Tlachinollan' (2010), Inter-American Court of Human Rights (2012).

Prior to her attack, Inés and Fortunato participated in OPIM, an organization that fought for the rights of Indigenous people. This organization was formed after the Masacre del Charco,[3] when 11 Indigenous people were killed by soldiers. In particular, OPIM struggled for justice against military abuses in Indigenous communities. When Inés joined the organization, she was able to learn about women's rights. Eventually she began to share this knowledge with other women in her community, so that they would know when and how to denounce intrafamilial violence before the authorities. Over time, Inés became recognized for this work in her town.

Together with the leader of OPIM, Inés and Fortunato caught a ride on the back of a pickup truck—the only transportation available—into the closest town, Ayutla de Los Libres. They went to the local authorities, and Inés reported what had happened to her. She told the official in the Public Ministry that she had been abused by Mexican soldiers in her town.

Her experience was anything but straightforward. At that time, neither Inés nor her husband spoke Spanish. Growing up in a rural Indigenous community, they were only able to communicate in Me'phaa, a local language otherwise known as Tlapaneco. No one in the local public ministry spoke her language. And when she was eventually able to make herself understood with the help of her OPIM colleague, no one believed her. The authorities tried to have her undergo a physical examination to prove that she had been raped. The doctor was a man; Inés refused. She told me that government officials told her: "if a man raped you, why don't you want a man to do your exam?" She went to a different hospital, where she eventually allowed a female doctor to take some tests. She and Fortunato went back up the mountain to their community, but over the coming months, they faced multiple barriers to access justice.

The main barrier Inés faced was that the authorities wanted the case to be reviewed under military jurisdiction. At one point, the Public Ministry claimed to have lost fundamental evidence in her case. Inés told me that she was told repeatedly that she was a liar and that she was trying to take advantage of the situation in Mexico to get money. Over the years that followed, she was forced to make the long and expensive trip from her rural town to various cities, where she was denied proper access to justice repeatedly.

[3] See CNDH México (2023).

Moreover, both Inés, her husband, and the lawyers and civil society activists supporting them began to receive death threats. At times, they were followed, stalked, and had their houses under surveillance. Soldiers came to their house and demanded that they stop their legal processes. Inés' brother was tortured and murdered. Fortunato was beaten by a neighbor who did not want him to pursue Inés' case. It got to the point where the threats against the family became too scary; Inés and Fortunato made the difficult decision to send their children away for protection. The eldest went away to study at universities in other states. The younger children went to live with relatives in nearby towns in Guerrero. The threats became such that the Inter-American Commission of Human Rights authorized precautionary protection measures. The other Ambassadors told me that they were terrified during this time; one said: "when Doña Inés denounced, it got much worse. The army began cutting hoses and destroying our farmland as a punishment for what Inés was doing."

Inés' Fight for Rights

Inés described to me that it was her interactions with the psychologist that Tlachinollan made available to her that helped her to overcome her fears. She recounts how the psychologist told her—"Don't be afraid, be angry." And she was angry—angry with the soldiers who raped her, angry with the public ministry who didn't believe her and made her feel small, and angry that what had happened to her might happen to other women. She told me that she was afraid that what had happened to her could happen to her daughters, but she was determined to get justice for herself and for her family.

In May 2004, Inés—with the support of OPIM, Tlachinollan, and another civil society organization (CEJIL)—took her case to the Inter-American Commission for Human Rights. She made the case that the Mexican state had violated her rights to personal integrity, personal freedoms, due process, human dignity, protection of the family, private property, and judicial protection, as well as various articles of the Inter-American Commission to Prevent, Sanction, and Eradicate Violence Against Women (Convención Belem do Pará) and the Inter-American Convention to Prevent and Sanction Torture. In 2006, the Commission accepted the case, and in 2008 it published a report to ensure that the Mexican state offer a series of reparations. After three months of no action, the Commission recommended the case to the Inter-American Court.

Inés went to Washington, DC with her lawyers from Tlachinollan. She remembered that it was cold, despite the warm clothes she had been advised to take. Worst of all, she joked, "there were no tortillas!" Adopting a more serious tone, Inés described how her experiences in Washington were re-traumatizing. In the meetings she attended, she had to face high-ranking officials in the Mexican army. Even years later, they told her—to her face—that she was lying about what had happened to her.

Yet, Ines' years of dogged pursuit of justice were ultimately successful. On 30 August 2010, the Inter-American Court declared the Mexican State responsible for violating Inés' rights. Two years later, in 2012, the Mexican government held an International Act of Acknowledgement of Responsibilities for Inés. She told me that when the Sentence was emitted, she felt *tranquila* (calm). "I never felt *happy*," she said, "but at least I knew that they were listening to me."

"I DON'T WANT WHAT HAPPENED TO ME TO HAPPEN TO ANYONE ELSE."

Perhaps the biggest "win" for Inés was the Court's order that the Mexican state provide her with the resources to build a community center for other women who have suffered or are suffering gender-based violence. For her, the most important element of this reparation involved ensuring access to services in the region's local Indigenous languages. In this way, no woman would have to suffer alone because she doesn't speak Spanish. Yet, when I visited Inés and her family in 2022, they had only recently received the funds for reparations, after repeated pressure on the Mexican State (see Centro de Derechos Humanos de la Montaña 'Tlachinollan' 2020). Yet Inés was clear that she needed to continue in her struggle; "I knew that if I stopped my *lucha*, the Mexican justice system would stay the same forever, both for me and for other women," she told me.

To visit Inés and her Ambassadors in Ayutla, I had to take a nine-hour bus from Mexico City. First, we traveled down major highways; eventually we turned off onto smaller, winding roads that meander through small towns. The towns are sleepy, hot, and arid. Entering and leaving these little hamlets, I saw various community police organizations with their weapons, guarding their communities. Ayutla is a relatively big town, comparatively. It also has a special history; it is one of only a few towns in Mexico that is ruled by *usos y costumbres* (traditional law), rather than party politics. It has a spirit of social justice and citizens who fight for their rights despite the complex security situation at the nexus of organized crime, state violence, and local self-defense militias.

As I got down from the bus, Inés and one of the Ambassadors, Alberta, were there to greet me. Immediately, they took me to their community center. Behind heavy metal gates, the creamy yellow building looks new and fresh. On one side are the dormitories that will one day be filled with children from the rural mountain communities nearby. The hot pink walls of the basketball court frame the mountain range behind, where the moon was just beginning to rise. On the other side of the complex, the "Casa de los Saberes"—the house of knowledge. This building is where Inés and her staff attend women who are suffering violence.

The offices surround a cool courtyard, where maize and milpa are planted in the same way that you would expect to find flowers or traditional decorative bushes. One of the offices is reserved for lawyers. The next, for psychologists. On the other side, the offices for a nurse and a social worker, as well as Inés' own office space. Between these two hallways is a big multi-purpose room, where the women hold workshops and events for other women in their communities. And the most special part of this tranquil space: every woman who approaches can be served in her own, Indigenous language. As Inés told me: "I don't want what happened to me to happen to anyone else." For her, this means that it is of paramount importance that other women experiencing violence can tell their story, in their own words, in their own language, and be understood, heard, and respectfully supported.

Inés oversees the small team of professionals; in fact, two of them are her grown daughters. She also directs the *Embajadoras* (in Me'phaa, Gu'jun Etsun), the Ambassadors: "these women are my *fortaleza* (strength)," she told me. There are nine Ambassadors, women that have supported Inés through her struggles. These women have supported Inés throughout her long struggle. Some come from the same community, but others come from other small villages in the mountains. These women do not have the formal and professional training of the lawyers or psychologists, but they have the capacity to create safe spaces for women seeking help. They take it in turns to live at the community center and spent their days waiting in the reception area for women to arrive. When these women come, they greet them in their own language, and they reassure them that they're safe.

My field notes clearly describe, however, the constant presence of four security guards outside the Casa's heavy metal gate. At one point during my stay, a heavily armed truck filled with soldiers drove by the house. When I asked what they were doing I was informed: "they're looking for some *desaparecidos* (disappeared people)." I was not convinced that this was true. Ayutla remains a hot zone in Mexico's ongoing war on drugs and organized crime. While Inés tells me that she hasn't suffered any direct violence lately, there is an ongoing fear of violent retribution for teaching women about their rights. She continues to receive threats.

For Inés and her Ambassadors, the opening of the Community Centre in September 2021 is only the beginning of this new chapter, one that begins 20 years after the original crimes she suffered. Indeed, it has taken the Mexican Government years to make good on its Inter-American Court obligations to not only build the house, but pay for furniture, bills, and staffing costs. The amount of heel-dragging has been noticeable; the women I interviewed raised their eyebrows when I asked about whether the State was delaying on purpose.

By way of example, the absence of children in the northern building—the dormitories—creates a somewhat eerie feeling. Part of the Sentence dictates that the Community Centre will provide food and beds for dozens of children. The reason behind this: many Indigenous children in the region effectively enter into domestic slavery in order to go to school. Noemí, Inés' daughter, told me that it is common in the communities for families to come to the town and knock on doors until they find a family who is willing to take in their child. The child is responsible for cooking, cleaning, and other housework; in exchange, they are able to attend secondary school. They are isolated from their families and their communities and often suffer abuse at the hands of effectively unknown hosts. The dormitory for Indigenous children, then, will let them be children. They will be able to speak their own language, access hot meals, and play after their classes. They will avoid potentially abusive situations, isolation, and loneliness. For Inés, this is a fundamental way of securing the rights of women and children in her community.

In my conversations with Tlachinollan, it became clear to me that Inés' Sentence establishes a standard for other women in Guerrero. The sentence highlights that Mexico must: "ensure that services for women victims of sexual violence are provided by the institutions indicated by Mexico, including the Public Prosecutor's Office in Ayutla de los Libres, through the provision of material and personnel resources, whose activities should be strengthened through trainings" (Centro de Derechos Humanos de la Montaña 'Tlachinollan' 2019).

As Hernández Castillo writes, "in the face of...counterinsurgency strategy, organized indigenous and peasant women have responded with denunciations in national and international forums. Their voices have confronted the patriarchal semantics that intended to use sexual violence inscribed on their bodies as a form of colonization. This was the case with Inés Fernández" (Hernández Castillo 2019, 640). And indeed, Inés' remarkable leadership has had a ripple effect and lasting consequences for the women in her community. She made the difficult choice to fight for rights—for gender justice—in a hostile setting. When I asked her if she feels like a leader, she told me: "when I say something now, people believe that it is going to happen." She is a respected and trusted figure, and she was able to do what others were not able to do. She thinks that women see her courage, and saw that she never gave up, and this is what makes her a leader.

The *lucha* Continues: "No one in this region fights like Inés"

At eight in the morning, I am picked up in a truck by one of the lawyers from Tlachinollan. I sit in the back of the car with members of the team of professionals. In the open truck bed sit Inés, Alberta, and a few other Ambassadors. We take off in the rural mountains outside of Ayutla, driving up to the crest of the range, and back down the otherwise, into a stifling hot village. When we arrive, a siren goes off. The lawyer tells me that the local *Comisario*, town authority, is using the loudspeakers to call the townspeople. At first the town seems empty, but little by little, men and women start walking toward the house that serves as the government building. There is a roof made of dried leaves that offers shade from the relentless morning sun, and over the next half hour, the plastic chairs under the awning begin to fill up.

The women and men divide themselves into different sides of the space. Men on the right, women on the left. The women wear bright, patterned dresses. Every dress is the same style—just under the knee with a build in apron—but no two color combinations are the same. Everyone sits in absolute silence.

Eventually the town authority stands up and welcomes us, first in Spanish so that the lawyer and I can understand, and then in Me'phaa. He gestures toward Inés, who goes to the front of the space. She takes a deep breath and then begins to talk. While usually a soft-spoken women, I am surprised at the strength and clarity of her words; although I can't understand what she's saying, she uses certain Spanish words that give me insights into the conversation. One of the professionals sitting next to me translates that Inés is telling the women about her story, about the Inter-American Court sentence, and about the Community Centre. She tells them that they can come and visit whenever they want, and no matter what problems they're going through. She tells them that they will be able to talk to people in their own language and explain their struggles in their own words. She says that she understands that it's a long distance to travel to Ayutla and that not everyone has the extra money available; she gives them her personal phone number so that they can call her if they are in a crisis and need someone to come to the community to pick them up.

One by one, the professionals also make small presentations before the crowd. They use colorful, hand-drawn posters (many of the women cannot read) to explain what violence is. They tell the crowd that it's not just about physical violence, but also about emotional and psychological mistreatment. They use examples to explain the different ways that violence can manifest and also to highlight that women have rights. These rights mean that they don't have to suffer alone or in silence, like Inés did so many years ago.

As the morning wears on, Inés and her team finish up their talk. They distribute information pamphlets and their phone numbers to the women in the crowd. There don't seem to be any questions or comments, but the lawyer tells me that the women in these communities are shy and would never speak up publicly in a mixed-sex setting. One of the Ambassadors tells me: "no one in this region fights like Inés."

Inés seems satisfied with the morning's work. I ask her if she was happy with how the meeting turned out; in her quiet way, she smiles and nods. "But there are still many more women we need to reach," she tells me (Photo 3.1).

Photo 3.1 Inés Fernández, Julia Zulver, and Prisciliano Fernández outside Noemí's house in Ayutla de los Libres

References

Centro de Derechos Humanos de la Montaña 'Tlachinollan'. 2010. *Inés*. Centro de Derechos Humanos de la Montaña 'Tlachinollan', March 8, 2010. Available: https://archivos.juridicas.unam.mx/www/bjv/libros/10/4934/7.pdf.
Centro de Derechos Humanos de la Montaña 'Tlachinollan'. 2019. *Justicia Olvidada: La violência de género em la Montaña de Guerrero*. Centro de Derechos Humanos de la Montaña 'Tlachinollan', November 25, 2019. Available: https://www.tlachinollan.org/comunicado-justicia-olvidada-la-violencia-de-genero-en-la-montana-de-guerrero/.
Centro de Derechos Humanos de la Montaña 'Tlachinollan'. 2020. *De la Montaña a la Corte Interamericana: El pesado trecho de la justicia*. Centro de Derechos Humanos de la Montaña 'Tlachinollan', October 6, 2020. Available: https://www.tlachinollan.org/opinion-de-la-montana-a-la-corte-interamericana-el-pesado-trecho-de-la-justicia/.

CNDH México. 2023. *Masacre em El Charco, Ayutla de los Libres*. CNDH México, June 7, 2023. Available: https://www.cndh.org.mx/noticia/masacre-en-el-charco-ayutla-de-los-libres-guerrero-7-de-junio.

Hernández Castillo, Rosalva Aída. 2019. "Racialized Geographies and the "War on Drugs": Gender Violence, Militarization, and Criminalization of Indigenous Peoples." *The Journal of Latin American and Caribbean Anthropology* 24, no. 3: 635–652. https://doi.org/10.1111/jlca.12432.

Inter-American Court of Human Rights. 2012. *Fernández Ortega y otros vs. México*. Available: https://www.corteidh.or.cr/tablas/fichas/fernandezortega.pdf.

Segato, Rita Laura. 2013. *Las nuevas formas de la guerra y el cuerpo de las mujeres*. Mexico City: Editorial Pez em el Árbol/Tinta Limón.

Zulver, Julia. 2022. *High-Risk Feminism in Colombia: Women's Mobilization in Violent Contexts*. New Brunswick, NJ: Rutgers University Press.

CHAPTER 4

Ancestrality and the Fight for the Right to Self-Representation: The Political Struggle of Enslaved People's Great-Granddaughters in Brazil

Ivone de Mattos Bernardo, Malu A. C. Gatto, and Debora Thome

INTRODUCTION

Between the sixteenth and mid-nineteenth centuries, 6 million[1] women, men, and children were forcibly transported from Africa to Brazil without their consent or prior awareness. This figure represents over one-third of the total global slave trade. This brutal practice was driven by the demand for labor in sugar cane and coffee plantations. The Portuguese monarchy

---

[1] This is an estimation(Slave Voyages 2023). Although numbers are imprecise, all sources point to Brazil as the destination of the highest number of enslaved people in the world.

I. de Mattos Bernardo
Coordenação Nacional de Articulação das Comunidades Negras Rurais Quilombolas (CONAQ), Rio de Janeiro, Brazil

© The Author(s), under exclusive license to Springer Nature Switzerland AG 2025
J. Zulver, K. Stallone (eds.), *Brave Women*,
https://doi.org/10.1007/978-3-031-70702-5_4

benefited greatly from the revenues generated by these plantations, leading to the expansion of the slave trade. As Brazil transitioned to independence and established its own monarchy, the enslaved population continued to play a crucial role in supporting the country's economic development. The reliance on forced labor until (officially) 1988 makes Brazil the last country in the Americas to abolish slavery (Fujiwara et al. 2017).

In acts of resistance to this entrenched system, thousands escaped slavery and formed free communities, which came to be known as *quilombos*.[2] In the period when slavery was considered legal, the State defined *quilombos* as "a gathering of five or more 'fugitives' stranded in an uninhabited place" (Reis 1996, 18). But as spaces of resistance, *quilombos* were much more than gatherings of previously enslaved (and self-freed) people: they constituted spaces for maintaining alive not only people but also their cultural heritages. As illegal settlements, *quilombos* were always under the threat of attack (Reis 1996). Following the abolition of slavery in Brazil in the late nineteenth century, *quilombos* persisted and were re-signified as ancestral lands that honor cultural traditions and practices. More than a century after abolition, however, the descendants of enslaved peoples still fight for the right to claim these lands as their own (Silva 2019).

This is the fight of Ivone de Mattos Bernardo. Ivone, a Black[3] Quilombola woman, was born in the Quilombo Maria Conga in the city

---

[2] The origin of the word "*quilombo*" is in the Umbundu language, one of the languages spoken by the Bantu people, who lived in the region where Angola and Zaire are currently located. "The word quilombo means an association of men, open to all (without distinction of affiliation to any lineage), in which members were subjected to initiation rituals that removed them from the protective ambit of their lineages and integrated them as co-warriors in a regiment of men invulnerable to enemy weapons" (Munanga 1996, 60).

[3] Following Ivone's preference, in this text, we use the term "Black" to refer to "Afro-Brazilians," the latter a term rarely used in Portuguese. In Brazilian Portuguese, the term translates to "negro," which combines two of the official skin color (*cor de pele*) categories employed by the *Instituto Brasileiro de Geografia e Estatística* (Brazilian Institute of Geography and Statistics, IBGE): *preto* (black) and *pardo* (brown).

M. A. C. Gatto (✉)
University College London, London, UK
e-mail: m.gatto@ucl.ac.uk

D. Thome
Fundação Getulio Vargas – Cepesp, São Paulo, Brazil
e-mail: debora.costa@fgv.br

of Magé, in Rio de Janeiro State, Brazil. Her family is originally from the Quilombo Guiti, in Paraty (a municipality in Rio de Janeiro State). A graduate in Social Service and the first in her family to attend university, Ivone currently serves in the leadership of the National Coordination of Quilombola Articulation (*Coordenação Nacional de Articulação de Quilombos*, CONAQ), where she fights for the recognition of Quilombola territories and advocates for the representation of Quilombolas in elected office—a continuation of her prior activism as the president of the Association of Quilombo Remnant Communities in the State of Rio de Janeiro (*Associação das Comunidades Quilombolas do Estado de Rio de Janeiro*, ACQUILERJ).

It was while mapping civil society organizations engaged in efforts to elect people from marginalized groups to elected office that Malu and Débora—who are both academics—first came across Ivone and her work. Common to our trajectories is a deep commitment to greater diversity in political office and, in particular, to promoting the right of marginalized groups to represent themselves. In this chapter, we first provide a brief history of Quilombolas in Brazil. As we convey, Ivone's fight spans centuries and is also the fight of her ancestors. Then, we discuss how recent political developments motivated a strategic change in Quilombola activism, prompting ACQUILERJ—an organization that had previously sought to advance their rights by pressuring elected officials—to change gears and work to strengthen the political prospects of people in their own communities. In outlining how these efforts have, thus far, unfolded, we also highlight the high risks that activism—and efforts to attain elected office—impose on Quilombola women and their larger communities. Finally, we conclude with the certainty that, despite all the obstacles, Quilombola women such as Ivone will continue channeling the strength of their ancestors to fight for the rights of their communities.

CENTURIES OF FIGHTING FOR RIGHTS

Although Brazil abolished slavery in 1888, it was not until a century later, with the 1988 Brazilian Constitution established in the period post military dictatorship (1964–1985), that Quilombolas' rights to their ancestral lands were officially recognized and guaranteed (Rodrigues 2020; Leite 2000). However, the constitutional recognition of the rights of Quilombolas to their territories and cultural heritage did not automatically result in the implementation of these rights. Decree 4.887 from

November 2003 gave Quilombolas hope this would change. Aimed at addressing historical injustices and providing legal frameworks for protecting Quilombola territories, the Law regulated the procedure for identification, recognition, delimitation, demarcation, and titling of Quilombo lands. But more than 35 years since the establishment of Brazil's Constitution and 20 years since the adoption of Law 10.639, Quilombola communities still struggle to ensure that their rights on paper are guaranteed in practice (Feres Júnior et al. 2011).

According to the 2022 national census, the Quilombola population in Brazil is estimated to be 1.32 million people, accounting for 0.65% of the country's total population (IBGE 2023). Quilombolas are based in different regions of Brazil, although concentration is higher in some parts of the country, such as the Northeast and Southeast regions. Despite the constitutional recognition of their land rights, only 4.3% of the Quilombola population currently lives in territories where the land regularization process has been settled (IBGE 2023). This means that the majority of Quilombolas are still fighting for land rights and facing challenges in securing legal recognition of their territories. In the absence of the State's efforts to protect the rights of the Quilombola population—who, along with indigenous people (among others), are considered to be the traditional populations of Brazil (MDH 2022)—the Quilombola movement began to mobilize and organize themselves more effectively to advocate for their rights.

Early activism focused on influencing public debates and engaging with politicians to raise awareness about their struggle for the recognition of their rights to ancestral lands. Disillusionment with politicians' ability to represent their interests and the increased threat imposed by the election of far-right President Jair Bolsonaro (who occupied office between 2019 and 2022) motivated the Quilombola movement to strategically change their activism and increasingly work toward the effort of electing more Quilombolas, especially women, to political office.

While recognizing the need to occupy public office to secure their rights, this strategy also identifies the centrality of women's leadership within Quilombola communities. Quilombola men often distance themselves from discussions about the communities' local needs (Lima 2014), migrating to nearby cities for work while women remain in quilombos (ONU Mulheres Brasil 2017). As a result, Quilombola women are not only particularly vulnerable to the precarity of services that reach their territories and the challenge of asserting ownership of their lands, but are also the ones who often have to interact with public officials to fight for the rights of their communities (Mendonça 2008; Grossi et al. 2019). Women's leadership within *quilombos* is not only a product of migration patterns but also of the cultural inheritance of African matriarchal traditions (Silva 2019; Molina et al. 2022; Gomes et al. 2024). As the protagonists of resistance movements, Quilombola women are, thus, natural candidates for representing their communities' interests in public office. As Ivone explains, "Black women have a different way of thinking, and they need to occupy political office so they can create laws and public policies focused on this vulnerable group. Being Black, female, and Quilombola, we know exactly what we need; no one needs to tell us."

Ivone has lived through the struggles of the Quilombola movement and the changes in its activism. She was born in Maria Conga (which would later become officially recognized as a *quilombo*), from the hands of her grandmother, who had herself been an enslaved woman. When she was born, Ivone's mother worked as a housekeeper, and her father was a small farmer who, like his parents, planted okra. At that time, the *quilombo* where they lived had no electricity, running water, sanitation, or sewage. She had no access to a television, and her family learned about the news from the radio. Her fondest memories of her childhood are from her classes at the local school. At the age of 13, Ivone started to work as a nanny but did not quit school. Five years later, when she was almost graduating from high school, she became pregnant with the first of her four children and decided to get married to her first husband (years later, pregnant with her second child, she got divorced, re-married, and had two more kids).

During the first part of her adulthood, Ivone dedicated her time to taking care of her children and guaranteeing their survival by working many hours a day (and, sometimes, at night) as a security guard, a job that required her to carry a gun. Even though she was still living in the *quilombo*, she was not involved with the social movement. Ivone's activism on behalf of her community started only when she was 28 years old, when she began partaking in meetings of the neighborhood association of her *quilombo*, Maria Conga. During these meetings, she learned more about the activism of CONAQ, an organization that was working toward the recognition and preservation of Quilombola communities throughout the Brazilian national territory. Ivone got inspired and was ready to become more involved. Her first goal was to fight for better conditions for their territory. Twenty-eight years after she was born, not much had changed in her *quilombo*: they still had no electricity or paved streets; the land was located on a hill, vulnerable to the risks of heavy rain, and inaccessible to adequate public services. Understanding the need to demand improvements from politicians, Ivone agreed to take an official role in the neighborhood association; due to her caring and work responsibilities, however, she decided she could not lead the association herself but could serve in the role of vice-president.

In 1982, when Ivone and her neighbors decided to more proactively demand rights for their community, they knew they were the descendants of enslaved peoples, living on land previously occupied by their ancestors—but they did not use the word "*quilombo*" to describe their community. It was only a decade later, in 2003—after years of struggle with public authorities and knowledge exchanges with other Quilombola communities—that Ivone formally became involved with the Quilombola movement, participating in the foundation of ACQUILERJ, an organization established to empower contemporary *quilombos* in the state of Rio de Janeiro and support the national-level work of CONAQ.

As part of their work in promoting the development and ensuring the cultural preservation of Quilombola communities, ACQUILERJ identified 52 *quilombos* in the state of Rio de Janeiro. With the support of the voluntary work of Quilombolas from these communities, ACQUILERJ's initial efforts were focused on gathering the necessary documentation to claim their rights to ancestral lands with the State, as well as ensuring territories' access to public services, such as security and health. In addition to continuing to perform these activities, however, since the early 2000s, ACQUILERJ has also been involved in increasing its presence in institutional politics far beyond its work of advocacy. Trying to elect its own representatives to the municipal council, ACQUILERJ identifies people with potential for leadership within Quilombola communities and encourages them to run for office. Because of Quilombola women's prominent roles in leading neighborhood associations across *quilombo* communities (Mendonça 2008; Grossi et al. 2019) and their historical exclusion from formal spaces of power, ACQUILERJ's work to promote the greater presence of their members in political office has often meant encouraging Quilombola *women* to run for office (Photo 4.1).

Photo 4.1 Ivone discusses candidate support initiatives with other activists in an event in Belém, Brazil, where Malu and Débora learned about Ivone's work to promote the election of Quilombola women

The Rise of a Far-Right Government—And the Urgent Need for Self-Representation

Since its establishment in 2003, ACQUILERJ has ardently advocated for Quilombola land rights. Before delving directly into electoral politics, ACQUILERJ was committed to visiting various communities to comprehend their historical context and ascertain whether they bore remnants of past enslavement. This involved listening to accounts from the elderly, amassing pertinent documents, and conducting thorough research to substantiate their assertions. Oral and written histories then served as the basis for claiming land rights and cultural protection.

ACQUILERJ has always understood that having access to formal politics could help advance their demands. However, although some of its individual members made an effort to attain representation in the local legislature, the organization itself did not make a formal plan to have its members occupy public office. For example, in 2004, just a year after the organization's foundation, Ivone was invited by the right-wing *Partido Social Cristão* (Social Christian Party, PSC) to run for office. Excited about the potential to represent her community's interests in the formal arena, Ivone accepted the invitation. Now that she understands more about partisan and electoral politics, Ivone regrets the experience: she does not associate with the party's ideology and believes she was only invited to run for office in order to help the party comply with the nationally legislated gender quota (which mandates that at least 30% of candidates nominated to party lists should be women). Recalling the experience, she says: "Until the day before the election, I didn't have any money to campaign or any pamphlet to give voters information about my candidate number." Lacking the party's support and access to campaign funds, Ivone took a "do it yourself" approach: she printed five T-shirts with her candidate number (20222) and sat at a bar on the street, asking people to vote for her. Even though Ivone herself considered voting for another candidate, her strategy still got her 117 votes. They were not enough to get her elected, but other members of ACQUILERJ "did not give up on the idea."

In 2008, 2012, and 2016, another leader of ACQUILERJ, Bia Nunes, also ran for office. Despite her considerable endeavor and (relative to Ivone) higher levels of voter support, Bia Nunes also did not amass the number of votes necessary to be elected. Reflecting on these experiences, Ivone is acutely aware of the high obstacles to attaining sufficient partisan and voter support, especially as a Black Quilombola woman—a candidate profile that may be perceived as representing the rights of a small group and, thus, not attracting the support of a wide spectrum of voters.

For some time, these early experiences with electoral politics prevented ACQUILERJ leaders from seeking in elections a potential avenue for advancing their demands. More recently, however, this changed.

After 15 years of work primarily focused on advocacy and strategies to pressure elected officials on their behalf, the organization's leadership recognized the urgency of electing representatives expressly from their community who truly understood their needs and concerns. Specifically, they realized that, amidst the context of an overwhelmingly white and male political class, advocacy alone was not enough to bring about the desired change: political power played a crucial role in shaping policies and decision-making. The election of far-right president Jair Bolsonaro in 2018 and his subsequent actions while in office further underscored the urgency of this shift in strategy.

Even before being elected president, Jair Bolsonaro had already declared himself an enemy of Quilombolas (Rodrigues 2020). Aiming to signal alignment with his support base in agribusiness, during a public speech in 2017, Bolsonaro stated that, if elected, one of his policies would be to revoke laws that guarantee land rights to indigenous people and Quilombolas. In justifying this policy reversal, Bolsonaro used crass language and compared Quilombola people to farm animals: "I went to a *quilombo*. The lightest Afro-descendant there weighed seven *arrobas*.[4] They don't do anything. I don't think they are even useful for breeding anymore. And the government spends more than a billion *reais* a year on them" (Congresso em Foco 2017). Reinforcing his dismissal and lack of respect for Afro-Brazilian cultural heritage and sacred traditions, one of Bolsonaro's actions during his first year in office was to remove from the presidential palace the painting *Os Orixás*, which depicts four deities from *Candomblé*, one of the African diaspora religions present in Brazil (Angeletti 2020).

Ivone, who had previously been involved in government consultations over public policies for women, was particularly attuned to the Bolsonaro government's significant neglect of human rights and noticed a regression in policies previously being developed for vulnerable groups. As she says, Bolsonaro's threats toward the Quilombola population were not only rhetorical but also had on-the-ground policy implications, such as delays and interruptions in the process of concession of land property rights—and only did not have more profound detrimental impacts because the Brazilian Superior Tribunal intervened and compelled the government to formulate a plan for public policies to support this vulnerable population. As Ivone recounts, seeing firsthand the negative impact of having a president who not only did not prioritize her community's interests but whose views and policies also threatened their rights and well-being served as a wake-up call and motivated ACQUILERJ to channel their efforts into the political arena: "We felt the need to have a Quilombola representative, because our agenda is being discussed in the legislature and we don't have our people to defend our agendas."

---

[4] A metric of weight used to measure cattle.

Driven by the realization that political power was necessary for enacting meaningful change and countering the detrimental effects of a far-right presidency, ACQUILERJ actively decided to add to its portfolio of activities the recruitment and training of Quilombola candidates. This was not unique to the Quilombola movement in Brazil. In fact, the perceived threat imposed by Bolsonaro's government also motivated other civil society organizations to mobilize to promote the greater representation of vulnerable groups in political office (Gatto et al. 2021, 29). By focusing on electing representatives from their communities, ACQUILERJ aimed to bring about change from within, ensuring that their voices were heard, and their concerns were addressed. This shift in their repertoire of action sought to allow the movement to have a direct influence on policy-making. This sentiment is poignantly encapsulated in Ivone's reflection about the organization's new aim:

> We have been trying for a long time to have a representative from our community. However, we now understand the necessity of incentivizing our people, mostly Quilombola women, to be candidates because many still are not motivated to get into politics. But we need much more. We need to have Quilombola candidates and for them to be elected.

> We always say that Quilombola women are at the forefront of their communities, but they don't present themselves as candidates. It has been this way throughout history, since communities dating back to slavery; it is women who structure, take care of, care for, and give guidance [to the larger community]. Now, we need to have the power of the pen because we have courage, willpower, and perseverance, but people need to believe in us and vote for us so that we can come to power, to be able to make public policies, and approve legislation.

FACING THE CHALLENGES OF SELF-REPRESENTATION IN AN UNWELCOMING CONTEXT

Undertaking this move toward institutional politics and political representation certainly holds value, but it is undeniably a challenging endeavor. The realm of politics remains a rugged terrain for marginalized groups in Brazil.

On the global stage, Brazil ranks among the countries with the lowest levels of women's representation in politics. Specifically, it holds the 133rd position in the global ranking, with a mere 17.7% of women holding seats in the lower chamber of the national legislature (IPU 2023). Despite granting women the right to vote as early as 1932, Brazil has struggled to effectively promote gender and racial diversity within formal politics. While the introduction of national-level gender quotas in 1997 was intended to bolster representation, it has fallen short in rectifying all the prevailing inequalities. The reservation of campaign funds for women and Black candidates instituted in 2018 and 2020 has also not addressed these gaps (Gatto and Thome 2020). Despite women constituting a majority of the Brazilian population (at 52%) and Black individuals accounting for 53% of the population, in 2022, only 26% of people elected to the Brazilian Chamber of Deputies were Black; Black women won only 5.6% of the seats.

If the gender and racial gaps in representation are stark, the lack of representation of Quilombolas is even more alarming: In Rio de Janeiro State, where ACQUILERJ operates, there is not a single Quilombola elected to any level of office. In other words, Quilombolas are absent from all the 92 municipal councils in Rio de Janeiro State and the state legislature. This absence of representation further perpetuates the marginalization of Quilombola communities and hampers efforts to address their specific needs and concerns.

When ACQUILERJ made the active decision to broaden its approach to political participation in 2022, it sought financial support to carry out activities to train and support people from their communities to run for office. ACQUILERJ is not operating in isolation in its endeavor to promote increased representation. There are over 50 civil society initiatives in Brazil working to aid marginalized groups in pursuing political involvement and election through training programs (Gatto et al. 2021, 141).

Candidate support programs offered by civil society organizations are a new phenomenon in Brazilian politics. Before the 2018 elections, candidate training schemes existed but were overwhelmingly provided on a fee-paying basis by private companies or were part of government-sponsored or internal partisan activities. Since 2018, however, numerous civil society organizations have started to offer non-partisan, free-of-charge programs designed to train and support people who have never run for office in this challenging endeavor (Gatto et al. 2021, 145). The programs carried out by civil society organizations to train and support political aspirants vary widely: most offer courses covering various topics related to elections and campaigns (such as the rules of the Brazilian electoral system and the important dates in the campaign calendar); some, however, provide less formalized and more ad hoc types of mentoring and support schemes, such as guidance and personnel resources to support one's campaign. Whether through competitive processes or the active recruitment of particular individuals, the first activity carried out by candidate training programs is selecting their participants. Although some programs are open to receiving applications from aspirants from all backgrounds, most target specific groups (Gatto et al. 2021, 145). This is the case of the program offered by ACQUILERJ, which selects representatives from within Quilombola communities—often, women who lead neighborhood association efforts and community services (Mendonça 2008; Grossi et al. 2019; Gomes et al. 2024)—to run for office.

Fostering Political Leadership Within Their Own Community

To create a robust network of politically engaged individuals and foster a sense of belonging and community, ACQUILERJ's strategy for honing leadership within its communities includes promoting in-depth discussions about politics, public policies, and the functioning of political parties. During these debates, the organization emphasizes the main policy areas affecting Quilombolas and discusses policy solution propositions. These discussions also involve highlighting the power of Quilombolas to influence the political process through two means: (1) by turning out to vote[5] and supporting candidates aligned with the community's interest, and (2) by potentially becoming candidates themselves, and having the opportunity of directly representing the needs and aspirations of the Quilombola communities in formal politics.

To assist their efforts with the latter, in 2022, ACQUILERJ recruited 52 volunteers—one from each of the 52 quilombos represented by the organization—to identify potential leaders within their communities. As Ivone elaborates, however, in their first year trying to incentivize greater levels of political participation in electoral politics, they ended up only launching one on candidacy:

---

[5] Although voting is compulsory in Brazil, penalties for non-compliance are relatively low. In any given election, the average turnout rate is around 80%, but this tends to be considerably lower in poorer areas (Speck and Peixoto 2022) —which is the case for many Quilombola communities.

We inquired about who was interested in becoming candidates. Subsequently, we worked towards identifying the specific positions they intended to run for. In 2022, we did not have people willing to run for all available positions. After many discussions, we opted to establish a collective candidacy for the Chamber of Deputies [the lower house of the National Congress]. Through this collective candidacy, we campaigned jointly for a single seat. I was among the members of the collective candidacy.

As Almeida (2023) and Gatto and Wylie (2025) convey, since people from marginalized groups tend to have lower levels of access to partisan support, collective candidacies[6]—which, by the sheer number of people involved, multiply the reach and the amount of resources available to a candidacy—can serve as a strategy for overcoming some of the common obstacles to greater diversity in representation, including partisan resistance. As an active member of the Workers' Party since 2008, Ivone knows well the challenges imposed by intra-party dynamics: despite her efforts to forge stronger connections mostly with leftist parties, she still finds a missing component—a lack of reciprocal engagement and the unwillingness of parties to integrate and champion Quilombola candidates and their agendas genuinely.

With the understanding that they could not rely on partisan support for electoral success, ACQUILERJ sought to devise its own electoral strategy. The first step of this was the selection of the people to integrate the collective candidacy. In choosing the primary candidate—whose name would be on the ballot—the organization considered who had the most established relation with institutional politics: they selected Bia Nunes, a member of their community who had prior experience running for office. In selecting a Quilombola leader with years of experience in party politics, ACQUILERJ recognized the distinct advantage her familiarity with party dynamics (an attribute that is still relatively rare within the Quilombola community) could warrant them. In an effort to strengthen her electoral chances,

---

[6] Collective candidacies are an electoral strategy whereby a group of people—and not a single candidate, as is most commonly the case in Brazilian legislative elections—pull resources to campaign together. This strategy is commonly employed by people from marginalized groups, who may have lower levels of access to partisan resources. This strategy is considered an informal institution since, according to Brazilian electoral legislation, candidates cannot be grouped together to compete for a seat; as such, although various people compose a "collective candidacy," electoral authorities only recognize the candidacy of the individual whose candidacy was officially registered by a party. (Almeida 2023; Gatto and Wylie 2025).

ACQUILERJ then selected another five women who declared their interest in running for office to support her candidacy. To extend their reach and tap into different electoral bases, ACQUILERJ strategically selected leaders from different areas of the state. Since women are key leaders in many *quilombo* communities (Lima 2014; Gomes et al. 2024), it is not coincidental that the collective candidacy also ended up being an all-women slate.

As with any other general election, the 2022 elections were a tough starting point for any outsider seeking election: the only offices available were at the state or national levels, and the threshold of votes required to win a seat was high. In spite of having attained a considerable number of votes (around 4000), ACQUILERJ's collective candidacy fell short of the votes required to attain a seat at the lower house of the National Congress representing Rio de Janeiro State.[7]

Despite the challenges related to the relationship with political parties and the struggles to access campaign funds, Ivone maintains a steadfast belief in the strategy of electing Quilombola women; as she, ACQUILERJ continues to believe that incentivizing and supporting the candidacies of Quilombola people constitutes the most effective means to address their demands and, particularly, advance the protection of their right to ancestral lands.

To remain committed to this objective, the strategy for the upcoming 2024 local elections involves an extensive outreach effort to visit and recruit candidates in several *quilombos*. Ahead of the 2024 elections, ACQUILERJ is seeking to devise a plan to make this work logistically possible: since *quilombos* are often scattered across remote rural areas and occasionally face challenging economic circumstances, it is difficult and costly to promote in-person activities. In fact, sometimes, the scarcity of resources necessitates a waiting period of up to four months before funds can be raised for a physical meeting. This is not deterring their efforts on candidate recruitment, however. As they wait for funding to support their activities, ACQUILERJ continues to conduct online meetings and discussions about their 2024 political strategy. Ivone explains there is no time to waste: "We have to start now because we are already in 2023, and we need to do this a year in advance. In 2024, we already have to have candidates who are ready to run. So, we have to start quickly, as quickly as possible."

---

[7] The only congressman elected by her party, PDT, was Marcus Tavares, who received 62,085 votes.

Part of the strategy for 2024 involves the provision of formal training programs to individuals who express an interest in becoming candidates. To recruit potential candidates, ACQUILERJ has devised a region-based strategy that centers on one-on-one discussions to persuade individuals about the importance of participating in formal politics. According to Ivone, however, a significant number of individuals have already declared their interest in competing for positions as mayors and city councilors in 2024. She perceives this surge in interest as a direct outcome of ACQUILERJ's persistent efforts in the preceding years to encourage their community members to consider becoming candidates to advance their larger community's fight for land rights. The organization's incremental and continuous work is now beginning to yield tangible results.

THE THREAT OF VIOLENCE

While numerous other candidate support initiatives encounter challenges and difficulties as civil society organizations, Quilombolas face a much more dire threat to their existence. Since their primary battle centers around securing land rights, they contend with distinct and dangerous adversaries, such as "*grileiros*[8]"—who assert ownership over a piece of land without providing any substantiating evidence of their claims and are often armed. Ivone is acutely aware that she, along with other members of ACQUILERJ, is under the constant shadow of this threat. In some instances, those who receive threats are compelled to leave the *quilombo* to ensure their survival. Be it as leaders of their communities or as candidates for public office, women are at the forefront of the fight for Quilombola rights (Mendonça 2008; Grossi et al. 2019). Ivone holds the view that women are especially vulnerable in these situations, as they are perceived to be less capable of protecting themselves and receive threats of violence that extend to their families. The struggles of Quilombola women leaders Ivone reports on extend much beyond Maria Conga and are observed in *quilombos* throughout the Brazilian national territory. As CONAQ Women's Collective (2022) explains:

> The violence against Quilombola women defenders is produced in the context of the struggle for territory, in the shape of overt threats, slander and

---

[8] *Grileiros* are illegal—and usually violent—land invaders who claim for themselves the right to the land, often through the falsification of land title documents.

defamation, as well as intimidation against their families. These practices of violence impact not only these women individually, but also the collectivity of the quilombo, as they intend to destabilize leaders, the community, and consequently the struggle for rights.

During the period when we were writing this chapter in 2023, Maria Bernadete Pacífico was brutally murdered in her own home. Mãe Bernadete, as she was known, was the leader of the Quilombo Pitanga dos Palmares (located in the metropolitan region of Salvador, in the state of Bahia). In addition to being known for her social activism, Mãe Bernadete was also a spiritual leader (*iyalorixá*). Having dedicated her life to actively advocating for the land ownership rights of the Quilombola people, Mãe Bernadete also sought justice for her son, who was murdered in 2017. While both cases remain officially unsolved, the executions have been primarily associated with disputes over ancestral lands. Due to their work leading efforts to protect Quilombola communities as part of CONAQ, Ivone and Mãe Bernadete have known each other since 2010. In 2022, they had the opportunity to spend more time together when they shared a room during a conference. At that moment, Mãe Bernadete was already fighting for justice for the murder of her son. Because of her political activism, Mãe Bernadete received constant threats, which led her to enter a government protection program. The brutal assassination of such a brave woman and organization colleague made Ivone even more aware of her own safety (and that of her group). CONAQ estimates that at least 30 Quilombolas have been assassinated in the last decade in Brazil (CONAQ 2023). The social activism of the Quilombola people already puts them in a position of vulnerability to violence. Entering politics adds a new layer to this—especially for women. Violence Against Women in Politics (VAWIP)—gendered violence directed at women because of their political activity as party members, candidates, or elected officials—stands out as one of the most pressing concerns, leading women to distance themselves from politics and discouraging them from becoming candidates (Krook and Sanin 2020). For Quilombola women, it is yet an additional source of potential violence.

In 2018, Brazil witnessed a widely publicized case of VAWIP involving Rio de Janeiro City Councilor Marielle Franco, a prominent figure in the Black and feminist movements. Assassinated while in her car returning from a public event, Marielle Franco's brutal case remains unresolved at the time of writing, with no judicial verdict five years later. Unfortunately, this is not an isolated instance, and cases of violence against candidates—particularly those from marginalized groups—are on the rise (Resende 2023). While in Brazil, there is no investigation into the vast majority of cases of VAWIP, scholarship indicates that this type of violence is often employed with the aim of scaring off and, thus, interrupting the political careers of people seen by traditional elites as "unbelonging" in formal politics (Krook and Sanin 2020). Anecdotal evidence featuring prominent women in Brazilian politics indeed underscores how such events can prompt women candidates to abandon their political aspirations (Gatto and Thomé 2024).

In deciding to run for office, Quilombola candidates such as Ivone are not only challenging the norms of a racist and patriarchal political environment but are also making a public statement about their intent to advance the rights to the lands of Quilombola people—an agenda that threatens the economic interests of powerful people (CONAQ Women's Collective 2022). This puts them at an even greater risk of violence. In fact, during the 2022 election campaign, the ACQUILERJ candidate leading the collective candidacy and a close friend of Ivone's also faced threats and intimidation when an unidentified vehicle obstructed her car on the road. Fortunately, her driver's attitude helped her evade the danger on that occasion. Following this alarming threat, she enrolled in a government protection program, which allocated police personnel to be stationed in front of her residence throughout the election period. Ivone does not feel safe to talk much about this but understands this episode as yet another attempt to silence Quilombola women activists.

As someone involved in shaping CONAQ's efforts in preparing candidates to run for office, Ivone is also thinking about how to increase her own safety as well as those of other Quilombola people. And, similarly to her ancestors, she knows that she cannot do it alone. Through the creation of support groups—a strategy other candidate support initiatives have also found effective (Gatto et al. 2021)—Ivone hopes to further empower Quilombola leaders, enabling them to navigate better the hurdles and complexities that come with political campaigns. As Ivone reminds us, there is strength and safety in numbers:

> We have a strong tradition of strong and brave enslaved women who were leaders, such as Tereza de Benguela,[9] for example, a Quilombola leader from

---

[9] For more on Tereza de Benguela, see Souza and Scalassara (2022).

the 18th century. Our strength has always come from the collective work. For this reason, we don't even say we are a 'group'. We say we are a 'collective.' All of our things are collective, our land ownership is collective. This happens because we strongly believe our strengths reside in collectiveness. When one of us is feeling discouraged, other women come and lift up this person. Collectiveness is our superpower: without the collective, it is impossible to move forward. Those who are behind me strengthen me.

Conclusion

Be it because of intra-party politics or the violence that Quilombola candidates are likely to face, the road for Quilombolas to achieve formal political representation is long and arduous. While ACQUILERJ hopes to reap the benefits of this strategy in the medium and long runs, they point to yet another challenge in their approach to self-represent their interests. Typically, people from marginalized groups begin their political careers by running for and occupying lower-level political positions, like city councilors (Gatto et al. 2021). However, in the case of Quilombolas, their agenda is often not the focus of municipal or state government debates. Instead, the discussions related to their main agenda—the right to ancestral lands—predominantly take place at higher levels of government, specifically in the National Congress and Senate. As Ivone conveys: "For this reason, we need our own voices advocating for our community at the highest levels of government."

Despite encountering a multitude of challenges, such as financial constraints, inadequate institutional support of ACQUILERJ, strained relations with political parties, the peril to their physical safety and lives, and, lastly, the long ladder toward national offices, Ivone remains resolute in her belief in a promising future for the organization she is part of and for Quilombola women in politics. Ivone holds a strong conviction that the emergence of a new leftist government, beginning in 2023, along with the renewed political mobilization of Quilombola groups, will create enhanced prospects for self-representation. She envisions a scenario where Quilombolas not only secure additional documentation to safeguard their land rights but also seize the opportunity to elect more representatives who hail from their own communities—and bring Quilombolas' realities, needs, and proposed solutions to light.

In the upcoming years, as she has steadfastly done in the preceding two decades, Ivone will continue to channel all her energy toward transforming the circumstances of Quilombola communities. Just like her predecessors, including her great-grandmother and relatives, she will stand alongside fellow Quilombolas in the struggle for an improved quality of life, wherein the law upholds their right to existence. And just like her fellow Quilombola women activists, she will follow the motto "*resistir para existir*" ("resist to exist"). Ivone has ideas, she has a strategy, she knows how to empower her community, and she, like her ancestors, will keep on fighting.

References

Almeida, Debora Rezende de. 2023. "Representação como participação: os mandatos coletivos no Brasil." *Revista de Sociologia e Política*, 31: e024.

Angeletti, G. 2020. "Jair Bolsonaro, long criticised for anti-black statements, removes a painting of Afro-Brazilian deities from presidential offices." *The Art Newspaper*, September 1, 2020. Available: https://www.theartnewspaper.com/2020/09/01/jair-bolsonaro-long-criticised-for-anti-black-statements-removes-a-painting-of-afro-brazilian-deities-from-presidential-offices.

CONAQ. 2023. "Violência e impunidade: pelo menos 30 quilombolas foram assassinados nos últimos 10 anos." CONAQ, August 18, 2023. Available: http://conaq.org.br/noticias/violencia-e-impunidade-pelo-menos-30-quilombolas-foram-assassinados-nos-ultimos-10-anos/.

CONAQ Women's Collective. 2022. "When a Quilombola Woman Falls, the Quilombo Rises with Her". *Capire*. July 25, 2022. Available: https://capiremov.org/en/experience/when-a-quilombola-woman-falls-the-quilombo-rises-with-her/

Congresso em Foco. 2017. "Bolsonaro: 'Quilombola não serve nem para procriar.'" Congresso em Foco, April, 2017. Available: https://congressoemfoco.uol.com.br/projeto-bula/reportagem/bolsonaro-quilombola-nao-serve-nem-para-procriar/.

Gatto, Malu A. C., Guilherme Russo and Debora Thome. 2021. +*Representatividade: relatório*. Instituto Update, December, 2021. https://www.institutoupdate.org.br/maisrepresentatividade/eleicoes-2020/.

Gatto, Malu A. C. and Debora Thome. 2024. *Candidatas: Os primeiros passos das mulheres na política no Brasil*. Rio de Janeiro: FGV Editora.

Gatto, Malu A. C. and Debora Thome. 2020. "Resilient aspirants: Women's candidacies and election in times of COVID-19." *Politics & Gender*, 16, no. 4: 1001–1008.

Gatto, Malu A. C. and Kristin Wylie. 2025. "Collective candidacy strategies and diverse representation in Brazil." In *Gendering Party Politics: Feminist*

Institutionalist Perspectives, edited by Elin Bjarnegård and Meryl Kenny. Oxford: Oxford University Press.

Gomes, Bruna, João Pedro Ramalho, João Pedro Sabadini, Júlia Zanon and Kézya Alexandra. 2024. "Matriarcado nos quilombos: 'Somos fortes pelas mulheres que foram fortes antes da gente'" Projeto Colabora. March 17, 2024. Available: https://projetocolabora.com.br/ods5/matriarcado-nos-quilombos-somos-fortes-pelas-mulheres-que-foram-fortes-antes/

Grossi, Patrícia Krieger, Simone Barros de Oliveira, Eliane Moreira de Almeida, and Ana Caroline dos Santos Ferreira. 2019. "Mulheres quilombolas e políticas públicas: uma análise sobre o racismo institucional." *Diversidade e Educação* 7, no. especial: 121–132.

Fujiwara, Thomas, Humberto Laudares and Felipe Valencia Caicedo. 2017. "Tordesillas, slavery and the origins of Brazilian inequality." Available: https://www.insper.edu.br/wp-content/uploads/2018/08/fujiwara-et-al-tordesillas.pdf.

IBGE. 2023. *População quilombola é de 1,3 milhão, indica recorte inédito do censo*. Instituto Brasileiro de Geografia e Estatística. https://www.gov.br/pt-br/noticias/assistencia-social/2023/07/populacao-quilombola-e-de-1-3-milhao-indica-recorte-inedito-do-censo.

IPU. 2023. *Monthly ranking of women in national parliaments*. https://data.ipu.org/women-ranking?month=8&year=2023.

Krook, Mona Lena, and Juliana Restrepo Sanín. 2020. "The cost of doing politics? Analyzing violence and harassment against female politicians." *Perspectives on Politics* 18, no. 3: 740–755.

Feres Júnior, João, Verônica Toste Daflon, and Luiz Augusto Campos. 2011. "Lula's approach to affirmative action and race." *NACLA Report on the Americas*, 44, no. 2, 34–37.

Leite, Ilka Boaventura. 2000. "Os quilombos no Brasil: questões conceituais e normativas." *Etnográfica. Revista do Centro em Rede de Investigação em Antropologia*, 4, no. 2: 333–354.

Lima, Karla Dias. 2014. "Reflexões sobre a Liderança Feminina na Comunidade Remanescente Quilombola do Tucum/BA." *Caderno Espaço Feminino, Uberlândia* 27 no. 1.

MDH. 2022. *Guia de Política Públicas para Povos e Comunidades Tradicionais*. Ministério de Direitos Humanos. https://www.gov.br/mdh/pt-br/navegue-por-temas/igualdade-etnico-racial/publicacoes/guia-pcts.pdf.

Mendonça, Marcos António Távora de. 2008. "A mulher na comunidade Quilombola do Curiaú no Amapá: Participação, empowerment e liderança." Dissertation. Instituto Superior de Psicologia Aplicada. Available: https://repositorio.ispa.pt/handle/10400.12/689?locale=en

Molina, Gabriela Leite, Elisa Yoshie Ichikawa, and Juliane Sachser Angnes. 2022. "O que Podemos Aprender com Mulheres Quilombolas? Um Estudo sobre

Práticas Cotidianas e o Processo de Territorialização, Desterritorialização e Reterritorialização de uma Comunidade Remanescente Quilombola." *Revista Latino-Americana de Geografia e Gênero* 13, no. 2: 17–37.

Munanga, Kabengele. 1996. "Origem e histórico do quilombo na África." *Revista USP* 28: 56–63.

ONU Mulheres Brasil. 2017. "Mulheres quilombolas: liderança e resistência para combater a invisibilidade". *ONU Mulheres*. September 12, 2023. Available: http://www.onumulheres.org.br/noticias/mulheres-quilombolas-lideranca-e-resistencia-para-combater-a-invisibilidade/.

Reis, João José. 1996. "Quilombos e revoltas escravas no Brasil." *Revista USP* 28: 14–39.

Resende, Leandro. 2023. "Brasil registra 114 casos de violência política em 2023, diz estudo." *CNN Brasil*, April 17, 2023. Available: https://www.cnnbrasil.com.br/politica/brasil-registra-114-casos-de-violencia-politica-em-2023-diz-estudo/.

Rodrigues, Cristiano. 2020. *Afro-latinos em movimento: protesto negro e ativismo institucional no Brasil e na Colômbia*. Curitiba: Editora Appris.

Silva, Silvane Aparecida da. 2019. "O protagonismo das mulheres quilombolas na luta por direitos em comunidades do Estado de São Paulo (1988-2018)." Dissertation. Programa de Pós-Graduação em História, Pontifícia Universidade Católica de São Paulo. Available: https://repositorio.pucsp.br/handle/handle/22324

Slave Voyages. 2023. *Dataset*. Available: https://www.slavevoyages.org/assessment/estimates.

Souza, Gabriele Gonçalves de and Kathleen Tie Scalassara. 2022. "A liderança das comunidades quilombolas por mulheres negras é um legado de Tereza de Benguela". *Brasil de Fato*. Available: https://www.brasildefato.com.br/2022/07/25/a-lideranca-das-comunidades-quilombolas-por-mulheres-negras-e-um-legado-de-tereza-de-benguela

Speck, Bruno Wilhelm and Vitor de Moraes Peixoto. 2022. "Participação eleitoral nas disputas nacionais, estaduais e municipais no Brasil (1998-2020)." *Revista Brasileira de Ciência Política*, e258449.

CHAPTER 5

"My biggest achievement...was to be myself." Trans Activism in Peru

Ana Flavia Chávez Pedraza and Janice Gallagher

INTRODUCTION

For much of her life, Ana Flavia has had to devote her energies to surviving. She now works tirelessly to ensure that other Trans people in Peru won't have to think only about their own survival—but will be able to thrive. She founded and leads the Peruvian Trans Movement of Arequipa, which runs a shelter for anyone who needs a safe place to stay—and especially for LGBTQ youth and migrants. In 2021, she came within several votes of becoming Peru's first Trans congresswoman in Peru.

This type of activism is not easy in a country where transgender identity is not legally recognized—and, controversially, was classified in May of

A. F. C. Pedraza
Arequipa, Peru

J. Gallagher (✉)
Rutgers University, Newark, NJ, USA
e-mail: janice.gallagher@rutgers.edu

© The Author(s), under exclusive license to Springer Nature Switzerland AG 2025
J. Zulver, K. Stallone (eds.), *Brave Women*,
https://doi.org/10.1007/978-3-031-70702-5_5

2024 as a mental illness.[1] In Peru, gay marriage is not legal, hate crimes are not criminalized, and perhaps, unsurprisingly, Trans Peruvians face widespread discrimination and violence based on their gender identity.

Ana Flavia and I met in March of 2024 at IGLI, the Inclusive Global Leadership Initiative—a conference of female-identified activists and leaders, which in 2024 was held for the first time in Latin America. I was struck immediately by Ana Flavia's spirit of struggle and solidarity. On her way into Mexico, she had to battle immigration officials who questioned her visit to Mexico, implying she was a sex worker—and also demanded to know why the name on her official Peruvian documents didn't line up with the name on her invitation to attend our conference.[2] The daily struggle to have her identity recognized and the outrage it provokes, I have come to realize, continuously fuels Ana Flavia's activism. In a pivot which turned this stressful interaction with immigration officials into an opportunity for organizational change, Ana Flavia pushed the organizers of the conference to be more prepared for and sensitive to the bureaucratic obstacles Trans people face when traveling. This ability to sow the seeds of change in moments of discrimination and adversity are central to how Ana Flavia has advocated for her community in Peru—by continuously pushing government officials, employers, and everyday citizens to make space for her as a Trans woman, and by extension for Trans people in all aspects of Peruvian daily life.

When I asked Ana Flavia if she would like to participate in this volume together, she responded "Obviously yes!…We are candles whose job is to illuminate!" While I haven't written about Peru nor Trans rights before, Ana Flavia's enthusiasm, energy, and spirit of solidarity convinced me that we needed to find ways to continue to work together. She interviewed me for her weekly syndicated television show, "Valientes" (Brave Ones), along with other members of IGLI. Then, I held a series of interviews with her to write this chapter. In this volume which highlights and champions brave women, Ana Flavia's energetic refusal to be silenced, to live her truth, and to help others do so as well is instructive and inspiring.

---

[1] See "Peru protesters slam new insurance law that deems transgender people mentally ill": https://www.reuters.com/world/americas/peru-protesters-slam-new-insurance-law-that-deems-transgender-people-mentally-2024-05-18/

[2] Peru does not recognize the rights of Trans people to legally change their gender from that assigned at birth. Ana Flavia's documents reflect the name and gender she was born with, rather than her current name and gender identity.

5 "MY BIGGEST ACHIEVEMENT...WAS TO BE MYSELF." TRANS ACTIVISM...

This chapter briefly contextualizes the struggle for LGBTQ rights in Peru and goes on to center Ana Flavia's journey into self-realization and activism. We see her realize as a young person that her gender assignment does not match her identity—and then witness her struggle to live this truth in her family, as a teenager, and into adulthood. The chapter concludes by highlighting the different ways Ana Flavia has worked to pave the way for other Trans people to survive and thrive in Peru.

Context: Hostility to LGBTQ Rights in Peru

As a region, Latin America has recently taken encouraging strides to guarantee the rights of LGBTQ people. Most countries in the region have decriminalized sex between adults of the same gender, legislation prohibiting discrimination based on gender identity and sexual orientation has become increasingly common, and same-sex marriage is now recognized in Argentina (2010), Brazil (2013), Uruguay (2013), Colombia (2016), Ecuador (2019), and Costa Rica (2020). Courts have been keys to these efforts, with the Inter-American Court of Human Rights (IACtHR), the court of the regional treaty body, mandating the legal recognition of same-sex marriage (2018), and the Mexican Supreme Court declaring bans on same-sex marriage unconstitutional (2019).[3]

Despite these advances in Latin America as a region, however, "Peru is miles behind its South American neighbors," according to Cristian González Cabrera, a Human Rights Watch researcher who focuses on LGBTQ rights in Latin America (as quoted by Glatsky and Taj 2024, in the New York Times). Peru has refused to recognize gay marriage, and its Constitutional Court ruled against recognizing same-sex marriages performed in other countries (2022), and has indicated that it is not bound by the IACtHR ruling. Adoption by same-sex couples is not legally protected, and recent hate crimes and hate speech legislation protecting LGBTQ people has been vigorously challenged.

Ana Flavia's organization cites the INEI (National Statistical and Information Office) statistic that 64% of Trans women in Peru engage in sex work; 96% report experiencing discrimination—but only 5% have ever reported this discrimination. The New York Times cite a 2021 study by

---

[3] For more on LGBTQ rights in Latin America, see: "The State of LGBTQ+ Rights in Latin America," written by Gabriella Farrell, 2021, https://www.wilsoncenter.org/blog-post/state-lgbtq-rights-latin-america-0

Mas Igualdad (More Equality), a Peruvian advocacy group, which found "among a sample of 323 L.G.B.T.Q. Peruvians, 83 percent said they had experienced some kind of verbal or physical abuse and 75 percent said they had been subject to discrimination."

In May 2024, the Peruvian government issued an announcement in an official newsletter which classified transgender identity as a "mental health problem" (Reuters 2024; González Cabrera 2024a). The organization Ana Flavia leads vocally denounced the government's position on Trans people—adding to national and international condemnation. While the government has subsequently sought to distance themselves from this unexpectedly explosive and controversial claim (González Cabrera 2024b), clarifying that the recent language designating transgender people as mentally ill was a misunderstanding stemming from their intention to expand access to mental health care, this follows a pattern of the governmental bias and stigmatization in terms of their action and rhetoric on gender and sexuality. For example, just last year a high-level Peruvian human rights official spoke of homosexuality as a "deformity"—saying that (Berrios 2023) "I am sure that if Jesus were here today, he would be by everyone's side (...). So, these deformities are debaucheries. These deformities do not contribute to institutionality, nor to the State. Therefore, we must correct these behaviors."

Early Life: The Struggle to Live Her True Self

Ana Flavia heard language similar to this inside of her own family growing up. After her mother died when she was a baby, she was subsequently raised by her wealthy and traditionally minded father—who was confused by how his "son" was acting at a young age. When Ana Flavia was just seven years old, her father discovered her kissing another boy. After violently scolding the other boy, he confronted her—telling her that he was sick of hearing from others that she was acting like a girl. Ana Flavia recounts that he asked her, "'do you consider yourself to be a girl?' I was seven years old and my response was very simple; very clear. I told him yes – that I felt I was a girl."

Ana Flavia knew from when she was about four years old that she was in fact a girl–and when she realized girls and boys had different private parts, she began to pray to the Virgin María that she would wake up as a girl every day. She told me: "I was very clear that I thought like a girl – that I, in fact, was a girl, and would be a woman – but despite this, I had to pretend and repress this identity – I had to hide this beneath a facade of a timid, shy boy who was sad or confused."

At ten years old, Ana Flavia went to live with her grandmother after her grandfather passed away. Here, she experienced unconditional love: while her grandmother didn't quite understand her gender identity, she did have a stable loving home. She remembers: "She was a woman who treated me out of the love she had for me in her heart – not from prejudice."

At 14, however, she was living with her father again, and he kicked her out of her house, albeit in a distinctly upper-class and diplomatic way: he rented her her own apartment. There, she learned how to live independently. During the day, she attended a religious all-boys' school and endured brutal bullying. After being threatened by some of the roughest boys at school, she learned for the first time that she could use her ability to attract men to protect herself: in her words: "I began to pay for my security with sex."

After high school, Ana Flavia's family went through a difficult time financially. For the first time, she didn't have the safety net of their money and began to realize that the luxuries she was accustomed to—chauffeurs, private schools, a nanny, private piano lessons—were not how most Peruvians lived. She went to a public university and began to come out of her shell and live, for the first time, as a normal Peruvian.

Professional Journey: Limiting Options

In university, Ana Flavia struggled to find her way professionally. She considered being a priest—she had always been a fervent believer in Christ and Christianity—and entered into a monastery and began ecclesiastical study. She explains her decision:

> *Ana Flavia:* "So I said, I would like to hold Christ in my fingers. I would like to serve my fellow man, I would like to give them that hope that is God – that hope which I had for myself in my life…So what I have to do…is to be a priest. And what's more, I told myself, perhaps God allowed me to be born with a soul distinct from my body, perhaps so that this body could be integrated through the Eucharist. And I entered into seminary, and I was like a fish in water."

As she studied philosophy, however, she realized her "anthropological reality" was indeed that she was a woman—a realization that convinced her she couldn't continue in the seminary, in a place where her colleagues believed she was someone she wasn't. So, she returned to university. She was a talented student and pursued journalism in her studies. After being laughed at repeatedly during her interviews—her interviewees asked her how could someone like her interview a policeman? Much less a bishop or member of the church?—it was clear journalism wouldn't be an option for her.

As she looked for what would come next, she realized that sex work was one of the only options open to her. As friend after friend made the choice to support themselves with sex work, Ana Flavia found herself considering this as well.

> *Ana Flavia:* "I realized that we had the whole world against us - but we had every opportunity to be prostitutes, to contract HIV, to drown ourselves in alcohol, in drugs. I realized that it is so hard to take care of ourselves because we are so deeply alone - because we don't have any family. [For most of us], we have parents, but we don't have them. And something that I also realized, [was] that I was not born poor, but being Trans impoverished me…In other words, [my difficulties are] not only because I am Trans, I am a woman, but also because I am [now] poor – [and I am poor] because, in some way, I do not meet certain [professional] standards [necessary to have and keep a job]."

This realization, along with returning to her faith, helped her figure out what was next for her.

Ana Flavia realized that because of discrimination, she must give up the idea of having a typical "professional" career—that her gender identity put limits on what she could do professionally, so she would have to approach her career differently than others. She had always loved doing hair and makeup—and began to see these "hobbies" as a possible career. She threw herself into the world of hairdressing—and was soon quite successful financially. The money she made from hairdressing allowed her to pay for her gender transition—and also, to pursue studies in law.

An Activist Emerges

In 2015, Ana Flavia had an experience which would shift her sights toward changing how Peru treats Trans people. After buying tickets to go to a club with a gay friend of hers on a Saturday night, a security guard came up to her and told her that there had been an error—she had been sold the ticket, but would not be able to go into the club. Here, the insinuation was that she wasn't welcome because she was Transgender. Ana Flavia activated legal knowledge she had absorbed during her university studies: she began to film the encounter and called the police. When the police questioned the club owner, who happened to be a gay man, he held firm: he wouldn't let Ana Flavia in, he said, because he couldn't guarantee her safety.

She filed a formal complaint against the club—something she was confident would get them fined. While she was confident in this, the newspaper article reporting on this incident (Parillo 2015) noted the historic nature of what Ana Flavia accomplished: "This is the first case in the history of Peru in which state institutions oblige the respect of the rights of a transsexual, and get an entertainment establishment fined for the crime of discrimination.[4]"

Ana Flavia was enraged by the discrimination she had experienced at the hands of the club owner and reached out to the local LGBTQ organization, which supported her as she set up a protest outside the club. Ana Flavia also worked with lawyers to follow up on this discrimination, and since the club owner was clearly in the wrong legally, they moved toward a legal settlement. Ana Flavia insisted the club host a Miss Trans World pageant on a Saturday night—the same night of the week they had denied her entry into the club. When the owner tried to push to have the event on a Sunday – Ana Flavia asked him if he wanted to go trial. "No," he said. He would comply with her request: Miss Trans World was held at the same club that denied her entry, on a Saturday night, and throughout her home town of Arequipa, Trans people were no longer denied entry to nightclubs.

From that experience, Ana Flavia says, "my life in activism began – but I believe that I have been engaged in activism since I was in high school, because I was always being myself. And my biggest achievement – before being formally an activist – was to be myself. That *was* my activism. To be the same person in school, at home – even if they kick me out. Because my whole body screamed this." (Photo 5.1)

---

[4] "Joven transexual denuncia a discoteca ante INDECOPI." Elard Parillo, Published on June 17, 2015: https://www.google.com/url?sa=i&url=https%3A%2F%2Fissuu.com%2Fvis talibre%2Fdocs%2F1edi_240_vljun2015%2F2&psig=AOvVaw1XWBvPhhtIokeIkqdfKwct& ust=1719964609361000&source=images&cd=vfe&opi=89978449&ved=2ahUKEwjdpuf NhYeHAxV-pokEHbezA0EQjhx6BAgAEBk.

Photo 5.1 Ana Flavia participates in a body mapping exercise at the 2024 IGLI meeting in Mexico City where she and Janice met. (Photo by: Luzbeidy Monterrosa)

Founding the Arequipa Trans Movement and Shelter: Providing a Home

As Ana Flavia began to shift into activism, she kept reflecting on the fact that the owner of the club that discriminated against her was a gay man.

> *Ana Flavia:* "Being gay doesn't take away misogyny – [being gay] doesn't necessarily negate old-fashioned ideas, [being gay] isn't necessarily anti-machismo…I began to realize that also within the LGBT movements there was a lot of machismo, a lot of inequality. That Trans women [were considered] *putas o brutas* [whores or brutes]. And that's when I said no, I'm not going to associate with any LGBT community and I'm going to form a Trans women's movement."

As she talked with her Trans friends about what this movement would look like, they began to study the violence they had all experienced. For almost all of them, violence really began when they were thrown out of their homes—which is when nearly all of them began to work in prostitution to support themselves. Ana Flavia realized the central role of support and stability in her ability to pivot in her life and career trajectory. For her, her grandmother provided this—begging her to move back in when she was thinking of living on the streets and engaging in sex work to survive. She wanted to give to others what her grandmother had given to her.

From that realization, the idea for the first shelter for LGBTQ youth in Peru emerged. Ana Flavia and her friends decided that the shelter would be not only for Peruvians, but for LGBTQ migrants to Peru, who often arrived after being thrown out of their homes in other Latin American countries. They quickly established the shelter and began to link with other services and opportunities.

> *Ana Flavia:* "We began to generate Trans scholarships in universities, and we began to realize…that [we needed to help with] all the things that people needed to live their lives: the ability to find work…we began to organize the kids, to hold regional youth meetings…[We helped people] fill their bellies and make money…gave them psychological support."

But, Ana Flavia realized—they needed to do more than this. They needed to attend to the spiritual needs of people; to take seriously the need to care for their bodies—and help people address the gender dysphoria many felt.

During the pandemic, the shelter became a semi-permanent home for their many residents who couldn't or didn't want to return home. This was a tremendous strain on the shelter's resources, but Ana Flavia knew they needed to make it work:

> *Ana Flavia:* "So we were talking at the beginning of the pandemic and one resident said 'I am from Lima', [another said] 'I am from another area.' We have a Colombian, we had other Venezuelans. And we told them, 'we are going to get the tickets and permits so that you can return home – does that work for you?' But when they thought of facing the pandemic with their families, they didn't want to. They said 'No, Ana Flavia, because if I return, they are going to cut my hair. I will return to the same [discrimination that I left behind]. I will have to put up with them calling me a man that I am not. They see me in a way in which I do not see myself.'
>
> So, that's when I told them: 'I understand you, because I also know what it's like to be kicked out of the house, and I'm not going to tell you to go

home. I'm not going to tell you to go, I'm not going to tell you to go to a place where they mistreat you. So, we will sleep two or three to a bed, we will eat from a single plate. I don't know how we will do it, but we can't let you go alone, much less go to a place where they will mistreat you.' And then [the shelter] grew with much greater demand and strength, because we had to look for a bigger space."

Fighting the Fight

Today, Ana Flavia's vision of a refuge for LGBTQ youth is thriving: the shelter serves more than 3,000 people per year. Among their services, they address food insecurity, legal needs, psychological and spiritual accompaniment, rights education, and empowerment meetings. They also work to address the high rates of HIV among young Trans people.

Ana Flavia decided to run for Peruvian Congress in 2020. Out of a field of five candidates, she came in second, trailing the leader by only three votes. However, because Ana Flavia is recognized only as male under Peruvian law, she was unable to take advantage of a Peruvian law which promotes women's participation in politics. This law would have allowed her to qualify as a candidate under the requirements for gender parity.

Ana Flavia also continues to challenge the everyday discrimination she experiences. This comes in all forms, In January of 2020, for example, she left her identifying documents at a government office—an office which she needed to go to as part of her work to address violence against the LGBTQ community. A government worker posted a picture of her identity document to social media mocking her identity as a Trans person. However, Ana Flavia saw the post and came back to confront the workers. As a result, the offending party lost their job,[5] and Ana Flavia and her organization met with the bosses in charge of the regional offices where this happened. According to the local paper (Montaño 2020):

> During the meeting, the approval of a regional ordinance that sanctions discrimination against LGBT people was also discussed, in addition to promoting the involvement of Trans people in the regional government. The following week there will be a meeting at the Social Development management to discuss the issue.

---

[5] https://larepublica.pe/sociedad/2020/01/31/activista-lgtb-sufre-discriminacion-en-gobierno-regional-de-arequipa-lrsd

This strategy—vocally denouncing discrimination, protesting, and meeting with state officials–is Ana Flavia's approach to confronting the national law that regards being Trans as a mental illness as well. She plans to sue in courts, pursuing strategic litigation to hopefully establish precedent.

> *Ana Flavia*: "We're going to have to continue to publicize what happens to us– we have to say it every time, re-say it, and at the same time extend this strategic litigation that can help the international community to put pressure on the government."

For Ana Flavia, this is what being a Trans activist entails: "Putting one's body; one's back, into the struggle." She continues:

> *Ana* Flavia: "I think being a Trans activist means that you will suffer, with the hope that others won't suffer from it. In a country where there is...no real objective exercise of the law...this is how it has to be, right? And, and in being so unprotected, I feel that I have assumed a role of exposing myself...where with one hand I receive all that violence, and with the other I also shoot back at them to say – 'And what's in it for my Trans sisters?'...I strive for a Peru where we're all free from violence; I strive for a Peru in which Trans Peruvians stop just surviving – but in which they can live and thrive!"

REFERENCES

Berrios, M. (2023, May 21). *Un defensor del pueblo a la medida de la contrarreforma que impulsa el Congreso*. Ojo Público. https://ojo-publico.com/politica/un-defensor-la-medida-la-contrarreforma-que-impulsa-el-congreso

Farrell, G. (2021, June 21). *The State of LGBTQ+ Rights in Latin America | Wilson Center*. Retrieved July 7, 2024, from https://www.wilsoncenter.org/blog-post/state-lgbtq-rights-latin-america-0

Glatsky, G., & Taj, M. (2024, May 26). Peru Issued a Decree Calling Trans Identity a 'Disorder.' A Backlash Followed. *The New York Times*. https://www.nytimes.com/2024/05/26/world/americas/peru-transgender-mental-health.html

González Cabrera, C. (2024a, May 15). *Peru Chooses Bigotry in Medical Services | Human Rights Watch*. https://www.hrw.org/news/2024/05/15/peru-chooses-bigotry-medical-services

González Cabrera, C. (2024b, June 27). *Peru Walks Back Anti-Trans Guidance in Health System | Human Rights Watch.* https://www.hrw.org/news/2024/06/27/peru-walks-back-anti-trans-guidance-health-system

Montaño, F. (2020, January 31). *Activista LGTB sufre discriminación en gobierno regional de Arequipa | lrsd | Sociedad | La República.* https://larepublica.pe/sociedad/2020/01/31/activista-lgtb-sufre-discriminacion-en-gobierno-regional-de-arequipa-lrsd

Parillo, Erard (2015, June 15). *Joven transexual denuncia a discoteca ante INDECOPI by VistaLibre—Issuu.* (2015, June 17). https://issuu.com/vistalibre/docs/1edi_240_vljun2015

Peru protesters slam new insurance law that deems transgender people mentally ill. (2024, May 18). *Reuters.* https://www.reuters.com/world/americas/peru-protesters-slam-new-insurance-law-that-deems-transgender-people-mentally-2024-05-18/

CHAPTER 6

Practices of Love and Care in the Women's Advocacy Network, Northern Uganda

Fatuma Abiya and Erin Baines

INTRODUCTION

In considering the question, "what does it mean to fight for women's rights in the 21st century?" we decided to foreground practices of love and care in the Women's Advocacy Network (WAN), a grassroots collective of conflict-affected women in northern Uganda. The two decade war between the government of Uganda under President Yoweri Museveni and the non-state armed group that eventually came to be called the Lord's Resistance Army (LRA) morphed into a transnational one, with militias, community defense councils, foreign intervention, and state and non-state alliances fighting by proxy (1986–2006).

The LRA's main "recruitment" strategy was to abduct men, women, and children to labor for and fight in their army. In LRA bases in Sudan, girls and women were forced into marriage with senior LRA commanders and to bear children. It is estimated upward of 65,000 persons were

F. Abiya
Youth Advocacy Network-Uganda, Gulu, Uganda

E. Baines (✉)
University of British Columbia, Vancouver, BC, Canada
e-mail: baines7@mail.ubc.ca

© The Author(s), under exclusive license to Springer Nature Switzerland AG 2025
J. Zulver, K. Stallone (eds.), *Brave Women*,
https://doi.org/10.1007/978-3-031-70702-5_6

abducted by 2008, the majority children and youth (Pham et al. 2008). Where so many people had suffered at the hands of the LRA, survivors and their children are often blamed for their actions and so face discrimination and exclusion, leaving them on their own to rebuild their worlds with their children. Close to 20 years after the end of the war, and despite various international and national court trials and humanitarian programs, the survivors continue to live precarious lives. The lack of housing and land for farming, food and economic insecurity, discrimination and stigma, and chronic illness, disabilities, and impairments compose the landscape of daily struggles in post-conflict Uganda. Evelyn Amony, a survivor of abduction, forced marriage and pregnancy and held in LRA captivity for 11 years, co-founded WAN to collectivize survivors as a way to support one another and to advocate for reparations. "Even if you have gone through difficult challenges, you can still do something good." Amony reflects and continues, "It doesn't stop you from moving forward with life... *You don't just give up on life*." By bringing women together as a collective, WAN provides a space in which to dream.

WAN members demand accountability from government officials, the military, and the men who harmed them. They travel back and forth to Kampala, the capital city of Uganda, countless times to speak to Ugandan officials, members of civil society, and representatives of the United Nations. They endlessly call for justice and reparation for their "time lost" and for their children (Anyeko 2021). They have traveled to Kinshasa, the Hague, New York, Geneva, Lagos, Freetown, and Nairobi to meet other survivors to collectively think of strategies for realizing justice and reparation. Despite ongoing political resistance to their efforts and the exhaustion of living in the margins, they keep moving, asking questions, insisting on answers, and looking for solutions. This endurance is nourished by their efforts to support each other when they are down and to celebrate one another's accomplishments, such as when their children graduate from school or they marry. The refusal to "give up on life" is a transformative praxis and insistence on reckoning. Love is a radical act of self and collective transformation and the fuel to keep *moving* (hooks 1989). It births and sustains *movements* seeking social justice and political accountability.

To prepare this chapter, Fatuma and Erin met to reflect on the ways WAN members flourish in the company of one another and on how the labors of love and care amplify their advocacy. This is the first time we have written together, but we have known each other since the early 2000s both in and through the relationships with the women of WAN. We write as witnesses and supporters and from different social locations and positions. Fatuma holds a deeply personal connection to WAN as a daughter of the collective and youth advocate for women's and youth rights. She was born to a mother abducted by the LRA and spent the first eight years of her life inside the armed group until their escape in the early 2000s. Fatuma's mother was one of the first members of WAN, founded in 2012. Accompanying her mother to those early meetings, she witnessed their efforts first-hand. As she grew into a young adult, she began to assume new responsibilities, helping them organize livelihood projects such as bead making and tailoring, and representing the organization in workshops related to questions of justice. As a child born of forced marriage, she often faced unique barriers herself, and slowly she and other youth with a shared experience formed the Youth Advocacy Network, housed at WAN.

Erin is a Canadian researcher who has collaborated with Evelyn Amony and WAN on documentation, advocacy, and memory projects for close to 15 years (Amony 2015; Baines 2017). Such projects center research as relational, fostering reciprocal and respectful relationships over time (Baines, with Amony and Okot, 2024) and working with communities to co-create research of relevance to their lived experiences. Collaboratively, we consider the complexity of victimhood and justice, everyday acts of social repair, and the transformative possibilities of story and storytelling. Such efforts are focused on different communities affected by war, including working with fathers to children born in the LRA, persons with disabilities, the mothers, their children, and families of the missing. These research efforts come together with other war-affected groups in partnerships with social movements and grassroots groups globally and have resulted in not only academic enrichment, but amplification of stories through knowledge exchanges, international delegations, and museum and art exhibitions.

Just as our relationship to one another and to WAN grew over time, so did our sense of responsibility to the stories we were told, including the desire to respond to their call to "do something," and to practice a "loving accountability" (Boer Cueva et al. 2024, 17–19). We write with commitment to a feminist politics that centers the lived experiences and knowledges of women who exist in the margins of war's end and engages with a transformative praxis of "radical compassion" (Olufemi 2020, 7). We draw on our memories, feelings, and encounters with women, some captured in our notebooks and others that live in our hearts.

In this chapter, we begin with WAN's origins under the shade of a mango tree and how care and love manifest in the everyday labor of being there for one another. Next, we consider how savings and loan initiatives and livelihood projects—in particular bead making and tailoring—not only provide resources but strengthen relationships and do reparative work. In the following section, we consider how practices of love and care manifest in the responsibilities of motherhood and in relation to their children. We then highlight moments of joy and celebration embraced by the women, such as births, weddings, or when a loved one who was missing is found. Love and care, we argue, birth movements and open portals to different ways of being together. In lieu of a conclusion, we present the Petition to the Ugandan Parliament filed by WAN in 2014. These are the stories of brave women in the twenty-first century.

Stories Under the Mango Tree

Fatuma: When women finally escaped the LRA, they painfully had little to call their own. It was hard to find work as many had lost the opportunity to study and equip themselves with the skills to acquire jobs. There was no land, as lineage and land rights customarily go through the man's side. Many felt alone. Their relatives had died when they were in captivity or scattered across the nation following the displacement of 1.8 million persons during the war. Others were rejected by their own relatives. Their very own mothers and fathers called them "evil" and accused them of being rebels. Some women were accepted back into their families but their children were not, and they were told to take them to orphanages. Many mothers say their children are their cowrie of hope, the reason for their optimism for the future. Thus, they decided to settle in the town areas and hustle for their children alone day and night just to live and breathe.

To support one another in livelihood, a small group of formerly abducted women started a savings and loan group called Rwot Lakica (God is Merciful). This group would later go on to create WAN. The idea of coming together as a group came to the women after they realized no one was going to rescue them. It was time for them to get on their feet, get together, and support each other. Rwot Lakica used to meet every Saturday in Kirombe, a small village in Gulu District. I would go with my mom to help them. During the meetings the women made beautiful beaded necklaces, bracelets, and sewed purses and dresses to sell. As they worked, they told each other stories about what each had suffered during captivity and how life was at home. They realized that they were facing similar challenges: a shortage of housing, illness and impairments, and traumatic memories. One of the things that hurt them the most was the experience of stigma and rejection by their families and the members of the community. What people did not understand was what the women had suffered during captivity, how they were beaten and even killed for failing to obey the LRA's rules. They felt traumatized by the past and this was compounded by the rejection. They felt lonely and lived in poverty without the support of their families. Some tried to marry and start a new life; however, their children were also rejected by the newly found husbands. Many endured domestic violence. I must say that so many difficult stories were told during these meetings, but the healing process started in this group.

Between the ages of eight and ten years old, I used to sneak into the Saturday meetings like a thief. Children were not allowed to attend the meetings as the subject matter was too big for our ears. Even when some of the women came with their children, they were sent to play far away from the meeting. I was that stubborn child who did not follow the rules. I was so desperate to hear what the mothers would be discussing every week. They used to send me to bring drinking water and other things during the meetings, but after the first time overhearing their stories, I told myself that I would never miss another one. My mother would chase me away, but I kept on sneaking back, sitting behind the very mango tree where they gathered to work and talk. There, I sat and listened to them tell their stories, cry bitterly, and support each other. When they cried, I cried with them and when they laughed, I laughed with them. I wished I could have helped them. I wish I could have gone to their husbands and told them to stop beating them, but I was still a child. It was here that I found the drive to study hard and vowed to become a lawyer and a human rights activist. I told myself that I will fight for these women and protect their rights for as long as I live.

Brave women inspire brave women. Today I am living out this dream. I study law in Kampala, but I continue to return home to support them. Every moment I spend with them, I tell them that they are the most beautiful of God's Creation, that they are enough, and that they are very strong. I have made it my duty to tell them about their rights as women and as human beings. I am proud to say that the women are no longer the same as when they started meeting under the mango tree in Kirombe.

Erin: I met some of the women who returned with children, including Fatuma and her mother, in one of the rehabilitation centers that had been established to help those who escaped to become healthy again as they located and attempted to reunite them with their families. With the Justice and Reconciliation Project, we designed a methodology of storytelling to document women's gendered experiences of abduction and life on return. Before long, our devotion to working and learning with the women transformed into nearly two decades of collaboration. Working with Ketty Anyeko, Evelyn Amony and I met with Rwot Lakica in the late 2000s and proposed the project, *Ododo Wa*—our stories—to foster exchange among women in the group around their experiences of life in the LRA and since escape (Anyeko and Hoffmann 2020). Under the shade of the mango tree, they began to narrate stories and make connections between their experiences. Members agreed to record their storytelling sessions based on different thematic topics they collectively chose to narrate in the group. They expressed a satisfaction in the project, which they described as a sense of relief, source of meaning-making, and generator of unity and common purpose. It also forged relations of love and care that inspired other women. Word of Rwot Lakica's storytelling and power spread, and soon more women approached and asked to join the group. Rwot Lakica grew until it was suggested new groups form in different communities, and so the Women's Advocacy Network came into being in 2012. After *Ododo Wa* as a research project was completed, Anyeko and I gave each participant a copy of a life history book and we continued to collaborate to support the formation of WAN, accompany them in advocacy, and join them in the process of learning through exchange and reciprocity in research projects. Today, WAN employs different strategies of seeking "to make a life for themselves" as a radical act of survival and imagination which we explore below (Photo 6.1).

Strategies of Love and Care

Fatuma and Erin: Many of the women in WAN were once strangers to one another until they found themselves facing the same circumstances after their escape. They are not related by blood, but they love and support each other as if they all breastfed from the same mother. As relatives, they hold certain accountabilities to one another, such as the responsibility

Photo 6.1 An example of WAN's bead and needlework. Gulu, Uganda. (Attributed to Diana Ajok, used with permission, 2023)

to call on one another when they are struggling and the responsibility of members to respond to that call. Should a member's relative pass away, for instance, WAN will call for an emergency meeting of members to discuss a way forward. It is not compulsory but it is a culture in the WAN that each member will make a contribution to help the family in pain. After everyone has made their personal offering according to their means, then WAN as an organization will make the largest contribution. These offerings can be in the form of money, food, or other commodities. Most members live modestly, on or under the poverty line, but this does not stop them from supporting their colleagues in dire times and doing what they can.

Some women find that they do not have food to feed their children at the end of the day. In such situations, members contribute food and money and it is given to rescue their sisters. Sometimes the committee passes a rule that everyone will contribute a certain amount of food for a member who is badly off. For example, the committee can say that everyone must contribute two cups of beans or two kgs of flour, and everyone who is able will make that offering to save a colleague. WAN members will help organize funerals, cooking, cleaning, and caring for children. Most importantly, they offer comfort and give hope to their sisters. Women from different families, who met during captivity, now hold each other, cry with each other, and remind each other of the battles they have already won.

Visitation by members is one of the strongest tools used by the WAN women when supporting one another. Usually, all members go to visit each other in difficult times, however sometimes members are selected by the group to comfort their peers. For example, if the group has been informed about a situation where one member is going through a family conflict such as domestic violence, members are selected by the organization to go to said families to find out more about the situation. The family sits down, and the conflict is resolved. In cases where a conflict cannot be resolved, a report is brought back to the group where members come up with other ways to solve the problem, such as involving other leaders. WAN members therefore are leaders and mediators. Each response to a person in need is an act of love and care.

Talking and sharing among themselves when they are down helps the women heal and grow. For Margaret, "Had it not been for my sisters from this group, I would have committed suicide long time ago. Listening to people who went through the same horrible past and are still fighting gives you more reasons not to give up." For Monica, "When I lost my son, my sisters from WAN stood by me even more than my own family members. I cannot imagine life without WAN."

Members of WAN refer to each other as sisters. You often hear someone say that in their case, water is thicker than blood and that they feel closer to one another than their own relatives because of the bond they share based on what they went through in captivity. In 2019, Fatuma and Erin traveled to Palaro to meet WAN members and learn how belonging to the network shaped their lives. We met Christine who recalled meeting Evelyn, shortly after her escape from the LRA.

> When I had just returned from captivity, I was so lonely, without anyone acknowledging my presence. But because of the strong relationship that we had from captivity, the Chairperson came all the way from Gulu town [after learning I had escaped]…she didn't know [the whereabouts of] our home, but used to hear from captivity that our home is in Palaro. She took her own time to come and fin[d] me but unfortunately, she failed to find me because [I was away]. She came again the second time to find me. We are not related but we knew each other from captivity. She sent a message to me that I should come and meet her and I responded by coming and meeting her. She

found me in a very poor state. I couldn't sit alone and I could not imagine that I would be alive to-date and I believe that when she looks at me today, she is so grateful for her efforts. I had nothing completely; she started calling me, advising me and including me in the group, pulled her own money and gave it to me to buy clothes and yet she is not related to me. This made me conclude that we who have returned from captivity are all related to one another, we are brothers and sisters.

The love and care between WAN members make life and the struggle to reclaim it possible when so many other forces align to render life impossible. Listening to Christine above, we began to understand how such interpersonal relationships culminate into a collective force, and as such, how they challenge structures of oppression and dispossession that would rather they disappear. It is the love that they have for each other and their children that keeps them breathing. It teaches their children to keep moving. Fatuma reflects "I grew up seeing these women; I grew up hearing some of them say, 'I can't do this anymore'." And their friends saying "we know you can do it."

In their work with communities affected by conflict and displacement in Uganda and Colombia, respectively, Roxani Krystalli and Philip Schulz (2022) argue love and care should be taken seriously by scholars. Some of the problematics of the study of war is the reproduction of categories that erase the complexity of life, the agency of persons who live with the memories of war, and the reduction of their experiences to that of a suffering victim. By centering love and care, we might measure a new kind of politics and "illuminate different pathways for understanding the remaking of worlds in the wake of violence" (2022, 3), as well as approximate an understanding of how people "make sense of and respond to violence as well as imagine and enact a life in the wake of it." Inspired by bell hooks, love is an action of care, accountability, and reciprocity and so is entangled in the constellations of relationships and relationalities that make such acts meaningful in material and affective ways. Of course, such acts take the shape of the landscapes they are situated within, but the concept of love and care take us toward the entanglement of emotions, actions, and practices that make life possible. Despite the devastation of violence, or perhaps because of it, love and care endure as sites of refusal, or remembering, and of forging new pathways to the future.

Through our own scholarly and activist work, we have understood love and care as the assumption of responsibility for one another, where one person comes into being in relation to others to whom they are held to account and to whom others are accountable. For instance, the efforts of the mothers to make a life for their children through communal livelihood projects or in joining the effort to support someone who has just escaped the LRA, as many are only now returning home with children. If a political act, it is one of refusal. It is to say, I do not accept this. Through stories and storytelling, women demarcate what was possible and not possible within the LRA and clarify that the actions they took *were never* taken in agreement with the LRA's murderous agenda, but to live another day, to tell their stories of what happened and to call for a reckoning for the future of Uganda. As such, the concept of love and care offers ways to think with a transformative praxis of memory for the future.

Bead and Needle Work

Fatuma and Erin: WAN began with small-scale community savings and income generation activities, including making paper beads for the design of jewelry and needlework, sewing and tailoring. Small loans are another way women support each other in WAN. There are two types of loans. One is given to members by the organization, and members are expected to pay it back after a specific period of time with a very small interest rates lower than those of other institutions such as banks. Another type of loan pools together members' savings to support mothers facing economic challenges. For example, when it is time to pay school fees, most WAN women borrow from a member who has some money and later pay it back in installments. These types of loans have also helped in times of sickness. People borrow from each other to pay hospital and other related medical bills. Most members live in grass thatched huts, and so fires are always a possibility. In such cases, members are the first to pool together resources to replace what was lost and to get a mother and her children back on their feet. The beauty of such loans and emergency funds is that one does not have to pay interest. Loans have lifted so many women in northern Uganda.

Most of the women are gifted in different technical jobs such as tailoring, bead making, shoe making, and others; members are resourceful when it comes to helping one another find the products and services required for such enterprises. When the Chairperson is invited to attend any conference within or outside the district, she always informs members to bring some of their products (like the beads and other crafts) to sell. She takes samples of these products, sells them, and the money is given to the different product owners. These efforts have supported WAN members multiple times. When a member is given an order to make certain items in large quantities, she will inform all members, especially those who are experts in making said items. They then work together and share the income equally. For Florence, "sometimes when I have totally lost hope, I get a call from one of my sisters in WAN that there is work. Certainly, I start breathing differently." The ability of these women to remember one another every time they get such opportunities is generous and life-giving. The network the women have built among themselves is so powerful and unique. It is important to understand that building a network starts from where they are. Before one looks at people in other places, the question is: how do you build up and support those around you?

Erin: As we started writing this chapter together, I was reading Sadiya Hartman's (2019) *Wayward Lives, Beautiful Experiments*, a speculative writing on the life worlds of young Black women who moved to urban areas in Philadelphia and New York at the start of the twentieth century. Hartman writes against an archive that contains Black life by reducing it to a social problem and moral threat. She thinks about women's efforts to prepare for "the good life" and the desire to "get ready for freedom" (2019, 24) in the space of the urban slum. She writes of beauty as "a way of creating possibility in the space of enclosure; a radical act of creation" (33). I shared this with Fatuma, and we began to think about the radical possibilities of bead and needle work, how it offers a space apart from the grind of daily life for the women to converse with one another, share their doubts, and strike a plan to resolve problems. Such work might also be thought of as moments to be free, to concentrate on the craft, to take one's mind away from what once was, to dream of what might be. Savings and loans and income generation are often entangled in the sterile and detached language of development, humanitarian aid, and empowerment, but they are also made of hope, and the desire to feel less alone and to be part of something greater than one's self.

Inspired by Hartman, I thought about the Beading Memory Tapestry created by WAN members over six months in 2022 using thousands of hand-rolled beads, each stitched on an 8x6 foot piece of black fabric to compose a testimonial tapestry of their experiences at the hands of the LRA. I think of how they made something beautiful out of such painful memories and use beads—the stuff of their livelihood—to document the undocumented and as a reminder to others that missing persons are still missing. I think of bead and needle work as grieving and a way to remember those who did not survive. I think of it as an expression of solidarity and love for one another. I think of it as rewriting the archive for the future. From the artist's statement, "We tell our stories so that our children will know what we went through, and so that they will tell their children" (The Lobby Gallery 2023).

Fatuma and Erin: The practice of textile making, beading, embroidery, or weaving is commonly devalued as "women's busy work," but globally, the craft is repurposed by women to safely visualize memories of mass violence. After decades of occupation, guerilla warfare, and civil war, women in Afghanistan repurposed the art of handmade carpets—a craft that is passed from mother to daughter–to offer testimony, often with a sense of irony and humor. Anonymous, the carpets are sold on international markets, amplifying their stories. Women's feminized labor becomes political even as the carpet makers remain anonymous (Moallem 2018). Maddalena Tacchetti et al. (2023, 3) argue that textile making by Afro-Colombian and Indigenous women in Bojayá (Chocó), Mampuján (Montes de María), and Sonsón (Antioquia) are a form of memory labour and testimony giving that enact a loving reparation by "reclaiming socio-ecological damages in their communities and repairing injured socio-environmental ecologies through mundane processes and practices of care and solidarity." As a practice, weaving is a process of co-becoming and transformation of the tapestry and the weavers, where lived, felt, embodied, and sensed ways of knowing and being come into relation. Thinking with Coroma and Mampuján textiles woven in the Andes, Arlene Tickner and Amaya Querejazu (2021, 403–4) suggest:

> woven textiles illustrate their caring role in sustaining life in a broad sense: they are a source of material sustenance when sold, they support the emotional well-being of those who weave them, they nurture the collective 'social fabric,' and they help to maintain the life of the cosmos. Understood as a vehicle for relating and for making kin, care is also a 'vital requisite' in 'interdependent worlds,' (Puig de la Bellacasa 2012, 97) that acts to connect and to entwine being, feeling, knowing, and doing.

Weaving is not only a site for political contest and worldbuilding, but a way of coming to know other worlds. Tickner and Querejazu suggest the labors of textiles teach us "how to think about relations, how to relate in a pluriverse characterized by multiplicity, variation, and interdependence, and more significantly, how to communicate carefully and respectfully with other worlds even when we are unable to understand or even see them completely." This transforms the work of the academic from a Western-centric framework that reproduces categorical, binary, and abstract theory to one that is grounded and calls for a practice of "care and loving accountability" (Boer Cueva et al. 2024), rooted in emancipatory projects and commitments to political transformation.

Motherhood

Fatuma: Among the mothers of WAN, one child belongs to everyone. It is a culture among women to look out for each other and protect each other's children. When a WAN member finds the child of another misbehaving on the streets, it is her duty to call them out and discipline them. If children are disrespectful toward people in the community, the Chairperson calls a meeting with members and the parents to find a different way. If it's beyond her, then she can invite other members who are good at talking to such children and together they help change the lives of many children. Children born in captivity face many challenges, such as stigma and hostility from the community. People call us terrible names. Imagine parents beating their children just because they were found playing with children who were born in captivity, children like me. At school, every time there was a dispute involving a child born in captivity, we were considered guilty from the beginning. We do not know how to respond to such hostility. So many children end up becoming cold and others are rude to everyone, including their own parents. They feel like the whole world has rejected them.

In such situations, the mothers of the children inform other members about their children's behavior and members are selected to talk to the children. Some children drop out of school, but through the assistance of the members of WAN, they have been able to go back to school and their mothers are happy again. Sometimes children threaten to kill themselves because of a difficult home life. In those cases, women in better situations take them in as they heal from the pain—they help them go to school in other cities so they can start again. My own mother has taken in and cared for so many children as her own. The children of WAN are now becoming farmers, small business owners, nurses, pharmacists, social workers and lawyers. The work of care succeeds when a child realizes their dreams.

The Acholi society is a patriarchal one—therefore, children belong to the paternal family and it is the duty of every woman to ensure their children know their male relatives (Kiconco 2021). Knowing the paternal family means the child has an identity and will gain respect. Yet for the most part, LRA commanders never revealed their identity. Most of the women come back without knowing the family of the people who made them mothers. The challenges that come with a lack of land and identity led WAN members to engage in collective action. Members of WAN went to Ugandan military bases to ask for help, as so many former LRA commanders have now joined the military. Perhaps their pay could be docked to pay for child support?

These are some of the reasons why WAN members work hard to identify the paternal families of their children (Mutsonziwa et al. 2020). This process is locally referred to as child tracing, one that requires a maximum level of collectivity. WAN calls upon the network of women to help identify who the paternal clans are, and once this is established, they pull together a committee to meet the paternal families with the aim to unify them with their son's children. WAN members provide important testimony to the relationship that existed between the child's father and the mother and attest to the birth of the child. During meetings with paternal relatives, many issues arise. For example, a child may be rejected and told there is no land or space for them. It is the duty of the members of WAN to mediate the process and make sure that there is peace and joy at the end of the day. Where the mother or child is unable to talk for themselves, other women stand in for them. When an agreement is made by the paternal relatives to recognize and assume responsibility for the child/ren, celebrations are generally followed through overnight feast, dancing, and storytelling. We interpret these courageous, complicated efforts as working toward transformative justice to secure the future of their children (Baines and Oliveira 2021; Baines and Anyeko 2023).

On some occasions, children born in captivity escape alone, they are separated from their mother and father without information on who they were or how to find relatives. In such cases, a member will volunteer to foster the child, recognizing it could have been their lost child. Evelyn explains their connection with mothers who are still missing: "those are our sisters….and it is our responsibility to support their children in their absence." In the act of caring for another's child, the women's mourning is transformed into love. Motherhood as a praxis of love is the assumption of responsibility for all those who lost during the war. To date, WAN's membership grows to include other war-affected persons in need of belonging. Motherhood is more than blood. It is the love extended to their children and the children of the missing in the simple, but radical act of giving encouragement as they make their way through this world.

Joy and Celebration

Fatuma: There is nothing more joyous to every WAN member than the birth of a new baby. Children are referred to as one of the best gifts by God. The women understand the importance of this gift more than anyone else, and this is why the celebration is taken to another level. When a woman gives birth to a child, the women inform each other through text messages or by going door to door. Members then organize themselves to pay a visit to the new mother and baby at the hospital. They buy gifts for both the baby and the mother. Other women prepare for the baby's arrival at the mother's home, where they collect water and do domestic work to ensure the home is kept very clean. The compound is swept and all the rubbish is collected and burned. Some women volunteer to be in charge of bathing the baby, while others are in charge of bathing the baby's mother. A mother is treated like a queen when she has just given birth. Everything is done for her. This is a way of welcoming the new baby.

One cannot ignore weddings when talking about moments of joy and celebration among the women of WAN. Marriage is a commitment between two people who both desire and *choose* one another. People fall in love with the people they want and get married—whether religiously or traditionally—and as they deem fit. WAN celebrates women who get married to the people they desire, a right stolen away from them when they were forced to marry in captivity.

When a member announces her engagement, people come together, starting from the preparation activities and extending to the last day. Members make contributions in the form of money and food, and others provide services such as cooking, the organization of the event, and performances such as dances and songs to entertain the guests. Others are assigned to dress the bride and make her the most beautiful woman of the day. Some members volunteer while others are selected by the women to be maids of honor. Witnessing the same people who you went through the most difficult moments of your life with walk beside you in ceremony, supporting you, and making your day a memorable one means so much. The bride and groom are blessed with so many gifts, which may even consist of utensils, money, clothes, and others items to start a home. After the wedding, some members may stay with the bride for a few days, singing, dancing, and making that occasion unforgettable.

A deep wounding of the people in northern Uganda is the fact that so many people who were abducted by rebels are still missing. The International Committee of the Red Cross (ICRC) estimates that at least 10,000 people are still missing from northern Uganda. No word can explain the joy the women get when someone who has been missing returns. Each time a person comes back, everyone is happy. Members immediately organize to meet and to visit them, and later on the new women are also welcomed to WAN.

Erin: For bell hooks (2001), love is a site of the political, a remaking of community animated through relationships and an ethics of care in preparation for the struggle against intersecting forces of oppression. Darnell L. Moore (2018) helps draw the link by reflecting on Black love in the United States: "At the root of Black resistance – the collective struggle through which we might imagine and build a world more just, more free, more equitable, more magical – is love. Nothing but an unwavering love for Black people can catalyze and sustain the protracted struggle for Black liberation and its various iterations across time, like the contemporary movement for Black lives."

Love activates a sense of responsibility for the wellness of another implies a process of transformation and insists on a way of being together that upholds one another, "you just can't give up." At the root of WAN's struggle for reparations (Anyeko 2021) are everyday acts of love woven into tapestries, the joy of newness, and the struggle of living through another day.

Fatuma: If there is something I have learned from WAN it is that, we should not just sit and wait, we have to fight for our rights but keep in mind that, one hand cannot fight this battle alone. We need to work together as one. Fighting for the rights of women requires quite a lot of work but *it is possible*. Following the mass abduction of Chibok girl students by the non-state armed group Boko Harem in Nigeria, WAN wrote a letter to the survivors. "We were once you," one member reflected, before sharing where they have reached now, and a desire for them to take hope. Each time WAN members meet someone newly released at home, or travel to meet other survivors across the world, they do so in anticipation of another world, they are inspired and inspiring. Their strength transcends the urgency of daily survival and grows as it crosses new borders and links to other brave women.

Coda

Fatuma and Erin: By way of conclusion, we present WAN's Petition to the Ugandan Parliament drafted over several months of dialogue across WAN's membership in 2014, and arriving at a set of agreements and their travel to Kampala to present it in person. The day was a joyous one, with a sense of accomplishment they had reached this far, and were united in their demands. To date, there have been many studies, consultations, and presentations on reparations in Uganda with the mothers, and new funds and strategies have been planned. Policy change is slow and promises remain unfulfilled, but WAN is undeterred. They continue knowing love grows relationships, strengthens ties, and makes the work of activism a powerful force that cannot be stayed.

Women's Advocacy Network Petition to Uganda Parliament

February 24, 2014.
To: The Chairperson, Uganda Women Parliamentarians' Association (UWOPA).
Cc:

1. The Rt. Hon. Rebecca Alitwala Kadaga, Speaker of Parliament of the Republic of Uganda Kampala -Uganda.
2. The Acholi Parliamentarians' Association.

PETITION BY WOMEN'S ADVOCACY NETWORK TO THE PARLIAMENT OF THE REPUBLIC OF UGANDA SEEKING ITS INTERVENTION IN ADDRESSING ISSUES AND CHALLENGES FACED BY WAR AFFECTED WOMEN IN THE ACHOLI SUB REGION.
Madam Chairperson,
This humble petition is submitted pursuant to rule 29 of the rules of procedure of the Parliament of the Republic of Uganda.
Women's Advocacy Network on behalf of war affected women in the Acholi sub region presents this petition to you. We are seeking your support to lobby for the intervention of Parliament of the Republic of Uganda to address issues and challenges faced by war affected women in the Acholi sub region.

Madam Chairperson, we acknowledge and are appreciative of the efforts and input of this August House in articulating and bringing to the fore the issues and concerns of the people of Northern Uganda who have been greatly affected in all spheres of life by the conflict that spanned over twenty (20) years. We are especially appreciative of the role UWOPA continues to play to ensure women issues are taken into consideration and their rights are upheld in Uganda.

Madam Chairperson, we were adversely affected by the conflict between the LRA and Government in Northern Uganda. Some of us were abducted, tortured, raped, mutilated, forced to become wives of rebel commanders, provided forced labor in rebel camps and were also forcefully conscripted to engage in combat. We were forced to bear children under harsh and deplorable conditions. As a result, we developed health complications such as gynecological problems, chronic back problems, gunshot wounds and were exposed to traumatic experiences. We also gave birth to children in captivity who are being ostracized by the communities we live in.

Madam Chairperson, those of us who escaped abduction were forced to live in deplorable conditions in the Internally Displaced Peoples (IDP's) camps where we were often targeted for rape and sexual exploitation. We contracted HIV/AIDS as a result and also bore children out of rape. We continue to bear the burden of looking after our immediate and extended families in absence of our husbands who were killed in the conflict or are still missing and are unaccounted for.

Our current status Madam Chairperson, majority of us do not know the identity of the fathers of our children since the LRA commanders who sexually enslaved and abused us in captivity used pseudonyms, while the few whose identities are known, have refused to pay maintenance for the children they forced us to bear. We continue to face rejection and stigmatization from an embittered community and families that are not ready to accept children fathered by rebels.

Madam Chairperson, while most of the male combatants were integrated in the army and receive a monthly stipend, there was no such mechanism for the support and reintegration of the female victims apart from the amnesty package which did not take into consideration the children we came back with from captivity. We find ourselves re-victimized and forced to live in deplorable conditions.

Madam Chairperson, we are also vulnerable economically, socially, physically and psychologically. We missed out on opportunities of going to school and wasted a lot of our productive years in captivity. This hinders us from accessing formal employment, yet we live in a society where it is difficult for women to access land. This has relegated us to casual jobs that do not pay very well in spite of our everyday burdens and challenges inclusive of the cardinal responsibility of looking after our children that were born in captivity.

Madam Chairperson, we as Women's Advocacy Network are not sitting down and wallowing in our pain and misery but rather doing our part in our small ways to alleviate the challenges we are facing. We continue to hold dialogues in our communities aimed at reconciliation, fighting stigma and reintegration.

Madam Chairperson, we are confident of the role that the Parliament of the Republic of Uganda plays in addressing issues that affect the citizens of Uganda and are assured that our concerns will be discussed by the August house. Therefore, as the Women's Advocacy Network on behalf of war affected women in the Acholi sub-region, we request you to lobby the Parliament of the Republic of Uganda to:

- Adopt a comprehensive reparations policy that will help us alleviate most of our problems related to our social economic status thus reducing our vulnerability. The proposed reparations policy should offer individual and collective reparations to female survivors of this conflict as well as acknowledge, repair the harms suffered, restore our dignity and recognise our rights as citizens of this country. The proposed reparations policy should offer free accessible health care tailored to address women's health issues, livelihood skills to help us recover lost education opportunities and compensation for lost time.
- Prioritize the creation of an urgent gender reparations fund to cater for the immediate needs of war- affected women.
- Recommend for increased budgetary provisions for health services in war-affected areas, to ensure accessibility to reproductive and mental health services especially for children and women affected by the war.
- Recommend for increased budgetary allocation to the education sector to cater for war affected children in the Acholi sub region and particularly children born in captivity. This allocation should also be used to train teachers on how to handle such children that may be experiencing trauma and other conditions related to their past.
- Call for an accelerated finalization of the National Transitional Justice Policy and the establishment of a sound legal framework with

comprehensive, adequate and sustainable mechanisms which are key in addressing the concerns of war affected women.
- Ensure that the National Transitional Justice Policy that will be adopted is holistic and will include mechanisms to ensure full participation of war affected women.
- Recognize the special and unique needs of the children born in captivity whose fathers and patrilineal heritage is unknown and request for a review of the laws that require information and documentation on paternity to be amended.
- Call for strengthening of the Acholi cultural institution because it was also affected by the conflict yet it is a trusted body that can play a big role in addressing the reconciliation needs of its people.

Chairperson, we are available whenever called upon to shade [sic] more light on issues encompassed in the Petition. We remain yours the undersigned.

Presented by the Women's Advocacy Network (WAN) under the auspices of the Justice and Reconciliation Project, P. O. Box 1216 Gulu. Tel – 0471433008. Email: info@justiceandreconciliation.com.

References

Amony, Evelyn. *I am Evelyn Amony: Reclaiming my life from the Lord's Resistance Army*. Edited by Erin Bains. University of Wisconsin Press, 2015.

Anyeko, Ketty. *Lived justice: women's senses of justice, reparations and decision-making after wartime sexual violence in northern Uganda*. Diss. University of British Columbia, 2021.

Anyeko, Ketty, and Tamara Shaya Hoffmann. "Storytelling and peacebuilding: Lessons from northern Uganda." *Peacebuilding and the Arts* (2020): 235–251.

Baines, Erin. *Buried in the heart: Women, complex victimhood and the war in northern Uganda*. Cambridge University Press, 2017.

Baines, Erin, and Camile Oliveira. "Securing the future: Transformative justice and children 'born of war'." *Social & Legal Studies* 30.3 (2021): 341–361.

Baines, Erin and Ketty Anyeko. 'The Secret War': Silence, Testimony and Wartime Sexual Violence, *International Journal*, 77(4) (2023) https://doi.org/10.1177/00207020231168900

Baines, Erin, with Evelyn Amony and Benard Okot. "Unspeakable: reflections on relational approaches to research in post-conflict settings." Peacebuilding 12.4 (2024): 463–482.

Boer Cueva, Alba Rosa, et al. "A Decolonial Feminist Politics of Fieldwork: Centering Community, Reflexivity, and Loving Accountability." *International Studies Review* 26.1 (2024): viae003.

hooks, bell. 1989. "Choosing the margin as a space of radical openness." *Framework: The Journal of Cinema and Media* 36: 15–23.

hooks, bell. 2001. *All about Love: New Visions.* New York: William Morrow.

Hartman, Saidiya. *Wayward lives, beautiful experiments: Intimate histories of riotous Black girls, troublesome women, and queer radicals.* WW Norton & Company, 2019.

Kiconco, Allen. Children born of wartime captivity and abuse: politics and practices of integration in northern Uganda. In *International Child Protection*, 101–119. Palgrave Macmillan, 2021.

Krystalli, Roxani, and Philipp Schulz. "Taking Love and Care Seriously: An Emergent Research Agenda for Remaking Worlds in the Wake of Violence." *International Studies* 24 (1), 2022.

Moallem, Minoo. "The Intangible Stories of War Carpets: War, Media, and Mediation." Edited by Harp, Dustin, Jaime Loke, and Ingrid Bachmann. *Feminist Approaches to Media Theory and Research*, Springer (2018): 257–269.

Moore, Darnell L. "Black Radical Love: A Practice." *Public Integrity* 20 (4), 2018: 325–328.

Mutsonziwa, Tinashe BC, Ketty Anyeko, and Erin Baines. "Child tracing: locating the paternal homes of "children born of war"." *Development in Practice* 30.5 (2020): 635–644.

Tacchetti, M., Chocontá-Piraquive, A., Quiceno Toro, N., & Papadopoulos, D. Memorial reparation: Women's work of remembrance, repair and restoration in rural Colombia. *Memory Studies*, 2023, https://doi.org/10.1177/17506980231188482.

Tickner, Arlene B., and Amaya Querejazu. "Weaving worlds: Cosmopraxis as relational sensibility." *International Studies Review* 23.2 (2021): 391–408.

Olufemi, Lola. 2020. *Feminism, Interrupted: Disrupting Power.* London: Pluto Press.

Pham, Phuong N., Patrick Vinck, and Eric Stover. "The Lord's Resistance Army and Forced Conscription in Northern Uganda." *Human Rights Quarterly* 30, no. 2 (2008): 404–11.

The Lobby Gallery, *Beading Memory Exhibit.* Artist Statement. Vancouver, BC, January 17–31, 2023.

CHAPTER 7

Feminist Activism in Exile: Burundi's *Mouvement Inamahoro*

Marie Louise Baricako and Miriam J. Anderson

INTRODUCTION

In 1996, I learned about a meeting taking place in Geneva to create an organization focussed on women's active leadership roles in conflict resolution in Africa.[1] I determined that "I must be at that meeting." So, I called the lady who was organizing it and I told her "Listen, whether you invite me and pay for my ticket or not, I will be part of that meeting!" She said to me: "Marie Louise, come." I knew that by myself, I could not change Burundi, but working through an Africa-wide NGO we could change things. Burundian society is patriarchal, and most of its leaders did not have the

[1] This was the founding meeting of the organization *Femmes Africa Solidarité* (FAS).

M. L. Baricako
Mouvement Inamahoro: Femmes et filles pour la paix et la sécurité, Butare, Rwanda

M. J. Anderson (✉)
Toronto Metropolitan University, Toronto, ON, Canada
e-mail: miriam.anderson@torontomu.ca

© The Author(s), under exclusive license to Springer Nature Switzerland AG 2025
J. Zulver, K. Stallone (eds.), *Brave Women*,
https://doi.org/10.1007/978-3-031-70702-5_7

vision, strong purpose, and commitment to lead the country. They confuse politics with leadership and instead see politics as a source of personal wealth – Marie Louise Baricako on the founding of *Femmes Africa Solidarité*.

Marie Louise Baricako, president of a Burundian women's organization in exile, *Mouvement Inamahoro: Mouvement des Femmes et des Filles pour la Paix et le Sécurité* (*Inamahoro* or the Movement),[2] has been a women's rights activist since 1996 with the founding of the Women's NGO *Femmes Africa Solidarité* (FAS) in Geneva. The organization has worked to empower women leaders across Africa to promote conflict resolution and peace. It has been instrumental in the adoption of the parity principle,[3] the promotion of Security Council Resolution 1325, as well as lobbying for women's participation in Burundi's peace process, standing beside them in solidarity and supporting them throughout the peace talks until 2000. As a result of Burundian women's efforts and the support of organizations, such as *Femmes Africaines Solidarité* and UNIFEM (now UN Women), women gained access as observers to the Arusha peace negotiations and held an all-women's peace conference in 2000 where they were able to influence the final peace agreement (Anderson 2016).

The peace process was a watershed moment for women in Burundi. Prior to the peace negotiations, there were around 12% female legislators (Inter-Parliamentary Union 1993), but following the peace talks, women's rights activists remained engaged, entering formal politics and successfully enshrining a 30% women's electoral quota in the 2005 Burundian constitution (Anderson and Valade 2023). Once in formal politics, they maintained tight linkages with civil society (Anderson and Valade 2023). The result was a strong voice for women in Burundian politics between 2000 and 2015.

In 2015, however, President Pierre Nkurunziza, supported by the ruling party, the CNDD-FDD, ran for a third term believed by many to violate the 2000 Arusha Accords and constitutional term limits (Daley and

---

[2] *Mouvement Inamahoro: Femmes et Filles pour la Paix et la Sécurité* was formerly known as the *Mouvement des Femmes et Filles pour la Paix et le sécurité au Burundi* (MFFPS). It split into two organizations in March 2020 with one group retaining the original name. In September 2020, the other group, headed by Marie Louise Baricako, renamed the organization *Mouvement Inamahoro: Femmes et Filles pour la Paix et la Sécurité*.

[3] The African Union (AU) committed to the gender parity principle in 2002 that men and women should have equal levels of descriptive representation in all organs of the AU (Peace Women: Women's International League for Peace and Freedom 2012).

Popplewell 2016; Vandeginste 2015). Resistance to the government's consolidation of power was met by the arrests of journalists, persecution of dissidents within the president's own party, intimidation, harassment and killing of human rights activists, establishing and arming of youth militias, the *Imbonerakure*, who kidnapped and handed over dissidents to Burundian intelligence services (Daley and Popplewell 2016; Purdeková 2017).[4]

High-level resistance included a failed coup attempt (Vandeginste 2015) and an unprecedented threat by the African Union to use force to protect civilians (Wilén and Williams 2018). Civil society groups participated in anti-government protests (Daley and Popplewell 2016) and women played a prominent role, in one case holding demonstrations in the center of the capital, Bujumbura, while protests were banned (Saiget 2020). Over 400,000 people fled the country (UNHCR 2018), including many of the women who had been involved in the demonstrations. Burundian refugee populations increased significantly, particularly in East African countries, such as Rwanda, Tanzania, and Uganda (Gaffey 2017).

Inamahoro formed in the wake of the protests—a number of women who joined said that they did so because they saw the need for women to stand together in solidarity as they were being targeted. The women had their first formal meetings in Rwanda and Uganda in November and December 2015. They officially established the organization in January 2017 in Kibuye, Rwanda, by adopting bylaws and a constitution. It is currently composed of about 80 Burundian women, about 60 of whom live outside of Burundi, most as refugees. A number of *Inamahoro's* members had already belonged to women's organizations or had been engaged in women's advocacy when they formed or joined *Inamahoro*.[5] Others were younger women who became involved in women's advocacy for the first time, precipitated by the crisis. Later, other women joined the organization after meeting *Inamahoro* members while in exile.

This chapter is based on interviews between Miriam J. Anderson (MJA), a political scientist based at Toronto Metropolitan University, and Marie Louise Baricako (MLB), the president of *Inamahoro*. The interviews were conducted in 2019 in person in Rwanda; in 2021 remotely via Zoom; and in 2022 via WhatsApp voice memos and focused on MLB's feminist

---

[4] Most peace agreements do not hold for more than five years, but failed cases remain understudied (Anderson and Golan 2023).

[5] For a typology of motivations for joining *Inamahoro*, see Anderson and Eskandari 2024b.

advocacy work, how it has changed over time as well as the objectives, strategies, and challenges faced by *Inamahoro*. MJA and MLB met in Nairobi in 2017 when Miriam was conducting research on Burundian women in politics in the period following the 2000 Arusha Peace and Reconciliation Agreement (Arusha Accords). MLB told MJA about the new organization that she was leading, and the two of them discussed the possibility of collaborating on a project that would track its work longitudinally. MJA and MLB submitted a proposal, based on a participatory action approach, to the Social Sciences and Humanities Research Council of Canada (SSHRC) Insight Development grant program and were successful in obtaining funds to conduct the research. The project involved hiring a member of *Inamahoro* to create an archive of the organization's documents, jointly designing questionnaires, and interviewing members of *Inamahoro* in person in Rwanda in 2019 and via Zoom/WhatsApp in 2021 during the pandemic (Photo 7.1).

MLB's observations evoke themes from literature on feminist peace activism; the gendered nature of carework, transnational feminism, and strategic essentialism. After offering a brief overview of *Inamahoro's* objectives, strategies, and some of the challenges it faced during COVID-19, this chapter is organized around those themes.

Photo 7.1 Marie Louise Baricako and Miriam J. Anderson on a Zoom call

What Is *Inamahoro*? Objectives, Strategies, and Activities, COVID and the Movement

The Movement has three main objectives. First, through advocacy, it seeks a peaceful resolution to Burundi's political crisis. Second, it aims to build the capacity of its members to promote peace in Burundi. Third, it seeks to mobilize Burundian women and girls, beyond its own members, to participate in all aspects of crisis resolution and, in the longer term, democracy, the rule of law, and ethical leadership in Burundi. These objectives align with the organization's host of activities, which include radio and television broadcasts, lobbying public officials both publicly and informally, and providing various trainings for its members.

Inamahoro responded to the COVID-19 pandemic by engaging in humanitarian activities for the first time (Anderson and Eskandari 2023). It raised funds to provide emergency assistance for members and for non-member refugees to pay for food, medications, and funeral expenses. It financially supported child mothers, whose numbers spiked during the pandemic in the Mahama refugee camp in Rwanda, so that they could continue attending school. It also trained community health champions to educate refugees about the dangers of COVID and how to protect themselves through masking and social distancing. In this context it also played an important role in combatting disinformation about COVID promulgated by Burundian officials by addressing Burundians directly through its radio programing, social media channels, and holding information sessions among Burundian refugee populations (Anderson and Eskandari et al. 2024a). Finally, it lobbied UNHCR to provide full rations to single mothers and the Rwandan government to include refugees in its vaccine rollout.

Feminist Peace Activism

Inamahoro's expansive objectives and wide-ranging activities fit a feminist vision of peace. Feminist scholars have long argued that for women, and other vulnerable groups, violence relevant to them is far greater than that conducted on a wartime battlefield (Berry and Lake 2021; Tickner 1995;

El Bushra 2007; Wibben et al. 2019). As a result, peace and security are more than just the absence of war and entail an environment conducive to living happily and free of fear or threat; a feminist conception of peace includes positive rights and freedoms (Confortini 2006). As MLB remarks, "It is about an environment where you are able to use your potential, be successful without any hindrance from anybody."

The fact that most of *Inamahoro's* activities take place outside of a war-zone in a time designated as "post-war" is illustrative of the problematic conception of war and peace as binary opposites. Feminist scholars have pointed out the inaccuracy of the war/peace dichotomy and instead proposed that the ways in which women experience threats, violence, and insecurity in their lives could better be conceptualized as a multidimensional continuum as Cynthia Cockburn depicts, "[the continuum of violence is from the] personal to the international, from the home and the back street to the maneuvers of the tank column and the sortie of the stealth bomber: battering and marital rape, confinement, 'dowry' burnings, honor killings, and genital mutilation in peacetime; military rape, sequestration, prostitution, and sexualized torture in war. No wonder women often say, 'War? Don't speak to me of war. My daily life is battlefield enough'" (Cockburn 2004, 43).

Made up solely of women and girls, the gendered experience of insecurity is evident for *Inamahoro's* members. Women and girls often face different threats than do men and boys which include domestic violence, sexual violence, unwanted pregnancies, and fewer educational and employment opportunities. These lived experiences in insecure environments should be considered in our attempts to define in/security and war/peace (Sjoberg 2016, 56). *Inamahoro's* work is in large part a function of lived experience of insecurity during a time period when international actors have deemed Burundi a safe place to which to return (Anderson and Eskandari 2023). The struggles of Burundian refugees are exacerbated by an official international discourse that is at odds with the lived experiences of some of the most vulnerable victims of Burundi's political crisis.

As mentioned previously, the organization pivoted to providing humanitarian aid during the pandemic.[6] It raised money through members living in Global North countries who sought out donations from their communities. *Inamahoro* used these funds to provide cash to Burundian refugees

---

[6] For an overview of Inamahoro's work during COVID-19, see Miriam J Anderson and Eskandari (2023, 2024a).

who had increased struggles to feed their families due to lockdowns during COVID. Members also organized community information sessions to inform the Burundian population about the seriousness of COVID and how to protect themselves. In addition, *Inamahoro* sought to support child mothers in the Mahama refugee camp in Rwanda which saw a spike in child pregnancies during the pandemic.

Inamahoro's shift in priorities and activities during the pandemic also illustrate its broad conception of peace. It is unsurprising that an organization composed of women, many of whom are refugees, is concerned with the existential needs of refugee populations and shifted its activities to address them. From the vantage point of a Burundian woman refugee in Rwanda, threats are multiple, emanating from a variety of sources and found in numerous spaces.

CAREWORK

Feminists in International Relations have long lamented the absence of women in International Relations histories (Enloe 1989). Their absences are due, in part, to male-centered scholarship concerned with "high politics" where, traditionally, men have dominated. This scholarship has also been concerned with the resolution of battlefield violence, and therefore, other aspects, of armed conflict, or its aftermath have focused less on women's experiences during war. Often it is women who take the lead in caring for their families and communities during conflict. As Krystalli and Schulz remark, "in the midst and wake of violence, people also fall in love, forge social and intimate relationships, and extend different forms of care to one another" (Krystalli and Schulz 2022, 2). Focusing on relationships of care provides "a more textured representation of individuals' and communities' experiences, beyond a universalizing storyline that focuses on violence, suffering, and cruelty" (Krystalli and Schulz 2022, 3).

Much of *Inamahoro's* work falls into the category of "carework" which women, in general, are more likely to perform as opposed to men. As Marie Louise said in one of our discussions:

> What unifies the members of our organization are our common cause and solidarity. We really try to take care of each other. We don't remain indifferent whenever there is one of us who is facing a challenge. We try as much as we can to make sure that everybody is taken care of. Everybody is consid-

ered so that we get everybody to feel comfortable and that they belong. It's not easy but, we try.

Something that is striking about *Inamahoro* is the wide range of work that it does. As already discussed, *Inamahoro* formed in order to speak out against the growing authoritarianism and violence in Burundi. However, as humanitarian needs among the Burundian refugee population increased, they felt obliged to act and offer support to this increasingly vulnerable population. This approach is consistent with "women's [...] care practices [which] are crucial to sustain families and communities, during periods of active conflict as well as in the current post-war context" (Blomqvist et al. 2021, 241).

It is worthwhile to note that the carework in which *Inamahoro* engages is directed at some of the most vulnerable members of the Burundian refugee community, including child mothers who had unwanted pregnancies during school closures and lockdowns during COVID. Their interventions included raising funds for school fees for the girls, arranging care for their children while they attended school, and offering them psychological support. They also encouraged the parents of the child mothers' to not reject their daughters. The material and psycho-social assistance provided to the child mothers involves "caring relationships" which "feature sustained and/or intense personal attention that enhances the welfare of [their] recipients" (Zelizer 2010, 269).

Inamahoro's carework includes the formal and informal interactions that occur among its members who provide "mutual aid" to each other to help members pay for school fees and funeral costs, for example. Some members of the organization describe their relationships with other members as familial, referring to them as "sisters" and speaking of sharing everyday joys and sorrows. These interactions could be considered labor within an "expansive definition" since "housework, child care, advice giving, and school attendance all count as labor to the extent that they do in fact augment the use values of their performers and/or recipients" (Zelizer 2010, 269). The carework performed by *Inamahoro* increases the quality of life for members and the organization's recipients.

The organization has stepped in to augment the neglect faced by Burundian refugees. During the pandemic, Burundi was de-prioritized internationally. After Évariste Ndayishimiye assumed the presidency in 2020, Burundi was readmitted into multi-lateral organizations and the Burundian, Tanzanian authorities pressured Burundian refugees to return home. The de-prioritization by state and multi-lateral organizations was likely due to Burundi's lack of geo-political strategic importance to powerful states in the international system. It is also worthwhile to consider these decisions as analogous to the so-called Doctrine of Feelings where "[h]igh-status people tend to enjoy the privilege of having their feelings noticed and considered important" (Hochschild 2019). In this case, an organization such as *Inamahoro* is tending to the feelings and physical well-being of a population deemed marginal by powerful actors.

Transnational Feminism/Diasporic Politics

As is the case with many actors who have limited power, *Inamahoro* depends upon cross-border solidarities. MLB describes some of the benefits of belonging to a diasporic network as the ability to lobby a geographically diverse set of foreign actors:

> If women can gather in Kenya and speak to their media and speak to the parliamentarians about the challenges faced by women in Burundi, can you imagine what impact this would have on what Kenya does for Burundi? And we can replicate this dynamic across different countries. When we travel, we speak to our networks and are able to raise their awareness and obtain their support.

This is similar to what is known as the "boomerang effect" where activists seek international allies to support their bid to influence politics in their home state (Keck and Sikkink 1998). In this case, however, members of *Inamahoro* reach out not only to international actors, but also to fellow Burundians across borders. In addition to partnering with displaced Burundians to influence politics in Burundi, members of *Inamahoro* residing in the Global North have access to networks of relatively greater wealth allowing funds to be mobilized to support Burundian refugee populations. During lockdowns in refugee camps during COVID, *Inamahoro* sought donations through their membership, many located in the Global North, and successfully raised around 17,000USD which they distributed to Burundian refugees in the Mahama refugee camp and urban refugees in Rwanda, many of whom needed money to purchase essentials (Anderson and Eskandari 2023).

Having fled violence and authoritarianism in Burundi, exile provides the opportunity to speak out against some of the Burundian government's actions. This is a form of participating in politics which is used by persons displaced from authoritarian states worldwide—exile provides the possibility to engage in politics in a way that would be impossible from within the state of origin: "[w]hen political opponents, dissidents, and activists are unable to operate within the country of origin, the most significant politics for a state is likely to take place transnationally, across states and among dispersed national communities" (Betts and Jones 2016). *Inamahoro* seeks to influence the Burundian government through radio broadcasts, letters, and occasionally personal communications with Burundian officials (Anderson and Eskandari 2023). Such actions would pose higher security risks if attempted from within Burundi. In speaking freely about Burundian politics, *Inamahoro* is fulfilling the function of civil society, but from outside the country.

Exile allows for politics that could not occur otherwise. As MLB remarks, "Working in exile is a necessary strategy of the Movement. It is risky for Burundians living in Burundi to criticize the government. You can be arrested and even tortured. Our movement has brave people in Burundi who speak for women, peace, and security. It's not easy, it's not obvious but you will still have people who speak, who mobilize the community for peace. From this perspective the only people who can do much in terms of advocacy are us, because we are outside of the country." As Betts and Jones note, politics are often carried out in the diaspora who originated from authoritarian states since it is not possible to conduct politics freely within the state (Betts and Jones 2016).

Finally, leading an organization with a transnational and diverse membership presents challenges. As MLB remarks, "We come from very different backgrounds. We do not look at the situation from the same perspective because we don't share the same living conditions." In addition, she continues, "meeting over WhatsApp or Zoom is not the same thing as sitting together and being in the same room." However, despite the differences and challenges, MLB attributes the organization's success to "[members'] passion, [their] commitment, and [their] resilience. And the fact that we are standing together, even when things are hard." She also speaks of taking collective action as essential:

> We are also learning to look for partners – and we want to make this our standard approach – with whom we can collaborate on specific projects because sometimes it is not easy to work on some projects alone. And it is always more productive and more effective to move in groups than alone.

So, *Mouvement Inamahoro* alone can succeed, but it will achieve even more when it works in collaboration, in synergy with other organizations. This means Burundian civil society organizations, human rights defenders who are also in exile, other African women's organizations and networks like Gender is my Agenda Campaign (GIMAC), using FEMWISE AU women mediators' network (FEMWISE AFRICA), or even the Africa women leaders' network.

STRATEGIC ESSENTIALISM

MLB remarks on the central challenge of internal cohesion facing women's organizations in deeply divided societies: "How do we bring together people that fought and killed each other? Giving them the perspective of coming together and building together so that our future generations can live happily in Burundi and be prosperous? It is possible, but it requires leadership."

Too little is made of women's peace groups in divided societies. Women are often depicted as "naturally" peaceful. As such, the work of women's peace organizations in divided societies may fail to garner adequate attention. *Inamahoro* includes members of both Burundi's major ethnic groups—Hutu and Tutsi. Its members have diverse political affiliations, including former members of the current ruling party, CNDD-FDD; the former major Hutu party, FRODEBU; as well as UPRONA—which was the ruling predominantly Tutsi party from independence to 1993 (while Burundi was a single-party state). Overcoming ethnic divisions among people who have experienced inter-ethnic conflict and genocide over generations requires extraordinary measures. As MLB notes, "[a]t times – even within civil society organizations – we find people who are radically opposed to any reunification of ethnic groups. Because of their past experiences, they see working with members of the other group as a betrayal. They cannot understand that we are women working for peace, that we are not here for ourselves, or for our ethnic groups, or for our family, but that we are here for Burundi. In our vision of Burundi, we want all ethnic groups to come together to build Burundi together. That is success to us."

The bridge-building that the organization engages in is what the scholar Gayatri Spivak has called "strategic essentialism"—the collapsing of multiple identities in order to amass power over oppression (Anderson and Valade 2023; Anderson 2016). In this case, *Inamahoro* focuses on members' shared identity as women. Members are diverse in terms of age, political affiliation, ethnicity, socio-economic status, the length of time they have been away from Burundi, as well as past experience in politics, civil society, and even in militant groups.

In addition to identifying around a gender-based identity, *Inamahoro* seeks to change mindsets over what it means to be a woman in Burundian society. MLB says:

> For a long time, women have been considered second-class citizens: they cannot take the floor, raise their voices, or decide anything. We have been treated like children and excluded from decisions. That is why it is important that women be reminded that they have the same rights and duties as men. They are the citizens of their country and of their continents. Therefore, whatever concerns their country should concern them. Whatever concerns their continent should concern them. It is either take on this struggle or let things go on as they are.
>
> We are working to create a culture of women, to build a new mindset for women. We seek to ensure that the voice of women is as strong as possible so that nobody can ignore it. We want women to stop thinking as women and start thinking as citizens. Women are needed *as women* because the voice of women is not the same as the voice of men. Their voice is important and for it to be heard, acknowledged, and taken into account there must be many of us.

Conclusion

Fighting for women's rights for Burundian women both inside and outside of the country requires the work of many hands. *Inamahoro* seeks a Burundi where there is "respect for human rights, inclusive participation of the population, justice for all, and freedom to speak out against the regime in Burundi" (MLB). Although Burundi is "at peace" and in a "post-war period" according to mainstream definitions employed by decision-makers, the reality on the ground for ordinary Burundians is markedly different. As MLB highlights:

> Our big challenge is that we still need to deconstruct the official discourse, which says that all is well in Burundi when there is nothing that is well in Burundi. It's difficult, but we are still tackling it. And we just want our women – even as we are in exile – we want our women to continue standing as leaders and getting ready to lead more when they go back home, when we start reconstructing Burundi. In this way, women will be visible in terms of

their impact and their influence; so that their contributions are accepted and recognized. This is our dream. And I need really to make sure that I hold onto this dream until I see it materialize, until I see it in concrete action.

Understanding *Inamahoro's* responses to multiple threats can be conceptualized along a "continuum of activism" across four dimensions: time, space, scale, and type (Anderson and Eskandari 2023). *Inamahoro* is active during a time period that is officially considered "post-war." Following the resignation of President Nkurunziza in 2020, international actors readmitted Burundi into multi-lateral organizations. This adversely affected Burundian refugees as host countries pressured them to return. From the vantage point of the refugees, Burundi's international standing mattered little since violence, poverty, and repression remained threats. *Inamahoro* continued its activism during this time period, publicly calling for respect for the rule of law in Burundi, the release of political prisoners, women and girls' rights, as well as tending to the humanitarian needs of Burundian refugees. It mattered little that their country of origin was deemed to be "at peace."

Inamahoro's activism took place in many spaces. Their interventions included the intimate sphere, where they concerned themselves with child mothers in the Mahama refugee camp. They also operated in the public sphere, producing radio and television programming to influence political actors in Burundi. Similarly, the scale of their activism ranged from the individual to the international. They provided funds for funeral expenses and school fees, at the individual level, and also engaged with international actors such as UNHCR, host countries, and humanitarian organizations in lobbying for single mothers with refugee status to receive a full family ration and for Burundian refugees to be included in Rwanda's vaccine rollout.

Finally, *Inamahoro* deals with violence of multiple types. It addresses direct violence, by providing assistance to victims of physical and sexual violence. It addressed structural violence by raising funds to provide emergency humanitarian aid to refugees during lockdowns. It also attempts to change attitudes and beliefs about the role of women in society and in politics.

In short, *Inamahoro* exemplifies how fighting for rights in the twenty-first century is all-consuming and multifaceted, made so by the multiple threats faced by women and the failure of decision-makers and macro-level structural forces to work in the interests of the most vulnerable groups globally.

References

Anderson, Miriam J, and Madeline F Eskandari. 2023. "From Peace Talks to Pandemics: The Continuum of Feminist Peace Activism." *Global Studies Quarterly* 3, no. 2. https://doi.org/10.1093/isagsq/ksad025.
Anderson, Miriam J, and Madeline F. Eskandari 2024a "Fake News and Gendered Public Labor: Burundian Peace Activists Combat COVID-19 Disinformation" *International Studies Review*, 26, no. 4: viae041_8, https://doi.org/10.1093/isr/viae041.8
Anderson, Miriam J, and Madeline F. Eskandari. 2024b. "Solidarity, Activism, Aid: The Formation of Women's Peace Organizations in Times of Crisis" *International Studies Association Annual Convention*, Montreal. March 17.
Anderson, Miriam J, and Galia Golan. 2023. "Women and Peace Negotiations: Looking Forward, Looking Back" *International Negotiation* 28, no. 2: 157–175.
Anderson, Miriam J, and Marc Y Valade. 2023. "From Peace Talks to Parliaments: The Microprocesses Propelling Women into Formal Politics Following War." *International Negotiation* 28, no. 2: 279–305.
Anderson, Miriam J. 2016. *Windows of Opportunity: How Women Seize Peace Negotiations for Political Change*. New York: Oxford University Press.
Berry, Marie E, and Milli Lake. 2021. "Women's rights after war: On gender interventions and enduring hierarchies." *Annual Review of Law and Social Science* 17: 459–481.
Betts, Alexander, and Will Jones. 2016. *Mobilising the Diaspora*. Cambridge University Press.
Blomqvist, Linnéa, Elisabeth Olivius, and Jenny Hedström. 2021. "Care and silence in women's everyday peacebuilding in Myanmar." *Conflict, Security & Development* 21, no. 3: 223–244.
Cockburn, Cynthia. 2004. "The Continuum of Violence: A Gender Perspective on War and Peace." In *Sites of violence*, 24–44. University of California Press.
Confortini, Catia Cecilia. 2006. "Galtung, Violence, and Gender: The Case for a Peace Studies/Feminism Alliance." *Peace and Change* 31, no. 3: 333–367.
Daley, Patricia, and Rowan Popplewell. 2016. "The appeal of third termism and militarism in Burundi." *Review of African Political Economy* 43, no. 150: 648–657.
El Bushra, Judy. 2007. "Feminism, Gender, and Women's Peace Activism." *Development and Change* 38, no. 1: 131–147.
Enloe, Cynthia. 1989. *Bananas, Beaches and Bases: Making Feminist Sense of International Politics*, University of California Press.
Gaffey, Conor. 2017. "Burundi: Refugee Camps Desperately Need More Land for New Arrivals, Pleads U.N." *Newsweek*, 2017. Available: https://www.newsweek.com/burundian-refugees-tanzania-pierre-nkurunziza-554139.

Hochschild, Arlie Russell. 2019. *The Managed heart: Commercialization of Human Feeling*. University of California Press.

Inter-Parliamentary Union. 1993. Burundi Parliamentary Chamber: Assemblée national: Elections Held in 1993. http://archive.ipu.org/parline-e/reports/arc/2049_93.htm. Accessed May 19, 2024.

Keck, Margaret, and Kathryn Sikkink. 1998. *Activists Beyond Borders: Advocacy Networks in International Politics*. Ithaca: Cornell University Press.

Krystalli, Roxani, and Philipp Schulz. 2022. "Taking Love and Care Seriously: An Emergent Research Agenda for Remaking Worlds in the Wake of Violence." *International Studies Review* 24, no. 1.

Peace Women: Women's International League for Peace and Freedom. 2012. *Africa: In Pursuit of Gender Parity at the African Court*. Available: https://peacewomen.org/content/africa-pursuit-gender-parity-african-court.

Purdeková, Andrea. 2017. "'Barahunga Amahoro—They Are Fleeing Peace!' The Politics of Re-Displacement and Entrenchment in Post-War Burundi." *Journal of Refugee Studies* 30, no. 1: 1–26. https://doi.org/10.1093/jrs/few025.

Saiget, Marie. 2020. "Women in Burundi." Oxford Research Encyclopedia of African History. https://doi.org/10.1093/acrefore/97801902777 34.013.573

Sjoberg, Laura. 2016. "Centering security studies around felt, gendered insecurities." *Journal of Global Security Studies* 1, no. 1: 51–63.

Tickner, J. Ann. 1995. "Introducing feminist perspectives into peace and world security courses." *Women's Studies Quarterly* 23, no. 3/4: 48–57.

UNHCR. 2018. "Burundi Risks Becoming a Forgotten Refugee Crisis Without Support."https://www.unhcr.org/news/briefing-notes/burundi-risks-becoming-forgotten-refugee-crisis-without-support. Accessed May 19, 2024.

Vandeginste, Stef. 2015. "Briefing: Burundi's electoral crisis-back to power-sharing as usual?" *African Affairs* 114, no. 457: 624–636.

Wibben, Annick T.R., Catia Cecilia Confortini, Sanam Roohi, Sarai Aharoni, Leena Vastapuu, and Tiina Vaittinen. 2019. "Collective discussion: piecing-up feminist peace research." *International Political Sociology* 13, no. 1: 86–107.

Wilén, Nina, and Paul D Williams. 2018. "The African Union and coercive diplomacy: the case of Burundi." *The Journal of Modern African Studies* 56, no. 4: 673–696.

Zelizer, Viviana. 2010. "Caring Everywhere." In *Cultures, Technologies, and the Politics of Care*, edited by Eileen Boris and Rhacel Salazar Parreñas. Stanford: Stanford University Press.

CHAPTER 8

The Politics of Care in the Fight Against Domestic Violence: Community-Coordinated Safety and Collective Care in South Africa

Tarisai Mchuchu-MacMillan and Emma Louise Backe

INTRODUCTION

This chapter was co-authored between Tarisai Mchuchu-MacMillan, Executive Director of MOSAIC Training, Service and Healing Centre, an NGO founded in 1993 to provide care to survivors of intimate partner violence (IPV) in and around Cape Town, and Emma Louise Backe, a medical anthropologist who studies the politics and temporalities of care for IPV survivors. I statements are written from the perspective of Tarisai to center her role within MOSAIC, her feminist activism, and her larger involvement within GBV advocacy within South Africa. Direct quotes from MOSAIC

T. Mchuchu-MacMillan
MOSAIC Training, Service and Healing Centre, Cape Town, South Africa
e-mail: tarisai@mosaic.org.za

E. L. Backe (✉)
George Washington University, Washington, DC, USA

University of Cape Town, Cape Town, South Africa
e-mail: embacke@gwu.edu

staff and survivors are taken from the research Emma conducted as part of her dissertation fieldwork within the Western Cape's gender-based violence (GBV) sector.

When I think of leadership—the kind of leadership I try to model in my own work as a feminist organizer, parent, and woman in the GBV sector— I think of my mother who, as a single parent, managed to take care of the physical, emotional, and spiritual well-being of four children. Often the women, like my mother, that I looked to for guidance growing up in my community were hindered by norms that fostered inequality, inequalities which often manifested when these feisty female leaders entered into an intimate relationship. Patriarchal social and cultural norms would become apparent when male partners moved into a woman's home—he would take on the dominant role in which respect must be shown through reverence and, in any defiance to that, violence seemed to follow. Even in my own childhood, I remember my mother experiencing domestic violence, and how I thought that violence between my parents was just "the way it is"—after all, in South Africa there is a local saying, often used to justify violence in the home, "Democracy ends at my doorstep."

As an adult, my activism has been to eliminate the very kind of violence I witnessed growing up. In my penultimate year of law school at the University of Cape Town, we visited Pollsmoor Correctional Centre. During this visit, they took us to the juvenile section where all the under-18-year-olds stayed. These youth had no access to education materials, and the conditions were appalling, especially since I was only a few years older than them, and we came from the same township communities. This visit catapulted my activism within the South African prison system—I ran the Young in Prison project from 2008 to 2014, working with youth who ended up in prison and often came from home environments riddled with family violence. In ninety percent of the cases, we found that young people turned to crime and sometimes violence because of a breakdown in the home or experiences with family violence—mostly their mothers, aunts, grandmothers bearing the brunt of it.

This experience led me to question the foundations of South African society: the home and family. My assumption was that if the home and family are stable, violence-free and safe, it would produce better outcomes for children into their adulthood. This transformational model, however, needed a home environment in which women were also protected from violence, had their own shelters of care and support. I realized that my activism needed to focus on safety in relationships, the home, and the community. By joining MOSAIC Women's Training Service and Healing

Centre in 2019—one of the oldest NGOs in the country to work with the often-invisible survivors of intimate partner violence (IPV)—I wanted to change the narrative that violence within the home was normal, and to coordinate holistic, integrated interventions where survivors could access healing and empowerment throughout their life-course of recovery.

As an organization dedicated to providing legal and psychosocial services to survivors, MOSAIC relies on young feminist students to connect their practice to research and emerging evidence around GBV care. These young students from the University of Cape Town (UCT) gain understanding of the lived realities of survivors in South Africa and ensure that their research is reflective of these dynamics. It is this very blending of research and practice which connected the two of us in 2019—we met on an unseasonably warm winter day in Cape Town, at a panel on "Gender-Based Violence and the Implementation of the Domestic Violence Act," which brought together policy-makers, front-line activists, and researchers to discuss issues with the criminal justice system's response to IPV. After the panel, Tarisai laid out her initial vision for the SAFE platform, a collaborative, community-based approach to cultivating safety which resonated with Emma's activism in the US.

Like Tarisai, Emma came to work with survivors through the prison system. Volunteering with female inmates at the Dutchess County Jail as an undergraduate, she found that most of the women were mothers around her age, many of whom had ended up behind bars due to abusive relationships or family violence. Their incarceration spoke volumes about the failures of the social support net for survivors, the replacement of care with carcerality (Kaba 2021), insight that was only amplified by her time conducting research with the Gender, Health and Justice Research Unit at the University of Cape on the treatment of survivors with disabilities by South African police and court officials. This realization led to Emma's work as a rape crisis advocate and community educator in Washington, DC, where she trained others in trauma-informed care (Backe 2017, 2020). The convergence of backgrounds and interests between the two of us presented an unlikely opportunity to combine Emma's PhD research and background in front-line work with Tarisai's launch of the SAFE platform—to track the development of the initiative and use feminist, ethnographic research methods to document this nascent grassroots strategy.

In what follows, we lay out in more detail the systematic ways that DV/IPV are tactically excluded or overlooked in South Africa's response to GBV more broadly, producing fundamentally uncaring spaces for survivors. We draw upon Tarisai's experience as a Black South African woman, and Executive Director of MOSAIC, and Emma's ethnographic research on gender-based violence in Cape Town, South Africa, embedded within MOSAIC. In MOSAIC's 29 years of practice and research on the implementation of domestic violence laws by the police, magistrates, and clerks of the courts, we've found several systemic barriers that indicate a failure to protect DV survivors under the Constitution and the Domestic Violence Act (Artz and Smythe 2005; Rehse et al. 2021). These obstacles include a justice system that is often confusing, negligent, or hostile to intimate partner violence (IPV) survivors and ongoing beliefs among criminal justice staff that IPV is a "private" matter best dealt with by families. These glaring failures serve to inform MOSAIC's own work on a national and local level, and the organization's deliberate efforts to coordinate a more holistic, intersectional, and integrated model of safety premised on "commoning care" through collective responsibility and sentiment (Federici 2019; Pain 2021; Woodly et al. 2021). In diagnosing the deficits and structural barriers to care within the state's Victim Empowerment Programme (VEP), we also discuss how MOSAIC's SAFE Platform attempts to address these issues within the state response and build more locally oriented spaces of collective support. If violence is a shared social problem, it must be addressed through collective solidarity and commitment across and beyond the family (Photo 8.1).

Intimate Contexts and Structural Responses to "Victim Empowerment" in South Africa

After the end of South Africa's apartheid regime in the early 1990s, the country's transition to democratic governance was accompanied by the pursuit of gender activism within the government and civil society (Artz and Smythe 2007; Britton 2006; Hassim 2003; Lewis 2009). In this section, we first lay out post-apartheid legal and criminal responses to DV/IPV, drawing upon Tarisai's training as a lawyer in the sector and Emma's research within the Victim Empowerment Programme (VEP) through MOSAIC. We then move to discuss how the criminal justice system regularly revictimizes and alienates IPV survivors and how responses by government officials, police officers, and court workers are complicated by cultural attitudes around violence and patriarchy that fundamentally undermine structural mandates to care.

8 THE POLITICS OF CARE IN THE FIGHT AGAINST DOMESTIC VIOLENCE... 113

Photo 8.1 Tarisai Mchuchu-Macmillan and Emma Louise Backe

Bringing the expertise of anti-apartheid women's activists to bear within the newly created government in the 1990s, the country set out to create a national Constitution and state structure that would ensure that all South African citizens could pursue a life free from violence, particularly for women of color seeking justice in a country that had formerly treated them as second-class citizens (Hassim 2003; Meer 2005). These policies included the creation of the Domestic Violence Act 116 of 1998 (DVA 1998), which enshrined a set of state responsibilities to prevent domestic violence and assist survivors to obtain protection orders, creating a pathway for a survivor to pursue criminal justice should the perpetrator violate the conditions of their protection order (Artz and Smythe 2007).

At the same time that the Domestic Violence Act (DVA) was being rolled out, Rolene Miller founded MOSAIC in 1993. Throughout the 1990s and early 2000s, MOSAIC's early work to provide counseling and access to justice ran parallel to state efforts to better protect survivors. Through the organization's community mobilization efforts, Rolene drew upon the importance of sisterhood and friendship as crucial kinds of mobilization and care in township settings, forms of solidarity, and covert action historically employed by women during apartheid (Gasa 2007; Moolman 2009; Stevenson 2011; Wells 1998). A cadre of MOSAIC community workers—from the very communities where MOSAIC conducted their programs, and with their own, personal experiences of violence—shared knowledge and resources about where survivors could get help, drawing friendship networks into wider collectives of care. This approach to community-led front-line work, in both formal and informal legal settings, is critical to MOSAIC's approach to care—combining professional expertise with localized, grounded knowledge.

Alongside the Domestic Violence Act (DVA), the government also created the Victim Empowerment Programme (VEP). This VEP is, at least on paper, a constellation of services implemented by multiple government departments in collaboration with NGOs and community-based organizations to provide a continuum of care across the criminal justice system. Essentially, through the VEP model, survivors should be able to file a case with the police; receive transportation for medical care and counseling; apply for a protection order; and receive court support for other needs. However, despite the comprehensive vision for prevention and survivor care, different forms of GBV are not treated with the same care and seriousness as others, often with fatal consequences for women experiencing IPV/DV.

The VEP's continuum of care, and its rhetoric of "victim empowerment," is woefully disconnected from the lived experiences of victims who attempt to survive the perilous gaps between justice, care, and protection. In the words of one survivor who spoke to Emma, "this law is really failing us women a lot." Despite the country's progressive legislation, and its efforts at post-apartheid gender transformation, it is estimated that South Africa has one of the highest rates of domestic violence in the world, with almost half of female murders perpetrated by current or former intimate partners (Abrahams et al. 2013). Statistics South Africa (2020) reports indicated that one in five (or 21%) of ever-partnered women have experienced physical violence by a partner in their lifetime—divorced or separated women also have a higher likelihood of having experienced physical or sexual violence. These numbers also fail to capture the ways that this violence is both historically situated and normatively sanctioned in the country, even by the very duty-bearers who are supposed to protect survivors. The effects of colonization and apartheid have a direct influence on how violence manifests in South Africa, creating a pervasive culture where violence is often used to settle public and private disputes (Campbell 1992; Gqola 2015; Ratele and Suffl 2010).

In contemporary South African society, cultural and religious norms still inform popular beliefs that it is appropriate to "discipline" female partners and wives (Backe et al. 2022; Colvin et al. 2010; Gqola 2007; Morrell et al. 2012); that violence is sometimes an expression of love (Wood et al. 2008); and that domestic disputes should be handled within the family. Women are taught that it is their responsibility to protect the dignity of the family, even in instances of violence, thus further silencing survivors. These attitudes not only inform rates of violence, and survivors' experiences of support in their communities, but also how the VEP and the criminal justice system respond to their duties. As one former MOSAIC court support worker put it, "there are two sets of laws running parallel to each other in GBV. There's a South African law related to GBV like our DVA. And then we have the cultural laws. And these are operating in two silos, two straight lines with no possibility of intersecting with each other." Keeping these cultural dynamics in mind, we detail the ways that the law, the VEP, and the criminal justice system only further undermine rather than promote care for IPV/DV survivors.

First, and perhaps most importantly, from my perspective as a lawyer, DV/IPV is treated as a civil, rather than a pre-eminently criminal matter in the country. In accordance with the DVA, in IPV cases, when a survivor goes to the police to open a criminal case and the South African Police Services (or SAPS) find out that the case was committed by an intimate partner, SAPS will often refuse to open a case. Yet, if the same person was assaulted by a stranger, the police would readily go and make an arrest. Even if a survivor is able to get a Protection Order (PO), the warrant of arrest which accompanies the PO is only activated if the respondent breaches the protection order. This means that the only crime committed in terms of the DVA is for a breach of the protection order and not for a crime or act of domestic violence in and of itself. So, essentially, a perpetrator might commit multiple acts of DV against their intimate partner, but this violence is essentially only considered a crime if the survivor was able to work up the nerve go to court for a PO, or call the police after another incident of abuse. In MOSAIC's experience, we have witnessed thousands of cases where women are sent back-and-forth between police stations and courts while seeking assistance. The civil law remedies effectively make both the specificity and the prevalence of IPV invisible under the eyes of the law.

The police also regularly fail in their duties to respond to DV cases or provide the protections SAPS is mandated to carry out under the DVA. In the DVA, SAPS members are supposed to serve protection orders with warrants of arrest to the respondent (alleged perpetrator); make arrests if the PO has been breached; provide support from Victim Friendly Rooms; and connect survivors with medical care, legal services, and court referrals. Yet this promise of protection has largely floundered, leaving survivors at greater risk of retribution from their abusers. The police do not always respond quickly to DV reports, while SAPS training remains minimal and is largely deemed ineffective, particularly in equipping officers with an understanding of how to sensitively respond to survivors (Rehse et al. 2021; Spies 2019). Survivors working with MOSAIC within the courts have even expressed to Emma that when they report DV incidences, or seek help at the police stations, police officers encourage them to go and work things out as "these things happen in relationships." These patterns of deferral evidence a marked absence of care or urgency on behalf of survivors' sense of personal peril.

SAPS are also supposed to work hand-in-hand with the courts to ensure the enforcement of Protection Orders, but the justice system is similarly fraught for IPV survivors. Clerks and magistrates do not apply the law consistently and exhibit skepticism about different forms of DV—they are less likely to take cases of economic, psychological, or emotional abuse seriously (Artz 2004; Moult 2010). In MOSAIC's own court monitoring project (Rehse et al. 2021), there is a concerning lack of knowledge about DV among court clerks, even though clerks are often the first point of contact for survivors when applying for POs. If clerks have negative attitudes around who is "worthy" or "unworthy" of court assistance—replicating ideas of the "perfect victim"—or don't assist the applicant to write their statement correctly, then those survivors will not receive a Protection Order. In an attrition research report conducted by MOSAIC and Lillian Artz (2006), applicants often made repeated attempts to secure a PO from the courts, in some cases going to court three or four times. Applicants eventually gave up trying to get legal assistance because the process was so onerous. This failure to quickly and sensitively respond to DV within the legal system has led to survivors dying with Protection Orders in their hands.

The attitudes of police officers, magistrates, and court clerks also reflect more systemic beliefs about DV/IPV in the country, the personal politics that inform legal implementation. In our research on the co-occurrence of violence against women and violence against children, first responders like police officers, clerks, and social workers revealed just how deep these socio-cultural gender beliefs go: "the cultural thing is when men feel they have more power, the women need to submit, the woman need to do whatever men ask them to do and they have been robbed of their identity if the women don't" (Mathews et al. 2022). Persistent cultural attitudes about the privacy and normalcy of IPV, coupled with the lack of adequate or effective training, have meant that when survivors report DV, police officers and clerks discourage survivors from going through the criminal justice system at all. Essentially, the formal government duty bearers respond based on their beliefs rather than what the law dictates, further weakening survivor support systems and serving to reprivatize the harms of IPV, rejecting collective and governmental responsibility.

Throughout MOSAIC's work in the courts, with police stations, and on the ground with survivors, it is increasingly clear all of the ways that the criminal justice system—and those that execute it—fail to take into account the lived realities and threat that survivors face. In a sense, survivors attempting to escape abusive relationships must instead navigate a system where they are held captive by an unresponsive state, reproducing yet another cycle of harm. The high levels of GBV and the slow pace of systemic responses highlight the need for feminist collective action. While MOSAIC staff could try to make the VEP more accommodating to survivors, our programs also had to focus on the more localized systems of care survivors accessed *outside* of the system.

Commoning Safety and Care—MOSAIC's SAFE Platforms

As a young African Feminist, learning and listening when I attended various collaborative spaces within the Western Cape's GBV sector, I was frustrated by the continued refrain that the justice system was failing, as if the system operated outside of people within the system itself. I came to the conclusion that the government employees were responsible for the system to work—if you have an un-trained, under-resourced person with harmful gender norms and beliefs, then the system would never work to serve survivors. As a key linchpin between government and civil society, and an organization founded on the importance of interpersonal relationships, I realized that MOSAIC needed to bring the same spirit of collaboration and sisterhood to bear within this system. Domestic violence is complex—it needs different stakeholders to actively respond and work together to ensure that care, security and justice are provided, drawing on the organizational politics that sustained us under apartheid, and continued to promote informal networks of care in the township settings where I grew up.

With these frustrations deep in my activist heart, I designed the SAFE Project. The aim was to create platforms within local communities to bring together multi-stakeholder first-responders such as the police, social workers, clerks, magistrates, NGOs, and traditional and religious leaders, each of whom interact with survivors in different ways, at different points of disclosure. Yet each of these actors were also crucial to understanding the local network of care that survivors navigate, both inside and outside the criminal justice system. I envisioned the SAFE Platforms as a coordinated referral pathway for survivors within communities, where every stakeholder knows the law, understands how to use it, and keeps survivors safe. The idea is to strengthen the system by strengthening the people who work within the system, carrying forward MOSAIC's initial model of partnership and localized, interpersonal care. As a researcher embedded within MOSAIC, Emma conducted participant-observation throughout the first year of SAFE. Just as MOSAIC staff members come from the communities they serve, Emma's approach to tracking and documenting SAFE relied on her sustained relationships within the communities, and the fact that the data she collected was continuously fed back into SAFE meetings and strategy documents.

In 2021, SAFE was launched in three communities–Mitchells Plain, Paarl, and Philippi–areas where MOSAIC has operated since the 1990s. MOSAIC served as the backbone support organization behind SAFE, conducting bi-monthly convening sessions where stakeholders worked together to identify common goals and challenges in addressing survivor needs, with the objective of improving survivor care on the ground. The convening meetings created space for stakeholders, including survivors themselves, to connect, build relationships, and recognize the support mechanisms that already exist in the community; identify referral pathways; and reinforce responsibilities within this constellation of actors. For instance, if a Protection isn't served, they could now follow-up with the police official who handled domestic violence cases or get in touch with a local safehouse to provide immediate —essentially, we realized that the functioning of the system relied on working relationships.

In the process of building trust, relationships, and even greater vulnerability among the community stakeholders, MOSAIC also provided training and skill-building to ensure that members of the SAFE Platforms could respond with care and empathy to survivors (Backe 2020; Krystalli and Schulz 2022; Ratele 2022). This process of carefully promoting closer, more interpersonal working relationships represents what Ticktin (2020) refers to as a "feminist commons." This feminist commons considers the ways that care work, often performed by women like my mother and myself, has long been undervalued, and how the "privatization" of homes often contributes to women's subjugation, and violence, in a patriarchal society. Feminist commoning, instead, "describes collective ways of organising and living that are in resistance to dispossession, including the forms of isolating that entail the loss of safe spaces and social networks" (Pain 2021, 12), and draws upon the models of mutual aid and community solidarity that have been central to South African feminist organizing for decades (Hassim 1998; Walker 1982; Wells 1998). This ethos informed our engagements in Mitchells Plain, Phillipi, and Paarl, as well as our approach to addressing the challenges that arose throughout the SAFE pilot process.

Flattening Hierarchies, Collapsing Siloes

One of the biggest challenges in SAFE has been getting all the different stakeholders to come to the table, particularly the government stakeholders with most of the VEP mandates to support survivors. Through the process of building each community platform, key government stakeholders were invited to the monthly meetings, including the Domestic Violence Coordinators at the police, court officials from the Department of Justice, and the social workers who handle DV/IPV cases. Yet getting these government stakeholders to respond to invitations and attend the monthly engagements has been challenging. The continued absence and excuses of the government stakeholders only served to reinforce the hierarchies and artificial systems of separation between state duty bearers and those working on the ground. Since the goal of the SAFE Platforms is to create mutual mechanisms of accountability—promoting more equal partnerships across those in the community—we had to leverage the convening power of MOSAIC and use our power to *call in* these stakeholders, essentially to push back on the contrived forms of state enclosure and segmentation that prevented us from working together.

To address this sense of siloing, we focused on in-person communication and site visits, collapsing the social distancing that had separated us during COVID. These site visits allowed us to create more familiarity and in-person rapport with the different stakeholders and permitted partners to share their own challenges. For instance, while blame might be apportioned at the police officers, the DV Coordinators shared their own issues with resourcing, the internal hierarchies, and power dynamics that they faced. This also allowed us to put a human face and a more nuanced understanding of the challenges for each stakeholder, whether they were a government department or a local organization. By building more interpersonal relationships, and illuminating the ways that each partner—even those in the government that seemed better resourced—dealt with institutional hierarchies that sometimes obstructed their work, we could highlight common challenges across all partners. Common challenges could create a sense of shared vision and direction for the platform that stakeholders could work through these obstacles together as a collective in a more egalitarian, even feminist, fashion.

Scarcity

Scarcity emerged as another key challenge across government and community partners. Despite government assurances to support the VEP and provide adequate funding to front-line organizations, most of the partners in SAFE struggled to make ends meet, even those in government departments. Across all three SAFE platforms, organizations spoke about the financial crisis that bedevils front-line organizations—survivors' ability to access services also depends on the financial survival of organizations delivering care. Scarcity also extended to staffing within the different partner organizations, and the availability of training to capacitate first-responders. The community partners who regularly helped to fill the gaps left by staffing issues, however, often went unpaid. Community groups were motivated by a desire to provide a sense of safety for the community, yet their labor and contributions to the community needed to be remunerated.

With the recognition that women's labor, and caring labor more broadly, has been historically undervalued, particularly under capitalism (Federici 2019), we worked to pool our collective resources and consider how to redistribute skills, materials, and training opportunities more equitably across all community partners, regardless of professional title. MOSAIC provided capacity-building around survivor-centered care and the legal frameworks related to victims' rights. As Emma helped to map out the relevant stakeholders within each community, we also identified the kinds of trainings these organizations could offer. We leveraged our relationships with the Western Cape Provincial Government to advocate for financial support—like stipends—for volunteers in the VEP, elevating the importance of their labor in the success of any victim empowerment initiatives. Recognizing the ubiquitous issue of resource scarcity, and competition over the limited funds available within the VEP, we also hosted workshops on grant proposals and identifying funding resources, thereby working to build the financial literacy, and sustainability, of our partners.

Aligning Timeframes

Scarcity of resources and staff leads to what some feminist economists have referred to as "time poverty" (Kes and Swaminathan 2006), or the absence of adequate time in a day to perform all the roles and duties expected of us. Time poverty is specifically gendered because it recognizes that women often are expected to take on the greatest amounts of informal labor within the home and to sacrifice any free time they have for their family members. We therefore had to account for time poverty through SAFE, setting monthly meetings and trainings that wouldn't conflict with other duties, including the limited time that parents and caregivers have in the day. Yet as an organization with a long history of organizing against IPV, we nevertheless recognized that we would be stuck in a perpetual cycle of crisis if we didn't invest in the kinds of structural, sustainable, even slow kinds of intentional engagement and preparation needed to do this work and not burn out (Adams et al. 2014; Berry 2022; Boonzaier and van Niekerk 2019).

Given the scale of violence against women in the South Africa, and the high rates of both intimate femicide and suicidal ideation among survivors, one of the central premises of MOSAIC, and the SAFE platform, is to build a positive future for women where they don't have to fear for their own safety, to advance a tomorrow that's better than today. This kind of future is not going to happen overnight. Relationship, trust, and movement-building take time, with short-, medium-, and long-term horizons of accomplishment to show progress. In each community, the vision of SAFE was tailored toward what would be necessary to achieve this kind of long-term change and how each group would measure change over time—not necessarily in span of a few weeks, or a few months, but over a broader sweep of years of dedicated coordination and care. By creating a shared vision within each platform, and drawing up a set of measurements we used among the stakeholders—some qualitative and some quantitative—to track our progress, we could also create tangible ways to document how safety was changing, the small victories along the way that could motivate us all for, in the words of Nelson Mandela, the long walk to freedom.

Conclusion

Considering the epidemic nature of GBV in South Africa, and the pervasive complexities of domestic violence in particular, operating "in the shadows" (Mlambo-Ngcuka 2020), MOSAIC's services remain eminently local through the SAFE Platforms, hoping that the deliberate efforts to strengthen the system is the solution that we have been waiting for. We recognize that in order to create a more just and equitable society for all survivors, each community also has its own local needs, its own localized network of advocates and change-agents. In order to cultivate a more responsive system for survivors, and a more caring and empathetic culture around violence, ending DV/IPV cannot be achieved by a single person or organization. In striving to cultivate a feminist commons within the space of the SAFE platforms, we also contribute to feminist understandings and practices around another South African tradition—that of ubuntu, a philosophy that intimately ties my life, my successes, my failures, and my humanity, to those around me. Ubuntu feminism (Diouf et al. 2023; Magadla and Chitando 2014), conjoined with a feminist commons, emphasizes our networks of mutual obligation and belonging, an interdependence that cultivates micro, meso, and macro conditions of care. It understands our care for, with, and on behalf of survivors as imminently relational, interpersonal, one that we can build in small but nonetheless meaningful ways. In so doing, our SAFE communities remind one another that by breaking down the proverbial doors that keep domestic violence invisible, we also invite collective care and reparation.

By tracking the pilot phase of the SAFE program and documenting data of what has worked in each community, Emma's research contributes to the evidence base on what works to contribute to this feminist commons, with the hopes of scaling up the SAFE platform to more communities in the country. The government's National Strategic Plan on Gender-Based Violence and Femicide (NSP GBVF) has a pillar dedicated to response, support, healing, and care, one that MOSAIC is helping to lead within the Western Cape. Within this NSP GBVF, there is an emphasis on the "power of going local"—locally oriented and responsive programming, but also local ownership of the initiatives that best suit each community. While the SAFE platforms at the moment are only in three communities, we hope to use the data we've gathered to help other collectives throughout the country. In so doing, we refocus on a vision of the future where democracy, and safety, start at all our doorsteps and continue the feminist work of our mothers and grandmothers.

References

Abrahams, N., Mathews, S., Martin, L.J., Lombard, C., and Jewkes, R. 2013. "Intimate Partner Femicide in South Africa in 1999 and 2009." *PLoS Medicine*, 10: e1001412.

Adams, Vincanne, Burke, Nancy J. and Ian Whitmarsh. 2014. "Slow research: thoughts for a movement in global health." *Med Anthropol* 33: 179–197.

Artz, Lillian and Dee Smythe. 2007. "Feminism vs the State?: A decade of sexual offences law reform in South Africa." *Agenda* 74: 6–13.

Artz, Lillian and MOSAIC 2006. *An Examination Into the Attrition of Domestic Violence Cases: Preliminary Findings.*

Artz, Lillian and Dee Smythe. 2005. "Bridges and Barriers: A Five Year Retrospective on the Domestic Violence Act, 2005." *ACTA JURIDICA* 200.

Artz, Lillian. 2004. "Better Safe Than Sorry: Magistrates' views on the Domestic Violence Act." *SA Crime Quarterly* 7:1–8.

Backe, Emma Louise, Bosire, Edna and Emily Mendenhall. 2022. "'Drinking Too Much, Fighting Too Much': The Dual "Disasters" of Intimate Partner Violence and Alcohol Use in South Africa." *Violence Against Women* 28.

Backe, Emma Louise. 2020. "Capacitating care: Activist anthropology in ethnographies of gender-based violence." *Feminist Anthropologist* 1: 192–198.

Backe, Emma Louise. 2017. "Engagements with Ethnographic Care." *Anthropology News.* 58:e81–e86.

Berry, Marie E. 2022. "Radicalising resilience: mothering, solidarity, and interdependence among women survivors of war." *Journal of International Relations and Development* 25: 946–966.

Boonzaier, Floretta and Taryn van Niekerk. 2019. *Decolonial Feminist Community Psychology.* Springer.

Britton, Hanna. 2006. "Organizing against Gender Violence in South Africa." *Journal of Southern African Studies* 32: 145–163.

Campbell, Catherine. 1992. "Learning to Kill? Masculinity, the Family and Violence in Natal." *Journal of Southern African Studies* 18: 614–628.

Colvin, Christopher, Joan Leavens, and Steven Robins. 2010. "Grounding 'Responsibilisation' Talk: Masculinities, Citizenship and HIV in Cape Town, South Africa." *Journal of Development Studies* 46, no. 7: 1179–1195.

Diouf, Emilie, Unifier Dyer, Asali Ecclesiastes and Marita Gilbert. 2023. "Our Ubuntu: A Black feminist turn." *Agenda* 37: 32–43.

DVA. 1998. Domestic Violence Act of 116 of 1998. South African Government.

Federici, Sylvia. 2019. *Re-Enchanting the World: Feminism and the Politics of the Commons.* Toronto: PM.

Gasa, Nomboniso. 2007. *Women in South African History: Basus'iimbokodo, Bawel'imilambo / They remove boulders and cross rivers.* HSRC Press.

Gqola, Pumla. 2015. *Rape: A South African Nightmare.* NB Publishers.

Gqola, Pumla Dineo. 2007. "How the 'cult of femininity' and violent masculinities support endemic gender based violence in contemporary South Africa." *African Identities* 5: 111–124.

Hassim, Shireen. 2003. "The Gender Pact and Democratic Consolidation: Institutionalizing Gender Equality in the South African State." *Feminist Studies* 29: 504–528.

Hassim, Shireen. 1998. "Family, Motherhood and Zulu Nationalism: The Politics of the Inkatha Women's Brigade." Feminist Review 43: 1–25.

Kaba, Mariame. 2021. *We Do This 'Til We Free Us: Abolitionist Organizing and Transforming Justice.* Haymarket Books.

Kes, Aslihan and Hema Swaminathan. 2006. "Gender and Time Poverty in Sub-Saharan Africa." In *Gender, Time Us, and Poverty in Sub-Saharan Africa,* edited by C. Mark Blackden and Quentin Wodon. Washington DC: The World Bank.

Krystalli, Roxani and Philip Schulz. 2022. "Taking Love and Care Seriously: An Emergent Research Agenda for Remaking Worlds in the Wake of Violence." *International Studies Review* 24: viac003.

Lewis, Desiree. 2009. "Chapter Eight: Discursive Challenges for African Feminisms." In *African Feminist Politics of Knowledge: Tensions, Challenges, Possibilities*, edited by Akosua Adomako Ampofo and Signe Arnfred. Nordiska Afrikainstitutet, 205–221.

Magadla, Siphokazi and Ezra Chitando. 2014. "The Self Become God: Ubuntu and the 'Scandal of Manhood." In *Ubuntu: Curating the Archive*, edited by Leonhard Praeg and Siphokazi Magadla. University of KwaZulu-Natal Press.

Mathews, Shanaaz, Makola, Lehlogonolo, October, Lauren and Neziswa Titi 2022. *Bridging the divide: Unpacking the intersections of violence against women and violence against children in two communities in the Western cape, South Africa*. University of Cape Town: Children's Institute.

Meer, Shamim. 2005. "Freedom for Women: Mainstreaming Gender in the South African Liberation Struggle and Beyond." *Gender and Development* 13: 36–45.

Mlambo-Ngcuka, Phumzile 2020. *Violence against women and girls: the shadow pandemic*. UN Women. https://www.unwomen.org/en/news/stories/2020/4/statement-ed-phumzile-violence-against-women-during-pandemic

Moolman, Benita. 2009. "Race, Gender and Feminist Practice: Lessons from Rape Crisis Cape Town." In *Women's Activism in South Africa*, edited by Hannah Britton, Jennifer Fish and Sheila Meintjes. Scottsville: University of KwaZulu-Natal Press.

Morrell, Robert, Jewkes, Rachel and Graham Lindegger. 2012. "Hegemonic Masculinity/Masculinities in South Africa: Culture, Power and Gender Politics." *Men and Masculinities* 15: 11–30.

Moult, Kelley. 2010. *Gatekeepers or rights keepers? Domestic violence court clerks and the administration of justice in South Africa*. American University ProQuest Dissertations Publishing.

Pain, Rachel. 2021. "Collective trauma? Isolating and communing gender-based violence." *Gender, Place & Culture* .

Ratele, Kopano. 2022. *Why Men Hurt Women and Other Reflections on Love, Violence and Masculinity*. Johannesburg: Wits University Press.

Ratele, Kopano and Shahnaaz Suffl. 2010. "Men, Masculinity, and Cultures of Violence and Peace in South Africa." In *An International Psychology of Men: Theoretical Advances, Case Studies and Clinical Innovations*, edited by Chris Blazina and David S. Shen-Miller. Routledge.

Rehse, K., Thobane, M., Gihwala, H., Artz, L. Waldman, J., Solomons, N., Maksudi, K., Karimakwenda, N. and M. Ngubane. 2021. *Protection orders must protect: exploring the implementation of the Domestic Violence Act (116 of 1998) at local magistrates' courts and police stations in Cape Town and the Cape Winelands*. MOSAIC Training, Service and Healing Centre, Cape Town.

Spies, Amanda. 2019. "Continued State Liability for Police Inaction in Assisting Victims of Domestic Violence: A Reflection on the Implementation of South Africa's Domestic Violence Legislation." *Journal of African Law* 63: 53–77.

Statistics South Africa. 2020. *Crimes against women in South Africa, an analysis of the phenomenon of GBV and femicide: An overview of the prevalence of crimes against women in the country and the conditions that exacerbate GBV leading to femicide.* https://www.parliament.gov.za/storage/app/media/1_Stock/Events_Institutional/2020/womens_charter_2020/docs/30-07-2020/A_Statistical_Overview_R_Maluleke.pdf

Stevenson, Judith. 2011. "'The Mamas Were Ripe:' Ideologies of Motherhood and Public Resistance in a South African Township." *Feminist Formations* 23: 132–163.

Ticktin, Miriam. 2020. "Building a Feminist Commons in the Time of COVID-19." *Signs Blog*, Accessed January 9, 2024 Available: http://signsjournal.org/covid/ticktin/.

Walker, Cherryl. 1982. *Women and Resistance in South Africa*. Monthly Review Press.

Wells, Julia. 1998. "Maternal Politics in Organizing Black South African Women: The Historical Lessons." In *Sisterhood, Feminisms and Power: From Africa to the Diaspora*, edited by Obioma Nnaemeka. Africa World Press, Inc.

Wood, K., Lambert, H., and Jewkes, R. 2008. "Injuries are Beyond Love": Physical Violence in Young South Africans' Sexual Relationships." *Medical Anthropology* 27: 43–69.

Woodly, Deva, Brown, Rachel H., Marin, Mara, Threadcraft, Shatema, Harris, Christopher Paul, Syedullah, Jasmine and Miriam Ticktin. 2021. "Critical Exchange: The Politics of Care." *Contemporary Political Theory* 20: 890–925.

CHAPTER 9

Transformative Activism: Women's Peace Efforts Within Conflict-Affected Populations in Georgia

Ekaterine Gamakharia and Magda Cárdenas

INTRODUCTION

The war in Abkhazia took me away from a happy childhood, made me feel the bitterness of loss and forced me to confront many challenges... The war and its consequences determined the path of my future life! [It] crafted me as woman activist for equal rights, who fights against war, who fights for steady and long-lasting peace!
—Ekaterine Gamakharia, Women Fund "Sukhumi"

This is the story of Eka, as she likes to be called. Eka was born and spent her childhood in the Georgian city of Sukhumi until the start of the war between the Georgian government and the separatist forces from Abkhazia in 1992. This conflict has been characterized as "frozen," as no peace agreement has been reached—despite a ceasefire enacted in

E. Gamakharia
Sukhumi, Georgia

M. Cárdenas (✉)
Uppsala, Sweden

© The Author(s), under exclusive license to Springer Nature Switzerland AG 2025
J. Zulver, K. Stallone (eds.), *Brave Women*,
https://doi.org/10.1007/978-3-031-70702-5_9

1993—leaving political and territorial disputes unresolved. The unresolved disputes over the breakaway territory of Abkhazia can be tracked back to Georgia's independence from the Soviet Union in 1990 and a political agenda in Tbilisi that limited the inclusion of minority ethnic groups. Sukhumi later became the capital of the *de facto* territory of Abkhazia, an area that sadly has witnessed the persecution of the Georgian population. Since 2009, the Geneva International Discussions (GID), a formal negotiation platform co-chaired by the OSCE, UN, and EU, has been in place; however it has not produced meaningful results in terms of conflict resolution. Despite the efforts in confidence-building measures, important challenges remain. One main challenge is the continued presence of Russian troops in the border areas, which increases locals' deep-seated distrust and constrains their freedom of movement.

Eka's earliest memories occurred in the diverse city of Sukhumi, where Georgians, Abkhaz, Armenians, and Greeks, among others, lived together. Her view of the world dramatically changed when, at the age of 13, the war forced Eka and her family to flee and find a new home in Kutaisi, the second largest city in Georgia. Living in Kutaisi, with its traditionalist outlook, was a big contrast from her childhood in multi-ethnic and multi-linguistic cosmopolitan Sukhumi. Displacement forced Eka and her family to confront new challenges such as the stigmatization of internally displaced persons (IDPs). In response, her mother, Alla Gamakharia, felt moved to transform the living conditions for displaced families in Sukhumi. Beyond providing support to IDPs through humanitarian responses and facilitating reconnection with family members who remained in Sukhumi, Alla also felt a call to promote women's rights and women's participation in peace efforts. She created an organization, Fund Sukhumi, to put her vision of developing women's capacities as paths of mobilization toward gender equality into action.

Like Eka and her mother Alla, many other internally displaced women in Georgia have tirelessly campaigned for their rights and for women's participation in all spheres of policy-making. Such activism takes place despite a patriarchal mindset that has historically shaped all social and political structures, relegating women to secondary roles. These women have had to find alternative channels for peacebuilding and are committed to transforming everyday life for the conflict-affected population. In doing so, they have launched themselves into a broader field of action, emerging as agents of peace.

This chapter details the story of Ekaterine Gamakharia's activism. It delves into her personal experience of displacement and her journey of becoming an activist. By reflecting on her personal journey, the chapter reflects more broadly on how to make the voices of conflict-affected populations heard. Further, it explores the dynamics and challenges of women's peace activism in Georgia. Such activism is grounded in everyday, local realities and personal stories, but also has the ambition to make long-term social and political transformations, including influencing decisions and policy-making. By analyzing Eka's story and her work as a peace activist, this chapter offers an empirical contribution to ongoing debates on feminist peace, gendered agency, and what it means to be a brave woman.

This chapter draws on interviews and conversations between Eka and Magda Cárdenas. Eka and Magda met in 2019 in Tbilisi, during Magda's PhD fieldwork. During their first interview, there was an immediate connection through their shared interest in empowering women activists and advancing the Women, Peace and Security Agenda. This was the beginning of many conversations about feminist peace, the challenges that women peace activist face in Georgia, and their role in creating long-lasting reconciliation. An inspiring exchange of opinions and reflections has been maintained through Skype and phone messages since Magda finished her PhD.

In this chapter, we first talk about the story of Eka, narrating her journey from displacement to her rise as an activist. The second part of the chapter discusses the practices that characterize her role as an activist, as well as the goals and political stances underpinning such practices. In the third section, we analyze the challenges that women activists still face in Georgia. Finally, we reflect on the broader contribution of this case by acknowledging the similar lessons and experiences that apply to women activists in other contexts.

Emerging as an Activist

Displacement and the Journey to Women's Empowerment

Stories, emotions, and memories shape our understanding of the world as well as the paths we envision for conflict resolution and achieving peace. Based on a feminist narrative analysis, this chapter allows Eka's voice to take the lead and explores a particular form of activism through her account of personal experiences and interpretations of memories

(Autesserre 2012; Sosulski et al. 2010; Wibben 2011). Eka's journey as an activist started at an early age when she reflected on the effects of war, the challenges of displacement, and the need to take action to transform the lives of conflict-affected population. To understand such journey, we need to know Eka's account about experience of the war, and, more specifically, of displacement.

Eka: "The story starts on the 21st of September 1993, the last day I saw my home. On that day, my mother and I were hiding in a corner of our apartment under a seemingly endless and ear-deafening shelling and bombardment...It was the day, when fateful phone call brought the worst news in my life – my 36-year-old uncle was killed and we had to immediately leave the city and make our way to a relatively safe village located east of Sukhumi where my father and my brother were waiting for us to say a last goodbye to me beloved uncle. This tragic day was followed by a cascade of unforgettable painful events imprinted in my memory forever: the fall of Sukhumi; massive expulsion of Georgian population from their homes; long, cold and devastating path through the mountains to a safe place and to a new life; the death of my second uncle in a combat; the wounding of my third uncle which confined him forever to the wheelchair; and then start of new life in a new place and constant struggle for survival...That time I did not know where life would lead me, but I did know that I never wanted to see a war again."

These experiences of loss and alienation were shared by many other women. However, displacement is not a homogeneous experience (Kabachnik et al. 2010; Lundgren 2015; Cárdenas 2022a; Datta 2022). The personal experience of Eka and her family as well as their encounter with other IDPs illustrate this argument.

Eka: "Unlike many other IDPs, who lived in abandoned administrative buildings, hotels, kindergartens, and schools which were not adapted for long-term accommodation, my family was relatively lucky, in that we were hosted by my father's friends. I did not experience what it means to live with extended family members in crowded rooms without our own kitchen and bathroom, without heating or working sewage systems, with leaking roofs and cracked walls. I did not have to miss school because of a lack of school utensils or proper shoes and clothes. But I vividly felt all the deprivations around me, and knew that ours was a daily fight for survival in the face of uncertainty. Even as a I child, I could feel a sense of disempowerment, whereby we could not be certain about tomorrow and all the decisions affecting us were made without us."

Although displacement can be experienced in multiple ways, there is a common feature in the resistance to social stigmatization and the limits of the category "victim" (Baines 2015), which is typically associated with passivity and powerlessness (Bickford 1997). By exploring Eka's view of displacement not as an event, but as key to her personal growth and identity, we can engage with and contribute to ongoing academic discussions about the category of victimhood and how such a category can disenfranchise agency (Bickford 1997; Helms 2013; Krystalli 2021). Eka narrates how her initial reaction to social stigmatization was to reject her identity:

Eka: "I did not want to be a guest in my own country and be called a 'refugee' or 'internally displaced', a 'homeless outsider'. I recall vividly how intensely I wanted to get rid of this 'refugee label'. I did not want others to know that I was an IDP, I wanted to assimilate and disappear into the host community. However, later I realized that by denying that I was an IDP, I was also denying my emotional connection to my hometown Sukhumi and my native Abkhazia."

The stigmatization Eka experienced as an IDP created a need for her to escape from that label and assimilate in her new context and community. However, this feeling was followed by a sense of responsibility and the need to vindicate her roots:

Eka: "I wanted to prove to myself and others, that as an IDP from Abkhazia I am not weaker but stronger than everyone else, that I am not a 'homeless beggar' as some would call us. IDPs are strong-willed 'warriors' who can rebuild their life from the scratch. Indeed, I believe that displacement became a mobilizing factor for me. I was aware of the responsibility that we had to claim our place in society and to strive for the recognition and enjoyment of our rights."

Eka's story and choices regarding the path of women's activism has been highly influenced by strong role models. Among them is Alla, her mother, who is also one of the most prominent activists in Georgia. Eka always remarks how she has been inspired by Alla's goals, and as a young activist she followed her lead in the work with IDP communities and women. Yet, Eka has built her own path to activism:

Eka: "From my childhood onwards, I was surrounded by strong and intelligent women. At the top of this list was always my mother. She was my ideal of a women leader, who despite all hardships has always stayed on the course she set, who despite all losses and deprivations, was never afraid of starting life anew, creating a dignified environment around her family and her community. She never stayed indifferent when someone needed assistance and support. She was never a silent watcher when action was needed."

Together with several other displaced women leaders like herself, Alla established one of the first IDP women organizations in Western Georgia, which they called Women Fund "Sukhumi." The Fund reflects the diversity that was once one of the distinctive features of Sukhumi. The women who gathered to create this organization had different professions, came from different parts of Abkhazia, different nationalities, and none had a prior experience of NGO activism. However, there was a common pain derived from displacement, and they all shared the strong commitment to support people in need. Reflecting on these shared goals and challenges, Eka explains "I recall how my mother, as a leader and role model, and chairperson of Fund Sukhumi, provided me with a space of passion and guidance. She was always the roadmap in my life journey."

Women activists who have directly experienced the effects of the armed conflict often face the challenge of harmonizing their goals of activism, empowerment, and commitment to memory without being constrained by the category of "victim." These same women victims also become agents of peace, as research from different conflict contexts such as Bosnia, Rwanda, Colombia, and South Asia has revealed (Manchanda 2001, 2005; Berry 2018; Kreft 2019). Indeed, Eka's experience—as well as the experiences of other internally displaced women in Georgia who became activists—contributes empirical content to the debate on women as agents of change whose "active participation in peacebuilding changes the meaning of peacebuilding itself" (Shepherd 2016, 125).

Eka argues that the main idea that motivated her and other women to engage with the work of Fund Sukhumi as activists was the refusal to be defined by the category of "victims":

Eka: "We all strived to become agents of change, truly empowered, and well-recognized as advocates for the rights of IDP women and gender equality, promoters of peace and driving force of progressive social change. The path was full of failure and disappointments, accompanied with achievements and satisfaction. As members of a small regional NGO, with little to no experience in fundraising, program management, or English language skills, we had to struggle even to be noticed. Therefore, we had to work twice harder just to become visible and recognized."

Such peace activism is transformative. Women who experienced the effects of the armed conflict have been working together to provide specific responses to everyday needs and humanitarian challenges, but beyond that, their ultimate goal is to create the conditions for women to be empowered and meaningfully participate in every aspect of society. This transformative activism highlights women's awareness of their rights and women's agency to influence changes in society. This empirical finding also gets inspiration from the literature on critical and transformative agency, initially explored by McNay (2003) and further developed by Björkdahl and Selimovic (2015), in which women's agency is driven by fundamental reflections on gendered relationships and their commitment to transform them. Likewise, Manchanda (2001) highlights the need to overcome the category of victim and move toward women's agency in peacebuilding. She argues that in the process of surviving the conflict, women acknowledge new spheres of action and "informal power" which encourage mobilization not only against violence but also against all forms of inequality.

NAVIGATING ACTIVISM: PATHS AND STRATEGIES

From Immediate Needs-Based Assistance to Women-to-Women Diplomacy

The transformative activism portrayed in this chapter also challenges unequal gendered power relations, which paint women as secondary actors in peace efforts. These narratives speak of women as operative—but not strategic—actors in humanitarian efforts (Cárdenas 2022a). However, growing evidence documented in different contexts demonstrates that women are strategic partners in peacebuilding initiatives (Olivius 2019). This has been the case in Georgia, and particularly in the story of the women of Fund Sukhumi. The way in which they have shaped this organization illustrates the role of women as peace agents. Fund Sukhumi evolved over time from providing immediate assistance to empowering women to ensure their participation and make their voices heard at all decision-making levels, eventually allowing them to influence and inform public policies (Cárdenas 2019, 2022b).

The initial purpose of the Fund Sukhumi was to address immediate basic needs of IDP women living in the Imereti Region (western Georgia). These women had to adapt to the new social conditions without adequate support from the government. In particular, the organization focused on their psycho-social rehabilitation. Eka analyses the evolution of the organization and how it reflects a more ambitious view of what their role in the conflict could be:

Eka: "With the support of different humanitarian organizations, including local women's groups, Fund 'Sukhumi' started providing the food, clothes, and household supplies and undertaking medical check-ups of IDP women and their family members. More than a thousand families were supported by the assistance. However, we realized that responding to immediate basic needs through humanitarian actions would not ensure long-term positive changes in IDPs' lives and would not guarantee their resilience. The need for social, political, and economic empowerment of women to change their position in the family and society, to create a possibility for advancing their status and agency, became clear. We realized that it was important to transform their role from mere passive recipient of assistance to someone who engaged in decisions concerning their present life and the future. As women are best able to support themselves and their families when they are financially self-sufficient, Fund Sukhumi started equipping them with the necessary skills for entrepreneurship and providing with the small business grants to lift them up from poverty and allow not only to survive, but also to contribute to their confidence and increase their opportunities in life."

In addition, women and girls engaged in series of trainings on leadership, communication, and advocacy skills, at the "School of Women Leaders," established by the organization. From early 2000s, Fund Sukhumi created the community leader women-led hubs—Women's Support Centers—in more than ten cities in Western Georgia. Such centers bring together women community leaders who are trained to collecting information about the specific needs and concerns of IDPs and conflict-affected women and girls, as well as victims of the domestic. The data collected by the women is analyzed and used as evidence-based information for developing a relevant response strategy and to undertake advocacy.

The type of activism that Eka and her organization have embraced is grounded in everyday realities and aims to transform the structural barriers that inhibit women's role as peace agents. Thus, it embraces an idea of peace that contributes to the discussion of feminist peace as grounded in everyday sites of peacebuilding (Reilly 2007; Wibben et al. 2019; True 2020). Fund Sukhumi looks at peace as a process of social transformation of everyday and political structures in Georgia, in which women play a key role (Cárdenas 2022b).

The work of this organization gave Eka the opportunity to participate in a meaningful project in which she could not only help to respond to immediate needs, but also to collectively envision what the role of women in conflict resolution *could* be.

Eka: "When I was 13 years, I realized that I didn't want this to happen again, I was always against this war. At the beginning, all the IDP sentiments were very aggressive. People were caught up in aggression. They were caught up in the desire for retaliation, but I didn't agree. Despite the fact that conflict in Abkhazia has left deep scars in my memory, many times, I've been involved in people-to-people dialogues with youth and representatives of CSOs from Abkhazia and South Ossetia in different platforms and forums, mainly held in third countries. To keep dialogue with conflict divided society, to discuss openly all grievances and failures, learning from the past mistakes to avoid them in the future, were among the main priorities to Fund Sukhumi. We have been also actively working with IDP women and youth to help rethink the past, destroy images of 'enemy', reduce the tension between conflict divided societies, promote a culture of peace, and involve them in peacebuilding."

Women's activism and peacebuilding practices deployed by Fund Sukhumi allowed Magda to develop the concept of "women-to-women diplomacy" (Cárdenas 2019). This concept encompasses the promotion of women's agency as a key element of mobilization and peacebuilding practices. Women's own experiences of conflict become a basis for bridging divides, and women's visions of gender equality become a fundamental part of peace. Women-to-women diplomacy represents an alternative peacebuilding practice aimed at the social transformation of gender unequal relations and narratives. The journey of Eka's activism and the work of her organization reflect how such transformation has been envisioned in Georgia. They demonstrate how local initiatives make women's agency a stepping-stone not only for the enjoyment of the rights of conflict-affected populations, but also for their participation as peace agents. The way in which the agenda and practices of Fund Sukhumi have evolved reveals how the very notion of peace has evolved:

Eka: "I believe in the importance of advocating directly with local officials at the local government level through Fund Sukhumi. Together with affected IDP women, we actively engage to address their urgent needs and ensure that municipal programs and budgets prioritize their concerns. This initiative stems from my own experiences and determination to empower displaced women, ensuring their voices are heard in decision-making processes that directly impact their lives. Moving to the national level, our role in the consultative platform on Women, Peace and Security under the Office of the State Minister of Reconciliation and Civil Equality becomes crucial. My motivation for focusing on this area arises from witnessing the resilience and struggles of women in conflict, driving me to advocate for gender-responsive strategies, policies, and action plans that address their specific challenges. At the international level, through active participation in meetings and exchanges with global stakeholders, Fund Sukhumi strives to integrate gender-sensitive and community-centric perspectives into the agenda of the Geneva International Discussions. This global advocacy reflects my belief in the importance of global solidarity and cooperation in addressing the complex challenges faced by displaced women and communities affected by conflict."

Eka also believes in the importance of challenging the widespread association of women's activism with so-called *women's issues*, including sexual and reproductive health, child-care leave, domestic violence, equal work conditions, marital law, social welfare policies and education, and women's struggles for equal rights. Although these are crucial themes, the idea that women only mobilize for *women's issues* limits their possibilities of participating in political space and formal negotiations. This linkage further excludes them from spaces where discussions about national security, conflict resolution, demilitarization, and other political issues take place (Photo 9.1).

CHALLENGES

The type of activism that Eka and her organization embody is transformative not at the personal level of women activists, but when it comes to how their networks evolve. Navigating these arenas—and maintaining the ideas of everyday peace and women's agency at the core of Fund Sukhumi—poses several challenges. There are structural barriers and challenges for women's meaningful participation. Too often, women's organizations engage or participate symbolically, without any follow-up, tangible results, or real impact. Eka points out that women's participation is limited and that their engagement in peace efforts is only symbolic and further explains:

Eka: "For example, the consultations with the delegates and co-chairs of the Geneva International Discussions is fragmented and ad hoc. Civil society, especially women, including conflict affected, IDPs and grassroots

Photo 9.1 Eka Gamakharia speaking with women at a workshop about women's rights in Georgia

leaders, who live further afield – and typically in areas more directly impacted by the conflict – want to be heard. Not just sporadically, but on a regular basis, through established systematic consultation mechanisms and working group meetings. They want to see more structure in the operations aimed at responding to safety concerns of the population at the border zones. For example, they want a real chance to discuss and influence policy issues related to access to the health system, mobility, and an inclusive education system. Ad hoc consultations and 'tick-box' consultations undertaken by the government officials are counterproductive and create distrust in the process."

In the discussion of such issues, Eka highlights that there is still a widespread misconception about what women can contribute and what their interests, expertise, and capabilities are. Throughout her journey as an activist and peacebuilder, Eka has come to understand the following:

Eka: "Women are frequently seen as depoliticized subjects, a homogeneous group with a single voice that usually is asked to talk about 'women's issues'. Men have never been asked to comment only on 'men's issues'. Women should have an equal say in issues such as the national security, conflict resolution, demilitarization, and other political issues that concern not only men, but women."

This issue is reflected in a growing field of research aimed at countering essentialist arguments that suggest women should be responsible for social themes—or a *soft agenda*—without getting access to the core issues in the peace settlement (Rehn and Sirleaf 2002). Indeed, getting women involved in peace issues helps foster an approach to transformational peace that benefits women and all of society, in contrast to efforts that merely lead to a return to pre-conflict status quo (Joshi and Olsson 2021). By illustrating Eka and Fund Sukhumi's vision of activism, this chapter has engaged with such literature and illustrates the possibility for women to become key actors in humanitarian and peace efforts.

Another important challenge in the advance of women's activism in Georgia is funding. The lack of sustained funding poses obstacles to the work of women's organizations and their meaningful participation.

Eka: "It is not only the scarcity of funding opportunity on the ground, but also the *type* of funding that is problematic. Available resources disproportionately target state, International Organizations, and International Non-Governmental Organizations (INGOs); only small sub-grants are available to those delivering the actual services on the ground. This system is ineffective and inefficient. It is not only important to increase funding for local, grassroots women's organizations, but also to provide them with technical assistance. In addition, short-term, sporadic, and unpredictable funding prevents long-term programming and its potential for sustainable impact. This is particularly disruptive to peacebuilding work, especially actions related to informal peace processes and confidence-building, which inherently require sustained and predictable engagement. When activities are disrupted, connections between people – which had been so carefully built up over time – become interrupted and severed, and many interesting valuable actions and initiatives that require to be built on and developed are suspended or stopped."

The context of shrinking space for civil society is another matter of great concern for the advancement of women's peace activism in Georgia. A recent legislative effort made by Georgia's ruling party has labeled civil society organizations as "agents of foreign influence." This effort was aimed at limiting civil society's ability to operate freely or express opposing views. Indeed, a draft law on "Agents of Foreign Influence" was submitted to the Georgian parliament on February 20, 2023. It was intended to make all NGOs and media outlets that receive more than 20% of their funding from abroad to register as "agents of foreign influence" in an official registry. The draft law authorized the Ministry of Justice to investigate and monitor those organizations they deem to be agents of foreign influence. Activists worry that the law might also give the government access to personal data. The proposed law risks not only increasing the government's control over civil society and media, but could also serve to stigmatize civil society and shrink space for the human rights activists.

Financial resources are already scarce for civil society organizations, making foreign support their major source of income. Thus, the Law would target those actors playing pivotal role in filling the gaps of government when it comes to providing social services and assistance to the most vulnerable populations in the country, including children and women, people with disabilities, national and ethnic minorities, IDPs, and conflict-affected population.

Eka reflects upon women's crucial role in participating in protests against this law:

Eka: "Women have been at a forefront of protests against the 'foreign agent law'. However, women have also been targeted by criticism from a society poisoned by toxic masculinity. They are stigmatized for being active, for voicing principled words, and for taking action. Women are not forgiven for raising their voice against injustice and inequality. Perhaps this is what has made women stronger. This bitter reality and the resistant environment give women perseverance, and pushes them to raise their voice fearlessly. During the days of protest against the 'foreign agent law', I witnessed the tenacity, courage, and intransigence of many strong women who fought for their own rights and for the rights of other member of the society. Of course, we will never give up, and we will always be on the forefront of the battlefield for this cause."

Conclusion

This chapter has taken us on a journey of activism inspired by the idea of amplifying the voices of conflict-affected populations. The experience of displacement and the dilemmas of identity, belonging, and stigmatization were key in Eka's story. She has supported women IDPs, from the promotion of their rights to the transformation of their role in society as peace agents. This chapter sheds light on how the experience of displacement not only influenced her decision to become an activist, but also shaped the kind of peace that she envisions. By analyzing this trajectory of activism, this chapter contributes new arguments to ongoing discussions that challenge the idea of victims as limited to being mere recipients of policies. On the contrary, this chapter underscores the transformative potential of their roles.

Eka's story also reveals key aspects of women's activism in Georgia. The agendas and practices promoted by women's organizations extend beyond national boundaries and speak to a broader understanding of the root causes of the conflict. They share the goal of advancing the status of women. The activism embodied by Fund Sukhumi articulates a conception of feminist peace that focuses on women leading social transformation through everyday practices, relationships, and narratives (Cárdenas 2022b). By following this agenda, they transform into brave women.

References

Autesserre, Séverine. 2012. "Dangerous tales: Dominant narratives on the Congo and their unintended consequences." *African Affairs* 111, no. 443: 202–222.

Baines, Erin K. 2015. "Today, I Want to Speak out the Truth: Victim Agency, Responsibility, and Transitional Justice." *International Political Sociology* 9, no. 4: 316–32.

Berry, Marie. 2018. *War, women, and power: From violence to mobilization in Rwanda and Bosnia-Herzegovina*. Cambridge; New York: Cambridge University Press.

Bickford, Susan. 1997. "Anti-Anti-Identity Politics: Feminism, Democracy, and the Complexities of Citizenship." *Hypatia* 12, no. 4: 111–131.

Björkdahl, Annika. and Selimovic, Johanna. 2015. "Gendering agency in transitional justice." *Security Dialogue* 46, no. 2: 165–182.

Cárdenas, Magda Lorena. 2019. "Women-to-Women Diplomacy in Georgia: A Peacebuilding Strategy in Frozen Conflict." *Civil Wars* 21, no. 3: 385–409.

Cárdenas, Magda Lorena. 2022a. "Rooting, shifting and mobilizing: Women's peacebuilding across differences in Georgia and Myanmar." *Women's Studies International Forum* 91.

Cárdenas, Magda Lorena. 2022b. "Exploring women's vision(s) of peace: towards feminist peace in Myanmar and Georgia?" *European Journal of Politics and Gender* 5, no. 1: 7–23.

Datta, Ankur. 2022. "The life of labels: Refugees, displaced persons, and migrants." In *The Routledge Handbook of Refugees in India*, edited by Irudaya Rajan, 265–272. Routledge.

Helms, Elissa. 2013. *Innocence and victimhood: gender, nation, and women's activism in postwar Bosnia-Herzegovina*. Madison, Wisconsin: The University of Wisconsin Press.

Joshi, Madhav and Louise Olsson. 2021. "War termination and women's political rights." *Social Science Research* 94.

Kabachnik Peter, Joanna Regulska, and Beth Mitchneck. 2010. "Where and When is Home? The Double Displacement of Georgian IDPs from Abkhazia." *Journal of Refugee Studies* 23, no. 3: 315–336.

Kreft, Anne-Kathrin. 2019. "Responding to sexual violence: Women's mobilization in war." *Journal of Peace Research* 56, no. 2: 220–233.

Krystalli, Roxani. 2021. "Narrating Victimhood: Dilemmas and (in) Dignities." *International Feminist Journal of Politics* 23, no. 1: 125–46.

Lundgren, Minna. 2015. "Crossing the Border – An Intergenerational Study of Belonging and Temporary Return among IDPs from Abkhazia." In *Security, Democracy and Development in the Southern Caucasus and the Black Sea Region*, edited by Ghia Nodia and Christoph Stefes. Bern: Peter Lag.

Manchanda, Rita. 2001. *Women, war and peace in South Asia: Beyond victimhood to agency*. New Delhi: Sage Publications.

Manchanda, Rita. 2005. "Women's Agency in Peace Building: Gender Relations in Post-Conflict Reconstruction." *Economic and Political Weekly* 40, no. 44/45: 4737–4745.

Mcnay, Lois. 2003. "Agency, Anticipation and Indeterminacy in Feminist Theory." *Feminist Theory* 4, no. 2: 139–148.

Olivius, Elisabeth. 2019. "Claiming rights in exile: women's insurgent citizenship practices in the Thai-Myanmar borderlands." *Citizenship Studies* 23, no. 8: 761–779.

Shepherd, Laura. 2016. "Victims of Violence or Agents of Change? Representations of Women in UN Peacebuilding Discourse." *Peacebuilding* 4, no. 2: 121–135.

Sosulski, Marya, Nicole Buchanan, and Chandra Donnell. 2010. "Life history and narrative analysis: Feminist methodologies contextualizing black women's experiences with severe mental illness." *Journal of Sociology and Social Welfare* 37, no. 3: 29–57.

Reilly, Niamh. 2007. "Seeking gender justice in post-conflict transitions: towards a transformative women's human rights approach." *International Journal of Law in Context* 3, no. 2: 155–72.
Rehn, Elisabeth and Ellen Sirleaf. 2002. *Women, War and Peace: The Independent Experts' Assessment on the Impact of Armed Conflict on Women and Women's Role in Peace-building.* New York: United Nations Development Fund for Women.
True, Jacqui. 2020. "Continuums of Violence and Peace: A Feminist Perspective." *Ethics & International Affairs* 34, no. 1: 85–95.
Wibben, Annick. 2011. *Feminist security studies: A narrative approach.* London: Routledge.
Wibben, Annick, Catia Confortini, Sanam Roohi, Sarai Aharoni, Leena Vastapuu, and Tiina Vaittinen. 2019. "Collective discussion: piecing-up feminist peace research." *International Political Sociology* 13, no. 1: 86–107.

CHAPTER 10

"I'd rather create my own table than sit where I am not wanted." A Conversation Between Stella Naw and Jenny Hedström About Myanmar

Stella Naw and Jenny Hedström

INTRODUCTION

I dreamt I was at an outdoor event; I remember speaking to some activist friends. Then suddenly planes began flying over me dropping bombs. I ran, and I saw these schoolkids in their school uniforms. I tried to run with them; we took shelter under a tree. The bombs were everywhere. I woke up crying to the news about the latest shelling in Hpakant [in which the Myanmar Air Force launched airstrikes, killing at least 80 civilians and injuring 100 at an outdoor event]. —Stella Naw

S. Naw
New York, NY, USA

J. Hedström (✉)
Swedish Defence University, Stockholm, Sweden
e-mail: Jenny.hedstrom@fhs.se

© The Author(s), under exclusive license to Springer Nature Switzerland AG 2025
J. Zulver, K. Stallone (eds.), *Brave Women*,
https://doi.org/10.1007/978-3-031-70702-5_10

In February 2021, the Myanmar military took power in a coup d'état, ending a decade of political and economic reforms, and in an instant reversing the country's democratic gains and freedoms (Hedström and Olivius 2023). Within days, thousands of people turned out on the streets to protest the military in jubilant, creative, and colourful displays of collective action. Many of these protests were led by young women from ethnic minority communities, and the protest movement soon included feminist and minority demands aimed at upsetting old power structures and the Bamar stronghold of national politics. The military response was slow at first, but within a few weeks it turned violent. The first protester to die was a young woman, Mya Thwate Thwate Khaing, shot in head by military police (AAPPB 2022).

Stella Naw, a Kachin political analyst and human rights activist who has worked with Kachin women's groups, as well as the Kachin Independence Organisation's foreign affairs office, the political wing of the Kachin armed struggle, was at the forefront of the protests, helping the younger generation of activists strategise in the General Strike Committee of Nationalities (GSCN), an organisation set up following the coup to help coordinate the protest movements and their demands. Importantly, these demands were broader than simply wanting to end military rule; instead, the GSCN recognised that the coup was facilitated by military involvement in politics and history and enabled by the prominence and privilege of the majority Bamar population. Rejecting military rule was the first step; building a federal democratic union—a new Myanmar—based on equality and the right to self-determination became the end goal. An exiled government, the National Unity Government of the Republic of the Union of Myanmar (NUG), was established by ousted Myanmar officials and ethnic leaders in the fight against the military junta, and in May 2021, Stella joined the NUG as Deputy Minister for International Cooperation.

The recognition of minority rights emerged from the ethnic diversity and leadership of the movement and of the GSCN specifically; a unique protest group composed of youth leaders from the minorities and Bamar communities who recognised the need for political equality among all ethnic communities as the basis to political solution. Many have suffered violence and abuse at the hands of the Myanmar military—transition or no transition. In ethnic communities in Myanmar, wars have been fought for generations. The ceasefire between the Kachin Independence Organisation (KIO), a revolutionary organisation controlling areas of northern Myanmar known as Kachinland (or Wunpawng Mungdan), and the

Myanmar military was broken a mere two months after the first semi-democratic government took office in Naypidaw, Myanmar's capital, in March 2011. There have been multiple rounds of ceasefire talks held between the Myanmar military and the Kachin leaders over the past several decades as wars continue to be fought. The latest cycle of the war in Kachinland—which first was declared in 1961—had at the time of the conversation upon which this chapter is based, been ongoing for almost 12 years.

Over a hundred thousand people in Kachinland are displaced, but the camps where mostly women and children live have not received humanitarian aid since 2016 due to a Myanmar military blockage of international assistance to these areas. The Myanmar military has been accused of committing gross human rights violations in Kachinland, including but not limited to killings, sexual- and gender-based violence, arbitrary arrests, and forced labour, amounting to war crimes and crimes against humanity (Office of the UN High Commissioner for Human Rights 2018). After the coup, displacement increased, as did the arrival of young women and men from the cities deciding to arm themselves: thousands of People Defence Forces (PDFs) and new armed alliances have emerged, with veteran revolutionary groups like the KIO often hosting and training new young fighters. Fighting in Kachinland is now occurring almost daily, with the airstrikes against civilians in Hpakan (a remote town and centre of jade mines in Kachinland in northwestern Myanmar) recounted above, being the deadliest to date.

Stella has been involved in the struggle for rights and equality in Myanmar since 2011, when the war resumed in Kachinland. This chapter is based on a conversation between Jenny Hedström, a Swedish-based researcher who has spent close to two decades working with and researching gender and violence in Myanmar, and Stella Naw, a Kachin political analyst and human rights activist. It reflects on the struggles and joys of striving for feminist change within the Myanmar Spring Revolution, and what opportunities and risks institutions of power, like the NUG or the Kachin military, entail for feminist activism. They wrote the chapter collaboratively after Stella left Myanmar, thinking together in conversations online and sharing drafts over email. This conversation was born out of mutual respect and admiration for each other's work after they first met in 2016. The authors decided to set up the chapter in an interview format to reflect that the conversation happened between two different people, coming from different backgrounds, with different perspectives. They wanted to include their separate voices to honour this working dynamic and friendship. From this section onwards, we switch into our own voices.

"I HAVE AN OCEAN OF TEARS IN MY BODY": CONTINUITIES OF VIOLENCE AND RESISTANCE FROM KACHINLAND TO MYANMAR

Jenny: A feminist reading of Myanmar's transitional decade reveals both the insecurity of the transitional years and hints at the violence unleased in the military coup d'etat. As the late feminist scholar Cynthia Cockburn argues, different incidences of violence and different phases of war build upon and reinforce each other across time, often in non-linear ways (Cockburn 2004). This perspective emphasises how the violence experienced by women and members of minority groups, alongside the persistence of masculinised, military politics throughout Myanmar's transitional decade, enabled and facilitated the 2021 coup. This means that the violence unleashed by the coup is part of a broader continuum of violence that transcends the supposed divisions between pre-war/war/peace. Understanding this allows us to see how the acts of violence experienced by communities or individuals in Myanmar during the transition were not discrete or episodic events, but experiences informed by broader relations of power that normalised exclusion and legitimatised inequality (see Krook 2017, 2020). These relations of power both endorsed military, masculine might and exposed particular bodies—those belonging to women or ethnic minorities—to violence in the home and in the public sphere.

I would like to cite Esther Wah, one of the Spring Revolution leaders. Esther powerfully writes: "We have endured war, authoritarianism, exploitation, and chauvinism. But just as our nightmare did not start with the coup, neither did our struggle" (Wah 2021). You Stella, like Esther, comes from a community that has been fighting for equality for generations, a community for which the democratic transition in 2011 did not end up being about greater freedom but instead greater violence (see, for example, Sadan 2016; Saw Ralph and Naw Sheera 2020; The Karen Women's Organization 2010; Kachin Women's Association Thailand 2013). In other words, the violence after the coup is not new, and it is important to see the continuities of oppression and insecurity over time in Myanmar.

Otherwise, uneven empirical and theoretical attention to violence will continue to restrict our understanding of the present political moment in Myanmar, and how this might develop. Can you tell me a little of what happened in February 2021, and what your thoughts and experiences, as a long-term Kachin activist, were?

Stella: Throughout my lifetime I have seen so many different waves of conflict and violence. Even so I felt shocked when the coup took place [in Myanmar in February 2021], because this meant the conflict and violence occurred at the national level. I was in Yangon, the capital, at the time, and the way life was interrupted, normal day-to-day life just interrupted, in that sense it was more of a shock. Recently someone, a Bamar [majority community] activist, who joined the anti-coup movement said to another Kachin friend of mine that "this is our chance, we have to win, we have to put everything into this!". My friend just looked to her and said, that's how we have done things *always*. We have *always* had to put everything in to respond to the outbreak of war, military offences and for our survival.

This is part of our normal life, responding in a material and emotional way to this violence. That this happened now at a national level, and to the Bamar community, was surprising, and the way it interrupted everyday life so suddenly was shocking, but the how and the way it is happening is not surprising. We have seen it all. Of course, it is always sad when violence on this scale happens, not just to our own community, but to other communities as well. This brings more grief, because seeing the violence unfold in someone else's community, the pain is doubled. Because, you know, our community has been through this and still goes through this, and now someone else is also suffering. And that's why it is more painful to see this. I have an ocean of tears in my body.

I did not have a choice, not a question, to become involved in the protests against the military. For me—working for justice, working for rights, always—when anyone else's rights are violated I am going in. I had to do it. It was pure instinct. Joining the protest wasn't without its risks as members of the security forces started firing live rounds at protestors a few weeks into the protest. There was always a chance that I might not come home at the end of the day because so many people did not get to go home due to the arrest or killing. Even when you got to come home, there was a potential risk that local administrative personnel in our neighbourhood could also inform us to the security forces for the arrest. This also happened to many protestors who were arrested at home in the middle of the night. While both women and men protestors were leading protests those days, men acted as the physical shields of the protest groups and women took turns chanting on loudspeakers. For me, at the end of every long protest day the goal was to get home to my toddler son waiting for me at home; joining the protest was compelled by the injustice, and wanting to create a better future for my son and the future generation where they won't have to go through the same kind of institutional discrimination and physical violence that previous generations have gone through.

I wasn't so concerned about the elections being overthrown because the consecutive elections had happened since the country opened up in 2010 were very disconnected from our lived experience of renewed civil war. But the violence and the suppression that followed, and at such a scale, that concerned me. So, to me it was incredibly important; I had to go in and help wherever I could.

Marching along the crowd of young protestors, my blood was rushing: I felt all the energy in the world that one could imagine. With all that energy and feelings of solidarity, I choked up seeing bystanders cheering for us—the non-Bamar ethnic protest group holding diverse flags representing each of us. Those Bamar and urban people weren't looking at us as if "what special rights do they want? Trying to destroy the Union?", but they supported us.

It was during the marches, I felt seen and heard for the first time. There seemed to be a notable shift among the Bamar majority in understanding the plight of ethnic people; bystanders on the streets of Yangon cheered for the GSCN protest carrying various ethnic flights and chanted along with us for our call for Federal democracy. This was unthinkable prior to the coup where many Bamar Buddhists, the ethnic and religious majority of the country, saw the ethnic minority's call for political equality in the form of Federalism as an attempt to break up the Union and the Myanmar military as the protector of the Union.

People, Bamar and people living in urban areas in particular, seem to finally understand what it means to have one's political rights taken away from them. I also felt that for the first time that we have a shared feeling of injustice being done to us and through a common enemy—the military. Before the coup, they saw the Military as the protector of the Union. I saw a bystander woman weep as she did her three-fingers salute in the air. I smiled back at her with tears in my eyes with my own salute sign, the three-finger salute widely used in the protest movements for democracy, including in Thailand and Hong Kong.[1]

A Feminist Revolution

Jenny: A great deal of reporting on the Myanmar Spring Revolution has focused on the gendered symbolism of many of the protest activists, such as the use of female underwear and *htamein*-campaign to mock the military. These protests emerged from widespread beliefs in Burmese culture that women's underwear and menstrual blood have the power to detrimentally harm men's status and glory, with military leaders as well as foot soldiers being "notoriously superstitious" (Marlar, Chambers, and Elena 2023, 16). Similar to the 2007 Panties for Peace Campaign that the exiled women's movement spearheaded, the 2021 *htamein*-campaign (htameins are women's skirts) saw women across the country making makeshift barricades out of *htamein* and smearing the photos of military leaders with red paint. Women's involvement in the recent protests have also received a lot of focus, although women in Myanmar have of course always been key to revolutionary movements and resistance activities, even if their involvement have been overlooked and quickly forgotten (see Zin Mar Oo and Kusakabe 2010; Gagnon and Moo 2023; Naw K'Nyaw Paw and Quadrini 2023). What do you think will happen this time? How and when did feminist demands make their way into the Spring Revolution, and what sets this revolutionary moment apart from other revolutions in Myanmar?

Stella: The unique thing about urban youth protests this time is how the leadership hasn't centred around men. For youth or protest groups like the General Strike Committee of Nationalities (GSCN), it wasn't only about following men blindly but more about having the right people to lead in their areas of expertise, men as well as women. These were more than just symbolic leaderships—we witnessed meaningful joint-leadership and decision-making taking place between men and women. The advisory group to the GSCN had more female members than males and our voices

---

[1] Through protest actions, Myanmar youth—especially those living in exile—joined the Milk Tea Alliance, transnational network of GenZ young activists/netizens fighting against authoritarianism and fighting for democracy in Hong Kong, Taiwan, Thailand, India, and then later Myanmar. This became quite visible on social media, but it did not take off as a national thing.

really mattered in the decision-making process. That sort of process paved ways for a new norm of gender equality. When that type of environment was created, you see more trust and respect among collaborators. It was so different from how it runs with the older generation. It was obviously also different for different protest groups and I can only speak for my own experience and the youth group I was involved with. The reason I chose to work with GSCN was because of my previous working experience with several of the youth leaders from the group who understood the importance of intersectional identities, gender, religion, ethnicity, and class. They were few Bamar youth leaders who chose to work with Rohingya poets despite being a very controversial collaboration even during the period led by the Aung San Suu Kyi-led democratic government who defended the military at The Hague against charges of genocide of the Rohingya community in Rakhine state. After the coup, many youth, especially urban Bamar youth, have also spoken out about their regret and a new sense of understanding and empathy for what other ethnic minorities and Rohingya communities have gone through.

When my Kachin community asked me to become part of the technical advisory team to the KPICT (which the KIO is also a member of), I chose to remain with advising the youth group instead. The Kachin Independence Organization, political wing of the Kachin Independence Army (KIA), is known to be one of the strongest ethnic armies in Myanmar challenging the Myanmar military. Working with KPICT would mean I will also be part of the strongest groups that I belong to ethnically and it would also mean having more power in political negotiation. But sometimes it's not always about being with a stronger group or our own group; it is about where we feel we can really make an impact. So, the feminist representation and voices that came out of this revolution came from having a much more open-minded young generation, where men understand that the right people—regardless of gender—should lead in order to ensure the best possible strategic outcomes. Some of the youth leaders pioneered gender-sensitive policies in their rights-based organisations that included paid menstrual leave for female staff. Because they understood intersectionality, inclusivity was important to them if our collective vision was political revolution.

And so, for the women, to finally get the rightful opportunity to lead in the areas of our expertise as we resist the military regime, we were able to focus more and bring more of ourselves and our energy as we didn't have to spare or waste any in trying to convince our male counterparts that we can lead. That was unique; I never had that experience before.

Violence, Resistance, and the Struggle for Survival

Jenny: Gayatri Chakravorty Spivak writes: "While violence is not beyond naming and diagnosis, it does raise many challenging questions all the same. I am a pacifist. I truly believe in the power of nonviolence. But we cannot categorically deny a people the right to resist violence, even, under certain conditions, with violence. Sometimes situations become so intolerable that moral certainties are no longer meaningful. There is a difference here between condoning such a response and trying to understand why the recourse to violence becomes inevitable" (Evans and Spivak 2016). While the first few days and weeks of the protests really felt hopeful and jubilant, and the protests were peaceful, the military soon turned their weapons onto protestors. To date, close to 3000 protestors have been killed; many more have been injured or detained. The military's violence effectively shut down the broader protest movement on the streets; the protests then moved to the rural areas where young people began taking up arms to fight the military (Fishbein 2023). I know you saw a lot of violence. What were your reactions when the people you had been advising fled the cities for rural and so-called liberated areas to begin a violent revolution?

Stella: I often think of a conversation I had with young Bamar protestors in the General Strike Committee of Nationalities (GSCN). We were working together strategising around the protests, and then a few weeks into the coup, the military scale of the violence exploded. By then a lot of young activists had gone to "liberated areas" to take up training from the EROs (to become PDFs) to prepare themselves. They said to me: "the military is not human, we have to fight them with violent means." I told them I understood their feelings; that because of the armed struggle my community is still alive so I understand that armed struggle is important as a defence system, but it should always be used as a last tool. I told them: I do not want to encourage you to go, because I don't think anyone should have to do this. I asked them to hold on to the peaceful struggle for as long as they possibly could because once you turn violent, and it becomes an armed struggle, there is no turning back. I always advocate for peaceful turns, but when you are from a minority group, and you are being attacked, how do you survive without an armed defence? In order to resist and survive, in order to make these broader changes, you have to first survive.

Using violent means, it is a very reluctant choice. These young people felt cornered. Of course, they didn't want to do that, to take up arms, no one does, but what else could they do when the security forces are shooting at the innocent protestors? The so-called international democratic allies did nothing more than issuing statements on Facebook. After dozens were killed and thousands arrested, they were left with simply no other choice. I understand this, coming from a community where the armed struggle is the only reason why we even exist, but an armed struggle should always be the last resort. It's also a complicated one because we picked up arms to defend ourselves and to demand political self-determination and then once you engage in an armed struggle, it's hard to get out of it too. Part of the cost you pay includes your culture and community being militarised, more hierarchical, and gendered. Yet, it is what people turn to when they feel there is no other option left for them, when other strategies and mechanisms have failed. When we feel that we have no one to turn to, we are left on our own to defend our own community. As crackdown on the protestors intensified in the major cities followed by arrest and killing by the security forces, many youth and protest leaders fled into the areas controlled by the ethnic-controlled territories along the border areas with the strategy to fight back the coup regime. Their absence weakens the urban mass protests which then transformed into flash mobs guerrilla protests. Marching the streets with a few dozens of protestors holding banners before quickly dispersing, to avoid being caught by the security forces, became a new strategy for urban protests. Photos of flashmobs were primarily used to keep up the momentum of the resistance on the social media pages, reminding the world that resistance to the coup continues.

"I'D RATHER CREATE MY OWN TABLE THAN SIT WHERE I AM NOT WANTED": ON FEMINISM, ACTIVISM, AND MILITARISED POWER

Jenny: As long-term Karen activist Naw K'nyaw Paw puts it, women from minority communities in Myanmar have had to fight on three fronts: they have had to fight the violent, ethnic oppression of the Myanmar state targeting ethnic minority communities; the patriarchal practices of the ethnic revolutions; and the military campaigns executed by the *Tatmadaw* (the Myanmar military) (Naw K'Nyaw Paw and Quadrini 2023). This is of course not unique to Myanmar; across the world, women from indigenous and minority communities have had to contend with the intersections of colonialism, racism, and patriarchal politics (Knobblock and Kuokkanen 2015; Anthias 2014), helping us see how multiple layers of discrimination and difference intersect to expose members of subordinated groups to insecurity and violence (Collins 2017; Crenshaw 1990), and shaping their access to authority, justice, and power. What does it mean to you to be a Kachin activist as well as a feminist so close to military power?

Stella: The higher you get; the fewer women there are. So, once you are at the top, or speak to the top, they are almost all men. And often the women who sit at the table with other male leaders are often there not just because you have experience and intelligence you also need connections, so they are not so interested in changing things drastically. Those are of course also important voices, they carry weight. To be a woman, and from an ethnic minority community, I have faced multiple layers of challenges, but I never really considered myself a feminist until I worked with a lot of male leaders; when I looked around and saw "oh wow I am the only woman, or one or two women sitting here, and not even in the decision-making position" this forced to me to stop and think: what is the problem here? Why are there no women here? Why I am not comfortable, why am I the only woman at the table? I started thinking about that. Also, when I started to work more with leaders in my community, I had to change my entire wardrobe (to be taken more seriously) and my manner to be accepted. Even though no one told me to, but I just picked up on the fact that I had to change. The fact that rather than focusing on my knowledge and skills that I brought to the table, I had to pay attention to the way I dress or act less feminine to be accepted and seen as part of the group were. I felt the need to make it very clear that I was there to work for the same shared goals with all the male leaders there. I thought to myself, if it was a Kachin man in my place, I don't think he would have to go through that same kind of experience and preparation. This experience became very clear to me: that intersecting identities—gender, age, and class—simply determine who gets to be included or excluded in the decision-making spaces. Seeing who gets to have power simply based on that intersectionality and then others like me have to change so much of ourselves to get to be a part of this didn't feel right. I want to change that for everyone, to have equal access to opportunities including and especially in the decision-making spaces. That made me a feminist.

Being a minority and a woman, there are so many struggles to focus on, we have to fight only once and choose our struggles carefully. With the KIO, I am willing to work as allies in certain thematic areas but any closer to the military means that the feminist struggle will be co-opted, because to me, I feel like the military space is such a deeply patriarchal space. So, you have to draw the line when and where you will cooperate with or support them. I do not feel they will ever make space for women on an equal level. The women in the KIO and its armed wing the Kachin Independence Army (KIA) have no space to advocate for women's rights. So I can be an ally with the political goals of the KIO, to advocate for our rights as a Kachin community to be recognised and respected, but I can't work from inside.

Sure, in some instances, we can make changes from within, but with the military, I don't think so. I often have these conversations with other feminists in Burma, and I just don't think it is worth sitting at the table when you are so not wanted. Maybe we need to focus our attention on creating another table, where the energy and focus will be so loud and so present they have no choice but to notice us! Yes, I'd rather create my own table than sit at a table where I am not wanted. I want to focus on really mobilising the young generation, that is where the future is, we need people who think differently, who will challenge existing norms. What is the point of trying to make changes otherwise, if we were just to be part of sustaining and reproducing the same existing mechanisms?

On Leaving: Going Beyond Tokenism

Stella: I accepted the nomination to be a Deputy Minister on behalf of my Kachin community. So, before I left Yangon in April 2021, I was busy working with the strike committee. My community first wanted me to come and support the Kachin Political Interim Coordination Team (KPICT), established by Kachin organisations both from inside the country and the diaspora communities to advocate on behalf of the Kachin people after the military coup. I felt honoured, but I felt more useful where the youth needed me, with the strike committee. I was helping the youth connecting to different diplomatic missions, and other organisations, I was able to help them get connected and getting their voices out in a peaceful manner. I felt I could do a lot. I turned down the invitation to sit at the KPICT, because I was working with the youth.

But then I left, making that very difficult decision to leave, because they were arresting left and right, we would see military trucks in our street, arresting people, and so we had to make the decision to leave. I had all these digital documents on our Kachin armed struggle, and of course working with the strike committee I had all these strategy documents, so I was thinking that "oh, I really need to leave." If I am arrested with all these documents, it will put a lot of people in jeopardy. I also thought that I can do more if I have freedom. I left Myanmar, but it was a very difficult decision. After spending a lot of time in dangerous contexts and protests, the decision to leave the country came down to a strategic one. My expertise lies, less on the community mobilising, in the international advocacy, trying to influence international policy makers on their policies affecting Myanmar, especially on peace creation, human rights, and humanitarian issues. In order to do what I do best, I needed the space, safe internet connection and ability to travel to see people if needed. I have defined my role very clearly, where and when I can be most useful to the struggle. So, leaving the country at the time was the best option to continue doing my work.

Once I landed in Canada, I realised I had been nominated. My immediate response was no. I felt like I am already doing things in my own way, but they said it was a real chance for me to represent my community to make change, and this role is important to make change. I said, let me think about it. Of course I did some risk calculation. At this time everyone else close to me or living with me leading up to the coup was out of the city where we were living before. The possibility of anyone getting arrested close to me seemed low. I spoke to a few people I look up to as I made my decision and they guided me. I drafted a letter of condition for this job, for what I could and would do, and what I could and would not do and shared this with the relevant people at NUG.

At the same time the pressure was mounting from my community. I didn't hear back anything then I went to sleep and the next day they announced that I had been elected on Facebook. That's how I found out and I thought ok, I'll do my best and try to fill in the gaps in my own ministry and within the NUG. I thought that this would be a historic opportunity to find a way to communicate our concerns and grievances and to do this with counterparts from the National League for Democracy (the NLD, the political party in government in Myanmar before the military coup). During the so-called normal times, when we supposedly had democracy (not that people in the borderlands had democracy), we were never treated as counter parts by any party or governance institutions, we were never treated as equal. But now this seemed the chance for us to be treated as equal and to try to see how we can work together with NLD, how to move forward, and that is why I decided to go in. I knew it wasn't going to be easy but I braced myself to get to work. However, things did not turn out like I had hoped for.

I felt like, as in all political systems, decisions were always made before by other political actors so the important decisions were not made at the meetings. So many of the things I was hoping for that we would help convince each other to help each other and see other perspectives were not getting through. This remained me that if this is not a space where I can have genuine conversations and be able to make reforms and decision-making, this is not where I want to focus my energies on; again, it comes back to picking your battles. It was such a difficult decision though, at that point the crackdown, the intensity of the humanitarian crisis, the brutality of the military response, and also how would people see this—my community nominated me, so it was a hard decision. I thought it would be transformative to be in NUG, but it wasn't. It was hard decision to leave, to disappoint my community and also the idea of being an activist outside these structures of power means you have less potential for impact.

Freedom from All Forms of Oppression

Stella: Being a woman from a marginalised community, and also my position within the NUG, the roadmap for the NUG has always been to be the diverse face of the movement, and different from the past, that's why I was placed there. What they wanted the world to see, a diverse, progressive face, and I was ok with that being the purpose of the organisation, but I was not ok with being part of that "face" alone, politics of tokenism. A better representation and inclusive governance shouldn't be treated only as a strategy to win international support. It became very clear to me that a revolutionary government that doesn't see the importance of inclusion and acceptance in building unity to fight the authoritarianism and military dictatorship founded upon Bamar-Buddhist nationalism lacks willingness to transform a new political system. If I had known that they were only interested in inclusion of women and ethnic minorities for that purpose, I would not have gone in because I am not involved in this struggle to play politics.

Any system, regardless of whether it was being created in the time of revolution, that omits women's experience and roles in politics and in revolution will just end up reproducing a similar hierarchical structure that gives some gender, ethnic, racial, religious, or social groups more power over others. So, if we are really interested in creating a more just, equal, and transformative system, including women's political experiences and the roles they have taken is the first step towards envisioning a more transformative system. Including women isn't the end goal but only the beginning—an extremely important foundation! For a country as diverse as Myanmar to be stable, peaceful, and flourishing, we need to recognise the rights of ethnic (indigenous) communities to govern themselves. The central authority sitting in Myanmar's capital, with little to no knowledge of local contexts, micromanaging our affairs in education, health, culture, and resource management is doomed to fail in the governance. Only when local communities get to deliberate, design, and participate in their own governance, decision-making processes can become more localised and inclusive. Although women, traditionally, have always defended and taken care of our own communities as long as we have existed, men are the ones making all the national political negotiations representing the community who often doesn't get to have a say in shaping their future. Those who occupy leadership positions need to reflect the way communities are made up of, ethnicity, gender, religion, and sexuality. That's the only way when women and other marginalised groups can truly become part of the formal leadership structures.

Revolutionary Motherhood

Stella: In 2018, I met a female KIO officer at the maternity ward of the hospital in Laiza. She had just given birth to a baby boy. When she was asked if she wanted her son to be a KIA soldier as well, "as a Kachin citizen, I want him to continue fighting for our cause (I will be so proud of him), but as a mother, I wish he had more and safer options about his life." To be a citizen, a service member, and a mother, women can and will take on multiple roles as active political agents. So, their roles and experiences should be taken more seriously by anyone trying to understand or help resolve the conflict. So far, the history of conflict or political discourse are predominantly coming from men because that's where people (researchers or/and policy makers) are going to as legitimate sources of knowledge.

Focusing on the experience of women—of violence or leadership—as active and able actors and stakeholders can give us a more complete and fuller picture to understand the experience, struggle, grievances, and thus find a more inclusive and better solution. Also, what do we mean when we say revolution? International researchers always want to measure things through a focus on clashes, like things can be more or less violent. What nonsense. To understand revolutions we need to have a fuller picture of what revolutions are and who they are for. The armed part is just one small part of the revolution. The revolution is much longer term. It is intergenerational.

Being a mother has influenced the way I do activism. Before I became a mother, I always thought we have to understand the past to build a better future. But after becoming a mother, this took on a whole new level. I feel more urgency and the importance of getting it right this time. Getting it right means transforming a new and inclusive governance system may take longer time but we know this is the only political system that will accommodate and provide space and tools for Myanmar's diverse communities. Not doing it right would be doing the same thing, excluding people based on their identities, while expecting a different result. Becoming a mother means I am more focused on the future, but it also becomes a bit overwhelming, because we need to build a better future for these children, these little people. For me to understand feminism or sisterhood, or alliances with other women, it became more pronounced caring for each other, caring for our own family, and also caring for the community while we have to stand up to sexism and discrimination sometimes from men in our own community. Of not only wanting to create a better future but also the burden—if we don't do it right—how much worse it will become for them. So, I think for me our struggle becomes more urgent, so much more is as stake.

Both the emotional and physical labour of being a parent but also the opportunity of the added understanding of standpoint being a political activist and a mother shaped why and how I left Myanmar. I left Myanmar from its international airport, and by that point, several people had already been detained at the airport when they tried to leave the country. I planned it in my head that if they asked me difficult and sensitive questions, I would have no choice but to pinch my son and make him cry as a distraction. So, I carried my son wrapping him on my chest. Even after passing through the immigration gate, I couldn't relax until our plane landed in Malaysia for a layover. I felt like as much as I am fighting for a better future for my son and his generation, he also protects me in a sense that through motherhood I have learned so much to be more efficient and strategic. We need to think efficiently and strategically because this for us is an intergenerational struggle.

My son was born on Kachin State Day, and he was named after our hard-fought Kachin dreams for a future and federal democratic union: his name, Mung Jat, roughly translates as nations coming together. I still have hope that we will get there (Photo 10.1).

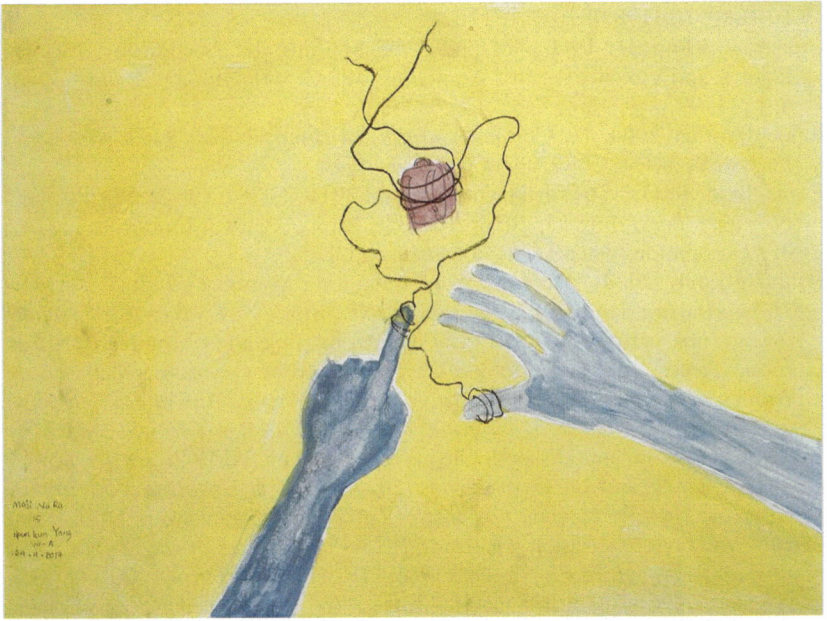

Photo 10.1 A painting created by Maji Nu Ra (15 years old), living in an IDP camp in Kachin State, Myanmar. The art exhibition was convened by Airavati, and can be seen in full here: https://www.airavati.net/wp-content/uploads/2019/04/ArtCatalogue181127.pdf

References

AAPPB. 2022. *Women Power in Spring Revolution*. Assistance Association for Political Prisoners, February, 16, 2022. Available: https://aappb.org/?p=20179.

Anthias, Floya. 2014. "The Intersections of Class, Gender, Sexuality and "Race": The Political Economy of Gendered Violence." *International Journal of Politics, Culture and Society* 27, no. 2: 153–71. https://doi.org/10.1007/s10767-013-9152-9.

Cockburn, Cynthia. 2004. "The Continuum of Violence." In *Sites of Violence: Gender and Conflict Zones*, edited by Wenona Mary Giles, and Jennifer Hyndman, 24–44. Berkeley: University of California Press.

Collins, Patricia Hill. 2017. "On Violence, Intersectionality and Transversal Politics." *Ethnic and Racial Studies* 40, no. 9: 1460–73. https://doi.org/10.1080/01419870.2017.1317827.

Crenshaw, Kimberle. 1990. "Mapping the Margins: Intersectionality, Identity Politics, and Violence Against Women of Color." *Stanford Law Review* 43, no. 6: 1241–99.

Enloe, Cynthia. 2004. *The Curious Feminist: Searching for Women in a New Age of Empire*. Berkeley: University of California Press.

Evans, Brad, and Gayatri Chakravorty Spivak. 2016. "When Law Is Not Justice." *New York Times*, July 13, 2016. Available: https://www.nytimes.com/2016/07/13/opinion/when-law-is-not-justice.html.

Fishbein, Emily. 2023. "Meet the Women Fighting Myanmar's Junta." *The New Humanitarian*, January 12, 2023. Available: https://www.thenewhumanitarian.org/first-person/2023/01/12/Women-fighting-junta-Myanmar-CNF.

Gagnon, Terese, and Hsa Moo. 2023. "Involved but Not Included: Karen Women's Care Work as Transformative Vision for Peace." In *Waves of Upheaval in Myanmar: Gendered Transformations and Political Transitions*, edited by Jenny Hedström and Elisabeth Olivius. Copenhagen: NIAS Press.

Hedström, Jenny, and Elisabeth Olivius. 2023. *Waves of Upheaval in Myanmar: Gendered Transformations and Political Transitions*. Copenhagen: NIAS Press.

Kachin Women's Association Thailand. 2013. *State Terror in the Kachin Hills: Burma Army Attacks against Civilians in Northern Burma*. Chiang Mai, February 28, 2013. Available: https://reliefweb.int/report/myanmar/state-terror-kachin-hills.

Knobblock, Ina, and Rauna Kuokkanen. 2015. "Decolonizing Feminism in the North: A Conversation with Rauna Kuokkanen." *NORA - Nordic Journal of Feminist and Gender Research* 23, no. 4: 275–281. https://doi.org/10.1080/08038740.2015.1090480.

Krook, Mona Lena. 2017. "Violence Against Women in Politics." *Journal of Democracy* 28, no. 1: 74–88. https://doi.org/10.1353/jod.2017.0007.

Krook, Mona Lena. 2020. "A Continuum of Violence." In *Violence against Women in Politics*, edited by Mona Lena Krook, 115–24. Oxford: Oxford University Press.

Marlar, Justine Chambers, and Elena. 2023. "Our Htamein, Our Flag, Our Victory: The Role of Young Women in Myanmar's Spring Revolution." *Journal of Burma Studies* 27, no. 1: 65–99. https://doi.org/10.1353/jbs.2023.0002.

Naw K'Nyaw Paw, and Maggi Quadrini. 2023. "Women's Leadership for Transformative, Feminist Change at the Grassroots Levelin Karen State." In *Waves of Upheaval in Myanmar: Gendered Transformations and Political Transitions*, edited by Jenny Hedström and Elisabeth Olivius. Copenhagen: NIAS Press.

Office of the UN High Commissioner for Human Rights. 2018. *Report of the Independent International Fact-Finding Mission on Myanmar*. OHCHR, September 18, 2018. https://www.ohchr.org/en/press-releases/2018/09/myanmar-un-fact-finding-mission-releases-its-full-account-massive-violations?LangID=E&NewsID=23575.

Sadan, Mandy. 2016. *War and Peace in the Borderlands of Myanmar: The Kachin Ceasefire, 1994–2011*. Copenhagen: NIAS Press.

Saw Ralph, and Naw Sheera. 2020. *Fifty Years in the Karen Revolution in Burma: The Soldier and the Teacher*. Ithaca: Cornell University Press.

The Karen Women's Organization. 2010. *Walking amongst Sharp Knives. The Unsung Courage of Karen Women Village Chiefs in Conflict Areas of Eastern Burma*. Karen Women's Organization, August 27, 2010. https://karen-women.org/2010/08/27/walking-amongst-sharp-knives/.

Wah, Esther. 2021. "Ethnics March Together General Strike- Nationalities Committee Against Coup." *Burma News International*, March 17, 2021. Available: https://www.bnionline.net/en/news/ethnics-march-together-general-strike-nationalities-committee-against-coup.

Zin Mar Oo, and Kyoko Kusakabe. 2010. "Motherhood and Social Network: Response Strategies of Internally Displaced Karen Women in Taungoo District." *Women's Studies International Forum* 33, no. 5: 482–491. https://doi.org/10.1016/j.wsif.2010.06.006.

CHAPTER 11

Pretty Purposed: A Social Justice Partnership for Black Girls in Virginia, United States

Nishaun T. Battle and Bianca Myrick

INTRODUCTION

There can never be too many programs and organizations that center the well-being and social development of girls. When Nishaun Battle began working as a Professor at a Historically Black College and University (HBCU) in the small historic town of Petersburg, Virginia, the ethnographer in her wanted to learn all about the culture of the city. Nishaun was born and raised in South Central Los Angeles and lived in Inglewood, California. Observing social and economic injustices within her own family and the community in which she resided, Nishaun knew early on that her purpose was to promote social justice. Growing up as a child of the 1980s, conversations among her friends—beginning as early as elementary school—included discussions of corporal punishment by family members (which we referred to as "whippings"), family members who had been

---

N. T. Battle (✉)
Virginia State University, Petersburg, VA, USA
e-mail: nbattle@vsu.edu

B. Myrick
Petersburg, VA, USA

© The Author(s), under exclusive license to Springer Nature
Switzerland AG 2025
J. Zulver, K. Stallone (eds.), *Brave Women*,
https://doi.org/10.1007/978-3-031-70702-5_11

murdered, or who was on drugs. Injustice based on race was normalized in Nishaun's mind, and she also observed gendered violence in her community. Whether it was communicated by violent verbal street harassment, or inappropriate comments about the anatomy and size of specific body parts on Black girls, Nishaun would soon surmise as a young girl that no one was going to protect Black girls like her.

She was not aware of, nor participated in any girl-centered mentoring or social development organizations growing up. However, as an adult with an awareness of the various non-profit organizations designed to instill self-esteem, leadership, and hope into girls, she felt encouraged to join in the philanthropic efforts of youth activism. Those formative years shaped the lens from which Nishaun began to make it her mission to fight injustice. The socioeconomic inequities that exacerbated the oppression, trauma, stress, hopelessness, violence, and other detrimental realities pushed Nishaun to try to identify and strategize ways she could help contribute her skills, talents, and passions toward creating a better society for girls in her community. Nishaun wanted to embody what she would later learn was a term in community activist circles called "servant leadership." She wanted to be an advocate and join with like-minded individuals who wanted to create an improved and sustainable environment for girls, while centering and acknowledging the unique racialized, socioeconomic position, and gendered experiences of Black girls.

It is important to note that the experience of Black girls is not a monolith. The various intersections of their identities shape their daily realities. The term coined "intersectionality" has been credited to scholar and legal activist Kimberlé Crenshaw (1990), who argued that institutional oppression must be examined by considering oppression as the intersections of race, class, gender, sexuality, and additional socially constructed identities that shape an overall societal perception and treatment of individuals. Crenshaw is not the first intellectual to study oppression from a multiple lens, as Angela Davis also studied race, class, and gender, Anna Julia Cooper—a nineteenth-century public intellectual—wrote an early examination of race, class, and demographic location, in her seminal book, *A Voice from the South* (1892), and Joyce Ladner wrote *Tomorrow's Tomorrow* (1971), which also provided an early analysis of the ways in which oppression impacts Black girls at the intersection of social violence based on their race, gender, and socioeconomic position.

As Nishaun began to notice several abandoned and dilapidated buildings in her neighborhood, she also envisioned community social justice spaces and opportunities for community revitalization. Nishaun believed those abandoned buildings could be transformed into community centers and that community and university partnerships could be formed, while forging student opportunities to help create mentorship-based models for local schools could emerge. Specifically, the student-mentor model developed was intended for only women students. Nishaun wanted younger girls to have the opportunity to aspire to and model young ladies who looked like them and had similar backgrounds and experiences. Nishaun, who did not have any mentors growing up in her childhood years, considers her work as a form of self-justice and community care.

A mutual friend, who also is a youth-based community leader, introduced her to Bianca Myrick, who is the director of Pretty Purposed (PP), a youth-based non-profit organization serving elementary and middle school girls in over ten schools in various neighboring cities near and in Petersburg, Virginia. Together, they began to think of ways to collaborate through a student-mentor model with women students from some of Nishaun's undergraduate courses. This was important to create a healing-centered engagement model, a model created by researcher and policymaker Shawn Ginwright. They also had several discussions about ways to improve collective efficacy and community wellness through mutually beneficial collaborations with organizations with similar missions. They both believe that if the community is well, the girls they seek to serve will be well, and vice versa. Bianca is a native of Petersburg, Virginia, who witnessed several forms of social injustices and, as a result, was determined to give back to the community that helped to shape who she was as a woman activist.

THE ROOTS OF PRETTY PURPOSED

Petersburg, Virginia, is a small city with a population of nearly 30,000 residents, and where the land-grant HBCU, Virginia State University is located. Bianca wanted to create a program that would specifically address some of the issues girls face due to various limiting city and structural realities for its residents. Bianca started Pretty Purposed during a time when she was out of work due to domestic violence. She always wanted to support and help her community grow by starting a program for girls, but she never thought she would have the time to do so as a mother and full-time educator. In 2014, she had the opportunity to sit back and focus on herself and the community. Pretty Purposed began as an organization designed to support girls and women that may be experiencing violence.

Bianca and Nishaun started with the mentorship component for girls. This program blossomed over the years, and currently Pretty Purposed is in 12 schools across 3 school districts and supports about 160 girls each year.

Pretty Purposed is a non-profit organization dedicated to inspiring communities to empower young women and girls. Through school and community-based programs that cultivate spaces of joy for girls, in addition to coalition development, social emotional learning, advocacy, and strengths-based educational curriculum, girls have a space to learn about themselves and grow. Pretty Purposed focuses on empowerment for all girls, but specifically centers Black girls due to the historical, racial, and gender-based disparities they suffer. Black girls are viewed and treated as being older than they are; this concept is reflected in a term coined by a Georgetown Law study on the treatment of Black girls—adultification. Black girls are suspended and discriminated against in schools more harshly than their white counterparts, as documented in narratives like the School to Prison Pipeline report and *Pushout*, a book written by Monique Morris. Girls involved in Pretty Purposed also experience economic challenges on a systemic level. The city of Petersburg, for example, is considered a food desert. There are no local grocery stores in the city of Petersburg, and therefore, if an individual doesn't have reliable transportation, they are subjected to eating processed foods that are unhealthy and may lead to future physical ailments.

Upon self-reflection, Bianca never considered herself as someone who had experienced domestic violence. Certainly, when she was in college, she knew there were parts of her relationship that were unhealthy, but not once did she think it was abusive. Bianca and her future child's father would graduate from the same undergraduate institution and remain together when she became pregnant. The relationship got progressively worse, and it wasn't until a domestic violence advocate gave her information that she realized that she was indeed in an abusive relationship. After separating, her child's father was so angry that he went to the police and alleged that she cut him (which was not true), and she went to jail for a few days. As a result of that unfortunate event, Bianca was forced to take a leave of absence from her job until the case was cleared. Hillary Potter, a criminologist at the University of Colorado Boulder, details the impact that intimate partner violence has specifically on women of color and the systematic barriers they often face as a result of their intersectional identities.

Bianca decided that it was necessary to start Pretty Purposed because there are few youth-based organizations in the city that center the development of girls. Girls living in the city of Petersburg face violence on a regular basis: they witness regular physical fights, police calls to come to elementary schools for violence, and interpersonal violence. The broader vision of Pretty Purposed, and the work that Bianca and Nishaun engage in regularly, is to create individual transformation in the lives of the participants, so that they can begin to model positive behavior and leadership among their peer groups, and communities for community collective care and efficacy.

Pretty Purposed not only cultivates spaces of joy for girls, but also views their engagement as an intergenerational exchange between girls and women. Pretty Purposed strives to change culture in schools, and works alongside educators to create spaces where girls can learn, lead, and grow. Joy is contextualized in several ways in Bianca and Nishaun's activist work. They define spaces of joy as both internal and external. Namely, spaces of joy are places where girls can come together and have their true authentic selves centered and celebrated. Individually, they have observed joy from comments made by girls in the program, attesting to any improvement in how they view life and the hope they have for their future. Many of PP's program facilitators in schools are counselors, social workers, or teachers. These individuals can create a multiplier effect because they serve as role models and mentors for girls, and their advocacy helps to build spaces of resiliency for girls and youth. Pretty Purposed fights for humanity, to be seen, to be treated with common decency, and respect. It wants to step in and offer advocacy to counter structural inequities that are sanctioned and present in our social institutions, primarily, our nation's schools.

ACTIVIST ENGAGEMENT: PRETTY PURPOSED

For about two years, Nishaun, Bianca, and a mutual friend who is also a youth program director, met monthly to discuss ways to build and sustain youth programming that will have a lasting impact in the lives of the girls in which we serve, their communities, and their families. Nishaun's research and activist engagement centers the well-being of Black girls and women. She is also a wellness consultant and collaborates with youth organizations to center wellness in both business practices and youth programming. She is interested in how joy can be an actionable emotion in the workplace and through community activism. Bianca also believes in modeling for her staff and board members the wellness platform she encourages for the girls in her program. At the fundamental level, there is an understanding between Bianca and Nishaun that self-care and wellness involve addressing institutional policies and procedures, to ensure that the staff's well-being places them in a space where they can offer the most effective programming possible. Nishaun draws from the work of scholar Stephanie Y. Evans, who has written extensively about the role practices such as yoga and other well-being practices in helping to save the lives of Black girls and women, who experience racism, sexism, misogyny, and discrimination. One of the ways Nishaun merges theory and praxis in her class is by involving her students in assisting with curriculum planning and workshop development for the Pretty Purposed programs. Nishaun primarily teaches criminological theory, research methods, and various electives, including "Black Women and Resistance" and "School to Prison Pipeline." Broadly, her research background explores spaces of justice that are created by and for Black girls and the relationship these have on the well-being of both Black girls and women. She investigates the role mentorship and wellness practices within these spaces help to foster identity and social development.

Students are encouraged to facilitate the workshops they created for the program. Bianca also provides paid internship opportunities to students, as an effort to promote a more equitable approach regarding internships and teaching our students the importance of not having their labor exploited. Pretty Purposed is an organization with intentional curricula and programming, designed to uplift young girls regardless of their race. As stated previously, the demographic of Petersburg, Virginia, is primarily Black, and as such, much of the programming *does* center Black girls. The curriculum is designed to raise their self-esteem and to teach them to advocate for themselves and others, while providing opportunities for exposure to cultural and social outings. Pretty Purposed encourages participants to learn and have fun in all social outings. These include, but are not limited to, bowling parties, escape rooms, theater plays, and more. Any social outing that takes place outside of crime-ridden, underfunded, hopeless community environments provide girls with the opportunity to see something greater than the social circumstances they may be forced to dwell in. Bianca and Nishaun both agree that when given opportunities, all girls will rise to the occasion to be engaged in activities that will help develop them into leaders in their communities. Bianca believes that:

"girls considered hood and ghetto are just one opportunity away from being your next civic leader if only given the chance."

Bianca knows her work is important because she has lived experiences within the community she serves. She is aware of how underserved communities that are labeled disadvantaged, ghetto, and hood can begin to take a mental toll on how Black girls view others in their community, as well as their visions for hope for their own lives. When a girl is constantly told in both indirect and direct ways that "you are a problem," it can lead to lateral consequences socially, mentally, and physically. This is a key concept in the looking glass theory presented by Charles Cooley, which is often used to contextualize the hopelessness many Black people begin to take on based on negative labels applied to them. The well-being of Black girls is at stake, and what Bianca and Nishaun have witnessed in this work is that they can help create a spark in the eyes of Black girls. The conversations that are held between the mentors and participants, and even conversations held between the girls, are qualitative ways that both Bianca and Nishaun have observed growth in the participants of Pretty Purposed. Additional measures to determine the effectiveness of the program are also conducted through yearly evaluations. Bianca has developed both questionnaires for parents and children and conducts interviews to assess growth among the participants of Pretty Purposed. Most of the participants in Pretty Purposed join the program through word of mouth via their friends, parents, and counselors and teachers who promote the program to students.

Pretty Purposed has programs designed to encourage girls to advocate for themselves, learning different methods of articulating lived experiences through storytelling and policy recommendations. Indeed, these programs have culminated in the girls testifying to lawmakers at the General Assembly on Advocacy Day in Virginia. Again, by taking girls out of dilapidated housing, poverty, and crime, they are afforded the opportunity to speak about their specific experiences. Girls have the opportunity to get on a chartered bus, enter the assembly professionally dressed, and walk up to the microphone to articulate the concerns that impact their peer group. This is a paid opportunity for eighth grade participants in the program.

Pretty Purposed brings together girls from fifth grade through to high school. Some of them come together in groups of 12 girls to participate in what is called a Girl's Circle. In these circles, there are structured and unstructured times to just talk. It may sound simple, but Nishaun and Bianca believe that by promoting positive communication, they can further affirm to participants that their voices are valued, and they recognize they are being heard and seen. The girls are active in the co-collaboration of their curriculum, which takes a holistic approach in addressing social and life skills.

The girls are also encouraged to engage in self-care. One of the hallmark activities is an annual tea party. The tea party is a time for the girls to gather together and be reminded of healthy eating habits, while simultaneously providing them the opportunity to embrace their own definition of girlhood. The opportunity to dress up with gloves, hats, and dresses has been a fun and uplifting part of the social engagement of the girls participating in the annual tea event. Nishaun and Bianca have had several conversations regarding their social upbringing as children. Nishaun often reflects on her unawareness of any type of mentoring programs for youth, debutante balls, Jack and Jill, or other high-society type of event prevalent in southern culture. Black elitism is just as harmful as white supremacy according to Nishaun. Drawing from the work of E. Franklin Frazier's *The Black Bourgeosie* (1957), Nishaun argues that programs for girls in marginalized communities are needed, because they are excluded from upper-middle class, bourgeoisie organizations. Nishaun does not believe it is fair that girls in low-income communities or girls who did not come from upper- or middle-class families should be socially penalized. These girls should be afforded the same opportunity to engage in cultural activities like anyone else, and this is why the tea party is so important to Black girls, like the participants in Pretty Purposed. Nishaun wishes she had had similar experiences growing up, so she is very determined to invite participants into a space of social etiquette.

One of the Pretty Purposed core values is to work with like-minded organizations in the community, including to generate collective funding. Bianca serves as the coordinator of the You GLOW GIRL Network, a multisector coalition centering wellness outcomes for all girls and young women through strategic partnerships with local youth-based organizations. Pretty Purposed does not discriminate against any group that is interested in programming. Social justice practices embedded within the culture of Pretty Purposed provide a vast collection of resources that can be shared across networks. Understanding that expanding awareness and leveraging financial resources by working together as a collective to impact policy and legislation is also a primary goal. What does this mean specifically? There are a plethora of non-profit organizations centered on helping improve the lives of the youth, which often results in several founders all

Photo 11.1 Bianca Myrick, founder of the Pretty Purposed program

scrambling to get minimal money here and there. This model of funding is not always sustainable. However, if organizations come together and attempt to apply for one large grant, it can be more effective than each organization having to fight for smaller monetary funding (Photo 11.1).

Challenges to Engaging in Activism for Black Girls and Strategies for Success

Throughout her career, Bianca has had to overcome multiple racial and gender barriers in order to carry out her work. For example, she has found it difficult to secure long-term and flexible funding, as these resources are often earmarked for organizations with majority white executive directors and board members. In fact, Bianca argues that white supremacy is deeply embedded within the fabric of philanthropy and that Black people and other people of color are often excluded from decision making within social and political circles. Bianca points out a study conducted by the Ms.

Foundation for Women, entitled "Pocket Change: How Women and Girls of Color Do More with Less," (2020) which highlights how youth organizations founded and directed by Black women and other women of color have less staff and bear the burden of taking on multiple tasks. Bianca states, "one day, we as Black women will be in the position to financially support ourselves, but until that day, we must fight with what we have."

Similarly, as a Criminal Justice educator, Nishaun has also experienced multiple challenges in the workplace. For example, she has found it complicated to convince department administration that collaborative work with criminal justice undergraduate students within community-based work should also be considered as a criminal justice internship. She argued that if students only receive internship credit for interning at traditional criminal justice agencies, including law enforcement, the courts, or the correctional system, that some students will be deterred from doing additional civil society work. While Nishaun was able to overcome this hurdle, there are so many hidden stories of violence that she has experienced working at an HBCU, which she argues are often proponents of white supremacy. Nishaun suggests that a deeper analysis should be held to discuss challenges faced within Black women activist circles. Nishaun has worked with passionate, deeply engaged Black women and women of color activists, but she has also experienced and observed performative activism among other Black leaders who lead from a deficit model to gain buy-in from their constituents for their own personal gain. In fact, she has experienced classism, Black elitism, and bullying, leading her to feel as if she is working on a modern-day plantation; the only difference is that the main oppressors have not just been Black individuals, but specifically Black women. The micromanaging and abuse of power can be unbearable at times. There is no escape or protection, because there is no way to report racial discrimination, so essentially, there is a feeling, and personal experience, of having no protection, nor anyone to report to. Nishaun is still unclear as to why Black elitism is still housed under the term white supremacy in certain spaces where discrimination is discussed. She also finds that it is a challenge to ensure consistent physical space for the girls in Pretty Purposed to enjoy their programs; easier access, guaranteed space would expand growth and awareness of youth-based programming for girls in Petersburg, Virginia.

There are no definitive narratives in the form of qualitative research that specifically address the lack of collaboration among youth-based leaders.

Nishaun argues that some Black youth leaders perform in front of the masses, but if they truly wanted to come together, they would. But as seen with Black elite organizations, they are often concerned with in-fighting and minimizing each other to accomplish a collective racial equity goal. There are several youth-based organizations in Petersburg and surrounding cities, yet, while there is an initiative to build and maintain a collaborative network of youth-based leaders, there has been limited activity on a collective initiative come to fruition. It is not clear whether this is due to a lack of trust when it comes to working with others, no awareness of all the programming in Petersburg, or simply an unwillingness to share information and resources. Through her personal experience of living in southern states for nearly 20 years, Nishaun believes Black southern culture—particularly in Richmond, Virginia, the capital of the confederacy—embodies a crab in a barrel mentality, in which there is the belief that there can only be a select few to be the vanguard of the Black community, and Black elites who embody white supremacy and exclusivity results in no real transformative community impact. There is so much literature on white supremacy, but Nishaun hopes that this chapter can spark a larger conversation that needs to be held with Black women activists. However, it remains the case that Black women leaders of youth-based organizations continue to find themselves behind in the philanthropy game of receiving and being in a position to provide sufficient funding to youth-based programs. From Nishaun's lived experiences and observation, although there is a significant number of youth-based organizations in one small neighboring town, there have not been any meaningful efforts to work collaboratively. Nishaun states: "she is not holding her breath on bourgeoisie Black leaders coming together."

Many youth-based non-profit organizations struggle to onboard and maintain executive board members and are overworked due to a lack of staffing. From a financial perspective, founders of non-profit organizations often find it difficult to identify board members who are in the position to donate a large amount of money for program initiatives. Therefore, founders are left with the task of fundraising, which can be a full-time job within itself. The biggest hurdle many women activists of color face when attempting to create a sustainable youth program is how to identify ways that they can provide non-financial support to organizations. Indeed, there are countless Black social and civic organizations who volunteer in tutoring, feeding the homeless, and offering educational and social development programs; but ultimately, money is what is needed for these programs to thrive.

Bianca and Nishaun both believe in using a holistic and integrative approach to help reach youth. Bianca is transparent in her discussions with relevant stakeholders and grant funding institutions about the challenges she faces, specifically those related to financial constraints. As an educator, Bianca also incorporates and reflects on up-to-date research and statistics about the dire conditions faced by many of the girls likely to join her program and across the country in general. Her grassroots approach not only seeks to amplify the voice of her organization, but she also explicitly uses her network to connect organizations who are willing to work together for the greater cause. Bianca employs a model of co-creation with the girls, so that she can include their experiences in her programs. This takes the shape of open communication and asking the girls for their input, citing and acknowledging their work, and collaborating in such a way that is productive and fruitful for all.

Pretty Purposed is currently finalizing its strategic fund development plan. Ultimately, the program needs additional financial resources in order to grow. In addition to being the executive director of Pretty Purposed, Bianca also dedicates her time to advocating for Black and Brown funding for small businesses and non-profits through the Black and Brown grant-based organization, Collective 365. Collective 365 is a philanthropic grant funding agency, founded by a Black woman activist, Fatima Marsh, and additional Black women and men activists, that specifically provides financial assistance to organizations that serve Black and Brown communities in the Washington, DC, Maryland, and Virginia areas. This collective realized that there were many stipulations and barriers for funding founders of community-based programs for people of color typically experience, so they created a solution. They believe that anyone should be able to give money, no matter the amount. They have raised over $50,000 in the past few years to assist Black and Brown community-based organizations. Pretty Purposed believes in the larger picture of helping to transform Black and Brown communities, therefore Bianca encourages other business to apply for funding and has been instrumental in assisting several new non-profit organizations that center girls, funding for their initiatives.

CONCLUSION

Youth-based organizations centering Black girls and girls of color should be prioritized in school and communities. They truly have the potential to create transformative and positive changes on individuals and communities. Small social circles allow girls to develop and maintain close-knit friendships and leadership opportunities that help shape their identity and promote high self-esteem. The main struggle with the growth and development of Pretty Purposed, and indeed so many other Black and Brown youth programs, is a lack of access to capital. Fundraising is an option, but if grant funding were distributed equally across racial lines, the energy exerted into raising funds for programs could be spent in more productive ways.

Nishaun believes funding should go toward co-op homeschools, small businesses, and start-up non-profit organizations, to help empower the future, rather than having their labor exploited. Accordingly, challenges faced by Black women directors of youth programming are usually based in similar patterns and issues around gendered and racial prejudice. However, there are so many Black women activists who are working together to fight for justice for Black girls.

There are strides being made toward a collective social justice mission for youth programs, but there is always room for further dialogue and action on the topic. Nishaun notes that the dinners held by authors Regina Jackson and Saira Rao of *Everything you already know about racism and how to do better, white women* would also be a good idea for Black women activists. Nishaun believes that when blame continues to be placed on white supremacy, white people, white men, and whiteness, Black people and people of color often miss the ways in which they promote the same injustices and inequities within their own communities. Nishaun believes the first step should be with Black women having real conversations about how they oppress their own.

Pretty Purposed grounds its practices for fundraising, programming, and recruitment with a grassroots approach. Bianca is transparent and authentic in establishing relationships with community members and individuals invested in the progress and positive development of youth—all youth—while acknowledging and centering Black girls. Relationships with the community for Pretty Purposed mean creating an inclusive space where all feel welcome, regardless of their intersectional identities. It means being open and transparent about the ways each person can learn to be a better person, for better communities. While financial assistance would certainly assist with sustainability and growth of Pretty Purposed, it does not hinder Bianca from hosting workshops and events in over ten schools in the Petersburg, Virginia, and nearby cities.

Challenges for scholar-activists relate to attempting to identify a way to document all the community engaged work they participate in. This is especially true of professors who work at teaching institutions. Nishaun has a 4/4 teaching load, meaning she teaches four classes each semester. Additionally, she is a consultant for youth-based non-profit organizations, is a business owner, and is a self-care coach and wellness educator. There is a plethora of scholar-activists who may never have the opportunity to write about all of the work they do, because they are overworked themselves. There are so many unheard stories of activism because often for scholar-activists, one role will take precedence over another. They may not be recognized in academia because they did not write about all of their accomplishments. However, this invisibility does not mean the work is not being done. There are many women activists with their boots on the ground, and their work should not be minimized because they don't reside in an ivory tower. Nishaun is firmly against elitism, including in academia, performative activism, and Black elitism disguised as white supremacy. Nishaun believes the focus needs to be on the progress of Black girls and their social development. She works diligently on both her community activism and scholarship and will continue to do so in an authentic and transparent manner into the future.

References

Cooper, Anna Julia. 1892. *A Voice from the South*. Xenia, Ohio: The Aldine Printing House.
Crenshaw, Kimberlé. 1990. "Mapping the Margins: Intersectionality, Identity Politics, and Violence Against Women of Color." *Stanford Law Review* 43, no. 6: 1241–1299. https://doi.org/10.2307/1229039.
Frazier, E.F. 1957. Black Bourgeoisie: The Book that Brought the Shock of Self-Revelation to Middle-Class Blacks in America. Simon and Schuster.
Ladner, Joyce. 1971. *Tomorrow's Tomorrow*. Lincoln, Nebraska: University of Nebraska Press.
Ms. Foundation for Women. 2020. *Pocket Change: How Women and Girls of Color Do More with Less*. New York: Ms. Foundation for Women.

CHAPTER 12

Conclusion: Brave Women in Afghanistan and Beyond

Farkhondeh Akbari, Kiran Stallone, and Julia Zulver

INTRODUCTION

Brave Women has presented unique chapters about the triumphs and challenges faced by women activists around the globe. From Burundi to Georgia to Colombia, it has revealed the ways in which women's journeys, although different in content, overlap in meaning and the overarching goal to protect, empower, and ensure the rights of women in all their diversity. The volume is the product of years of conversations and collaborations across continents. It was a project born during the pandemic, when we saw a "shadow pandemic" of gender-based violence take hold of the communities in which we all work. Indeed, one of the book's implicit

F. Akbari (✉)
Monash University, Melbourne, VIC, Australia
e-mail: farkhondeh.akbari@monash.edu

K. Stallone
Bogotá, Colombia

J. Zulver
Swedish Defence University, Stockholm, Sweden
e-mail: julia.zulver@fhs.se

© The Author(s), under exclusive license to Springer Nature Switzerland AG 2025
J. Zulver, K. Stallone (eds.), *Brave Women*,
https://doi.org/10.1007/978-3-031-70702-5_12

purposes has been to showcase the durability and steadfastness of women's bravery, even under new forms of duress.

It was also during the pandemic, however, that the Taliban forcibly returned to power, after 20 years of the US military intervention that used the protection of women's rights as one of its justifications (Akbari and True 2024). Julia and Farkhondeh met virtually during a conference on "Feminism in the Face of Failure" at the UNAM in Mexico City. Farkhondeh and her co-author, Jacqui True, presented their paper on how women's rights activists in Afghanistan create new strategies and counter-narratives, including a campaign to recognize "gender apartheid" in the wake of foreign policy failures by states promoting gender equality. Months later, Julia, Kiran, and Farkhondeh met online—connecting between Mexico City, Bogotá, and Melbourne—to discuss the possibility of a co-authored conclusion to the book. After learning how women in Afghanistan continue to fight for gender justice, resisting against one of the world's most brutal regimes for women, we felt a moral obligation to use this final chapter to shine a light on the country's brave women, particularly in this moment where hope is hard to find.

Together, we talked about the themes that emerged throughout the other chapters in this book. In particular, we asked: what does it really mean to highlight women's activism and amplify their voices, and why is it important? We discussed how crucial it is to shine a light on women activists' voices so that their causes are recognized, acknowledged, and supported. This recognition is critical to the endurance of women's rights resistance and legitimizes their activism. In the journey of women's rights activism, it is also key that women activists feel that they are not alone and their cause is global.

As we have seen from the chapters in this book, women activists are often fighting patriarchal norms and practices that deny their fundamental human rights. Turning a global spotlight on local women's activism in their respective communities empowers them. Women activists often encounter backlash from their homes, communities, and from the state itself. Providing international support and recognition of their activism can legitimize their cause by aligning the rights of women demanded by the local activists as a universal right. What follows is the product of a joint writing project that the three of us undertook to amplify the work of brave Afghan women, who are fighting for justice, against all the odds.

The Case of Afghanistan

The case of Afghanistan reveals the importance of highlighting and supporting women's fight for their rights, even in the most dire humanitarian and human rights situations. One of the most fundamental characteristics that defines the Taliban regime is restrictive policies against women and the violent treatment of women and girls. In March 2024, as this book was going through review, the Taliban regime continued a ban that prevents girls from attending school past sixth grade (Ahmadi and Ebadi 2022). This makes it the only country in the world with restrictions on girls' education beyond the age of 12. In addition, there are over 100 decrees and policies that restrict all aspects of women's private and public life, such as freedom of movement, tertiary education, and employment (apart from limited areas in healthcare and primary education), including a ban from working for the United Nations (USIP, n.d.).

And yet, there is space for micro-resistance and outright defiance even there. For example, women have opened underground schools across the country to educate the next generation of girls. They have come to the streets to protest, and they have adopted literacy and the arts to resist the Taliban's oppressive regime. When the Taliban announced the ban on women attending university, a girl protested alone by holding a poster with one word, "Aqra" in front of Kabul University – this means "to learn", which is the first word in the Quran (Shafaq 2022). Two sisters, who did not identify themselves for their safety, called themselves the "The Last Torch," wore blue burqas and sang for women's freedom as a form of undercover protest (Khamoosh 2024). They sang in a country that punishes musicians with arrest, and they "started a singing movement on social media" (Khamoosh 2024).

Over the last 20 years and even before the return of the Taliban to power, while having a pro-women's rights constitution and national policies, Afghan women and girls were engaged in consistent resistance against systematic social and cultural gender discrimination. They constantly navigated their way to access education and other opportunities. Especially in rural areas, where development and democratic progresses were limited, young girls were aware of their rights and pushed to change the norms in their households, their villages, and their communities by going to school and constantly negotiating their access to education.

Today, under Taliban rule, Afghan women are risking their lives to protest by raising their voices against the regime's extreme restrictions that have erased and dehumanized women. The international community, including states with feminist and pro-women's rights foreign policies, is failing to support women's rights activists. Diplomatic engagement with the Taliban by inviting them to conferences, capital cities, and meetings has given legitimacy to the regime (Theros 2023). This boosts the confidence and the morale of the Taliban in power and their gender-restrictive policies that face no accountability. In early 2022, Norway sent a private jet to the Taliban delegation to come to Oslo and present in high-level diplomatic protocol—all amid the gross human rights violations, including forced detention, torture, and abuse of Afghan women rights activists (Akbari and True 2024). So far, the many dialogues and engagements with the Taliban have resulted in no progress but regression of women rights in Afghanistan (Photo 12.1) (Maley and Jamal 2022).

Photo 12.1 Farkhondeh Akbari in Bamiyan, Afghanistan, in 2019. She stands in front of the empty niches of Bamiyan Buddha, a symbol of Hazara heritage, destroyed by the Taliban in 2001

12 CONCLUSION: BRAVE WOMEN IN AFGHANISTAN AND BEYOND

INTERSECTIONALITY AND WOMEN'S RIGHTS IN AFGHANISTAN

One of the themes that we have covered throughout this volume relates to the importance of adopting an intersectional approach when it comes to assessing women's bravery. That is to say, women are discriminated against not only for their gender but also for their race, ethnicity, sexual orientation or gender identity, geography, religion, age, among other factors. It is by studying these intersecting identities—and the ways in which women choose to be brave at the nexus of them—that we can further understand how they conceptualize and envision a gender-just future.

In Afghanistan, women face intersectional challenges that are similar to many of those faced by the women in the previous chapters. Fighting against the gender-oppressive regime of the Taliban is further complicated by the intersection of gender and ethnicity, especially for Hazara women. Hazaras are a marginalized and persecuted ethnic and religious minority group in Afghanistan (Ibrahimi 2017). The Hazaras welcomed the 2001 intervention as an opportunity for the recognition of equal rights and an inclusive peace for Afghanistan. Hazara women participated in elections in large numbers; they represented a large group of women in the national army and police force (Jardine 2021). However, because of the Hazaras' visibility in promoting democracy over the last 20 years, such as leading Afghanistan's civil society and initiating the largest people's protests and attending schools and universities, Hazaras in general and Hazara women in particular are facing double-edged discrimination under Taliban rule (Akbari and Moradi 2024).

The Taliban initiated a crackdown on Hazara women in Kabul and Hazara provinces by violently detaining, torturing, and committing other acts of gender-based violence (Special Rapporteur on the situation of human rights in Afghanistan 2024). The Taliban have used the excuse of "improper Hijab" use to justify their detention (suggesting that they did not follow their hijab or burqa rules); however, the Taliban's detention of women is also known to be ethnically fueled and to discourage the women protesters who are largely made up of Hazara women and girls (Nader and Ghani 2024). A report by Nader and Ghani (2024) highlights the Taliban's use of racial slurs combined with sexual harassment to target the young women from specific communities. An Afghan women rights activist stated in an interview that the Taliban burn the hands of women from Panjshir (the province that has armed resistance against the Taliban) and lash Hazara women (Akbari and True 2023). The different types of abuse based on women's ethnicity and political activism are not covered by the media or spoken about by the Afghan women rights campaigners. This flags a concern on the lack of understanding and awareness of the intersectional experiences of women under Taliban rule.

Historically as well as in the contemporary era, the intersectional discrimination against Hazara women has remained mute and unrecognized. Even over the last 20 years with the international pro-gender policies in Afghanistan, intersectionality in the gender discourse of Afghanistan was lacking. Therefore, the double-edged discrimination that women may face based on their intersectional identities has remained unrecognized and unknown to the public, policymakers, and women's rights activists.

After the Taliban's crackdown on Hazara women, Farkhondeh and her friend Kobra Moradi co-authored an article on the intersectional experiences of Hazara women in the Taliban's gender apartheid rule (Akbari and Moradi 2024). While the article resonated with and was received well by the Hazara women rights activists, the pair faced backlash from some of the Afghan scholars and women's rights activists for exclusively speaking about the Hazara women "at the cost of ignoring the experiences of Afghan women." The reactions revealed the lack of awareness about gender and intersectionality in Afghanistan. This is concerning, particularly given the Taliban's gender-repressive rule and further marginalizing ethnic minorities with a history of persecution.

Support as Legitimacy in Afghanistan

In Afghanistan's local dynamics, the support and solidarity received for women's rights causes and activities can go a long way. Solidarity could mean amplifying the diverse voices of Afghan women from inside the country, in exile or in the diaspora. Support could mean anything from donating to a local woman-led NGO to calls for the protection of Afghan women's rights, such as opening schools for girls, advocating for recognition of gender apartheid, and much more. On the other hand, the absence of a solidarity and support—at any level—can isolate Afghan women rights activists and their life-changing activities.

At the policy level, countries that have codified gender equality norms need to come up with more cohesive practical and political actions to address women's rights oppression under Taliban rule. Countries can dedicate visas and funding for scholarships for Afghan girls for education. Furthermore, supporting Afghan women entrepreneurs and businesses in international platforms is critical to support women-led households, as well as providing avenues for Afghan women's crafts in the international market. There are ways to work around Taliban rule to support women and girls directly through the mentioned initiatives. Additionally, supporting dialogue with diverse groups of Afghan women in exile and in the diaspora can help to understand the complex needs of Afghan women and find ways to support them inside the country.

As noted above, it is crucial to shine a light on the work of women's rights activists to reassure their cause, to ensure their struggle endures, and to energize local women activists and their activities. At the same time, women's rights and women activists are often politicized and their agency, space, and resources are bargained for politics, peace, and security or the "greater matters." The causes of women's rights activists are politicized, propagated, and dismissed in times of peace settlements. For example, during the US-Taliban Doha "peace deal" the women's rights agenda was deprioritized for the sake of reaching "peace" and "ending of war" with the Taliban (Akbari and True 2024).

Between 2018 and 2020, the US conducted 14 rounds of talks with the Taliban, in the absence of the democratically elected Afghan government and without a single Afghan woman representative. When an Afghan woman activist confronted the US Special Representative about Afghanistan negotiating with the Taliban and the fate of women's rights in the talks, he responded:

> I know I understand you, but we need to talk about the bigger issues first and then we need to get their agreements on certain things that pivot a way for, you know, for discussion. Like on women's rights. If we push them on these issues now, we can put the whole process at risk. (Zoom interview with Afghan woman leader, May 29, 2023, cited in Akbari and True 2024)

The deprioratization of women's rights and women's participation in any political decision, especially in peace processes, will have a severe impact on the rights of women and girls, as seen by the return of the Taliban to power and re-establishing "gender apartheid." Women's rights are not an afterthought, but need to be included meaningfully from the very beginning.

Brave Women in Afghanistan

We planned Brave Women to be a safe space for women activists to talk about resistance, resilience, struggles, heartbreak, and hope. We want it to reach a broad audience, one who may not have heard about the many cultures and contexts our contributors write about. The story of Brave Women is political, it is personal, it is communal, and it is emotional. It reveals the often muted and silenced stories that have always existed between wars and prospects for "peace." It gives women a chance to tell their own stories, in their voices.

Brave Women tells us about the dynamics of women's gender justice activism from across the globe, it draws on the patterns of similar struggles of women activists in their households, communities, grassroots, and national platforms. It is also a breathing space to find the rhythm for the local-global fight for women's rights and for solidarity.

Afghan women are the unexpected force on the frontline fighting the Taliban and their extremist ideology. This ideology has taken away their status as humans not only in society but also in their homes and private spaces. For Afghan women and girls, wearing a colorful dress—rather than a burqa—is now considered brave and an act of resistance. By acknowledging and respecting all acts of resistance and situating them in the context in which they occur, their bravery becomes evident. By putting their voices and stories in conversation with those of other brave women from all over the world, we hope their narratives build international solidarity and reach audiences who can contribute to a more gender-just world.

References

Ahmadi, Belquis and Asma Ebadi. 2022. Taliban's Ban on Girls' Education in Afghanistan. USIP, 1 April 2024. Available: https://www.usip.org/publications/2022/04/talibans-ban-girls-education-afghanistan

Akbari, Farkhondeh and Jacqui True. 2023. Gender Apartheid in Afghanistan: Foreign Policy Responses. Australian Feminist Foreign Policy Coalition, 10 April 2024. Available: https://iwda.org.au/assets/files/Gender-Apartheid-in-Afghanistan-and-foreign-policy-responses_AFFPC_Issues-Paper-12.pdf.

Akbari, Farkhondeh and Jacqui True. 2024. "Bargaining with Patriarchy in Peacemaking: The Failure of Women, Peace, and Security in Afghanistan." Global Studies Quarterly 4: 1–12. https://doi.org/10.1093/isagsq/ksae004

Akbari, Farkhondeh and Kobra Moradi. 2024. Hazara Women: How Gender and Ethnicity Intersect in the Taliban's Repression. *Just Security*, 7 March 2024. Available: https://www.justsecurity.org/93123/hazara-women-how-gender-and-ethnicity-intersect-in-the-talibans-repression/

Ibrahimi, Niamatullah. 2017. Hazaras and the Afghan State: Rebellious, Exclusion and the Struggle for Recognition. London: Hurst Publisher.

Jardine, Melissa. The world must evacuate women police in Afghanistan. *The Interpreter*, 23 August 2021. Available: https://www.lowyinstitute.org/the-interpreter/debate/afghanistan-after-america#:~:text=to%20support%20themselves.-,One%2Dthird%20of%20women%20police%20in%20Afghanistan%20are%20ethnic%20Hazaras,only%209%25%20of%20the%20population.

Khamoosh, Kawoon. 2024. Afghanistan's singing sisters defying the Taliban from under a Burka. BBC, 9 March 2024. Available: https://www.bbc.com/news/world-asia-68500111

Maley, William and Shuja, Jamal. 2022. "Diplomacy of disaster: the Afghanistan 'peace process' and the Taliban occupation of Kabul." The Hague Journal of Diplomacy 17, no. 1: 32–63.

Nader, Zahra and Fereshta Ghani. 2024. "'I was arrested for the crime of being a Hazara and a woman': The Taliban's 'bad hijab' campaign targets Hazara women." *Zan Times*. Accessed 3 February 2025, https://zantimes.com/2024/01/22/i-was-arrested-for-the-crime-of-being-a-hazara-and-a-woman-the-talibans-bad-hijab-campaign-targets-hazara-women/

Shafaq, Noor. 2022. Afghanistan: Woman protests Taliban's education ban with single word of God. BBC, 31 December 2022. Available: https://www.bbc.com/news/world-asia-64129401

Theros, Marika. 2023. "Knowledge, powe4r and the failure of US peacemaking in Afghanistan 2018–21." International Affairs 99, no. 3: 1231–1252.

USIP. (n.d.). https://www.usip.org/tracking-talibans-mistreatment-women

INDEX[1]

A
Aba Women's Riots, vi
Abkhazia, 127, 128, 131, 132, 135
Activism, vi–viii, 2, 3, 5–7, 12, 18–19, 39–41, 52, 59–69, 87, 93–105, 109–112, 127–140, 145, 152–154, 158, 164, 167, 171–174, 176, 178, 182, 184
Activists, vii, viii, 2–5, 7–9, 21, 28, 43, 53, 55, 60, 64–66, 69, 75, 79, 94, 95, 101, 102, 111, 113, 118, 127, 129–133, 136, 138–140, 143–145, 147, 149, 149n1, 151–153, 156, 164, 165, 167–178, 180–184
Afghanistan, 3, 82, 177–184
Afghan women, 178–184
Agency, 4–5, 12, 14, 79, 129, 131, 133–136, 172, 174, 183
Ambassadors, 23–33
Ancestrality, 37–55
Arequipa, 65–68

Armed conflict, 3, 7, 11–14, 99, 132
Arusha Accords, 94, 96
Authoritarianism, 2, 100, 101, 146, 149n1, 156
Ayutla, 24, 27, 29–33

B
Baricako, Marie Louise (MLB), 5, 94–96, 94n2
Belarus, 1
Black girls, 5, 163–176
Black women, 2, 41, 47, 81, 172–175
Brazil, vi, 5, 37–55, 61
Burundi, 3–5, 93–105, 177

C
Candidate training programmes, 48
Care, vi, 6, 18, 24, 41, 46, 62, 64, 67, 71–90, 99, 100, 109–123, 157, 165, 167

---

[1] Note: Page numbers followed by 'n' refer to notes.

© The Author(s), under exclusive license to Springer Nature Switzerland AG 2025
J. Zulver, K. Stallone (eds.), *Brave Women*,
https://doi.org/10.1007/978-3-031-70702-5

Care labor, 100, 121
Carework, 96, 99–101
Casa de los Saberes, 30
Civil society, 6, 26, 28, 39, 46, 47, 51, 72, 94, 95, 102–104, 112, 118, 136, 139, 172, 181
Collective, vii, 4, 49, 49n6, 50, 53, 54, 71–73, 79, 82, 84, 86, 89, 102, 109–123, 144, 150, 165, 167, 170, 173–175
Colombia, 3, 7, 9, 11–21, 61, 79, 132, 177
Conflict related sexual violence, 12
Congress, 20
Continuum of activism, 105
Continuum of violence, 6–7, 98, 146
Court clerks, 116, 117
COVID, 96, 97, 98n6, 99–101, 120
Criminal justice system, 111, 112, 114, 115, 117, 118

D
Decree, 39, 179
Diversity, vii, viii, 3, 39, 47, 49, 132, 144, 177
Domestic violence (DV), vi, 14, 16, 24, 75, 78, 98, 109–123, 136, 165, 166
Domestic Violence Act (DVA), 113–116

E
Entrepreneur, 183
Exile, 93–105, 149n1, 182, 183

F
Feminist, 3, 5, 52, 73, 93–105, 109–111, 117, 119–123, 129, 134, 140, 144–146, 149–151, 153, 154, 180

Feminist commons, 119, 122, 123
Fernandez, Inés, 23–33

G
Gender-based violence (GBV), 29, 109–112, 114, 115, 117, 118, 122, 145, 177, 181
General Strike Committee of Nationalities (GSCN), 144, 148–151
Georgia, 4, 127–140, 177
Girls of color, 175
Grant funding, 174, 175
Guerrero, 7, 23–33

H
Hartman, Sadiya, 81
Hazara women, 181, 182
hooks, bell, 72, 79, 86
Humanitarian, 72, 81, 97, 98, 100, 105, 128, 132–134, 138, 145, 155, 156, 179

I
Inamahoro, 5, 93–105
Indigenous, vi, 6, 8, 23–27, 29–32, 40, 45, 82, 153, 157
Inter-American Commission of Human Rights, 28
Inter-American Court of Human Rights (IACtHR), 8, 26n2, 61
Internally displaced persons (IDPs), 88, 128, 130–136, 139, 140, 159
Intersectionality, 5–6, 150, 153, 164, 181–182
Intimate partner violence (IPV), 3, 6, 109, 111, 112, 114–117, 120–122, 166
Israel, vii

J

Journalism, 64

K

Kachin, 144, 145, 147, 150, 153–155, 157, 159
Kachin Independence Organisation (KIO), 144, 145, 150, 154, 157
Kachinland, 144–149
Krystalli, Roxani, 79, 99, 119, 131

L

Land rights, 40, 43–45, 51, 54, 74
LGBTQ, 59, 61–62, 65, 67, 68
Liberia, vi, vii
Libya, v
Livelihood, 73, 74, 80, 81, 89
Localize/localization, 114, 117, 118, 122, 157
Love and care, 71–90

M

Magistrates, 112, 116–118
Memory, 16, 25, 41, 73–75, 79–82, 128–130, 132, 135
Me'phaa, 8, 23–33
Methodology, 7–9, 76
Mexico, 23–33, 60
Military coup, 3, 146, 154, 155
Motherhood, 74, 83–85, 157–159
Murad, Nadia, 2, 8, 9
Myanmar, 3, 4, 143–159

N

National Unity Government (NUG), 144, 145, 155, 156
Non-profit, 164–166, 170, 173–176

O

Organización del Pueblo Indígena Me'phaa (OPIM), 26–28

P

Palestine, vii
Peace agreement, vi, 13, 20, 94, 95n4, 127
Peacebuilding, 128, 132–135, 138
Peru, 6, 59–69
Political corruption, 17
Political leadership, 48–51
Political violence, 54
Pray the Devil Back to Hell, vii
Protection order (PO), 113–117
Protest, 2, 3, 65, 95, 139, 144, 147–152, 149n1, 155, 179, 181

Q

Quilombola, 5, 39–43, 45–55, 48n5

R

Racial politics, 47
Refugees, 5, 95, 97–101, 105, 131
Resistance, vi, 23–25, 38, 41, 49, 72, 86, 95, 119, 131, 146–149, 151–152, 178, 179, 181, 184
Revolution, 149–151, 153, 157, 158
Rwanda, 95–97, 99, 101, 105, 132

S

Same-sex marriage, 61
School of Women Leaders, 134

Schulz, Philip, 79, 99, 119
Self-esteem, 164, 168, 175
Self-representation, 37–55
Sex strike, v
Shelter, 59, 66–68, 110, 143
Silence, v, 4, 11–21, 33, 53
Social emotional learning, 166
Social repair, 73
Solidarity, vii, viii, 6, 60, 82, 94, 95, 99, 101, 112, 114, 119, 136, 148, 182, 184
South African Police Services (SAPS), 115, 116
Soviet Union, 128
Strategic essentialism, 96, 103–104
Sukhumi, 127, 128, 130–132, 134
Support and solidarity, 182

T
Taliban, 1, 178–184
Threats, 2, 3, 7, 18, 19, 28, 31, 38, 40, 45, 46, 51–54, 81, 95, 98, 99, 105, 117
Tlachinollan, 26, 26n2, 28, 29, 32
Transformative activism, 127–140
Transitional justice, 89, 90
Trans women, 6, 60, 61, 66

U
Uganda, 4, 5, 71–90, 95
UN peacebuilding, viii
US-Taliban deal, 183

V
Victim Empowerment Programme (VEP), 112, 114, 115, 117, 119–121
Victimhood, v, 5, 73, 131
Violence against women, 117, 122
Voice/voices, vi, 14, 32, 46, 54, 94, 95, 104, 129, 133, 135, 138–140, 146, 149, 150, 153, 154, 170, 174, 178, 179, 182, 184

W
War, v, vi, 4, 6, 7, 13, 18, 25, 31, 71–74, 79, 82, 84, 87, 89, 90, 98, 99, 127, 128, 130, 135, 144–148, 184
Women, v, 1, 4, 11–21, 24, 37, 60, 71–90, 93, 110, 127–140, 144, 165, 177–184
Women of Liberia Mass Action for Peace, vii
Women's political representation, 46
Women's rights, 1–3, 6, 8, 19, 25, 27, 71, 73, 94, 104, 128, 137, 154, 183

Y
Yousafzai, Malala, 8
Youth, 17, 59, 67, 68, 72, 73, 95, 110, 135, 144, 149, 150, 152, 154, 155, 164, 167, 170, 172–175
Youth activism, 164
Youth-based programming, 167, 172, 175

The manufacturer's authorised representative in the EU is Springer Nature Customer Service Centre GmbH, Europaplatz 3, 69115 Heidelberg, Germany. If you have any concerns regarding our products, please contact ProductSafety@springernature.com

Printed and bound by CPI Group (UK) Ltd, Croydon, CR0 4YY
23/03/2026
02076466-0003